Value Investing

Wiley Frontiers in Finance
Series Editor: Edward I. Altman, New York University

Value Investing

A BALANCED APPROACH

Martin J. Whitman

John Wiley & Sons, Inc.

New York • Chichester • Weinheim • Brisbane • Singapore • Toronto

Published by John Wiley & Sons. Inc. All rights reserved.

Published simultaneously in Canada.

This publication is designed to provide accurate and authoritative information in regard to the subject matter covered. It is sold with the understanding that the publisher is not engaged in rendering professional services. If professional advice or other expert assistance is required, the services of a competent professional person should be sought.

Library of Congress Cataloging-in-Publication Data:
Whitman, Martin J.
  Value investing : a balanced approach / Martin J. Whitman.
    p. cm.—(Wiley frontiers in finance)
  Includes index.
  ISBN 0-471-16292-2 (cloth : alk. paper)
  ISBN 0-471-39810-1 (paper : alk. paper)
  1. Investment analysis. 2. Securities. 3. Corporations—
  Valuation. I. Title. II. Series.
  HG4529.W53 1999
  332.6—dc21   98-44948

Printed in the United States of America

10 9 8 7 6 5 4

To my wife Lois

To my children and their spouses—Jim and Gillian;
Barbara and Dave; Tom and Mira

To my grandchildren—Daniel, Will, Nathaniel,
Lucien, and Raphael

Contents

Acknowledgments

This book has had a long gestation period during which I received the help of many people who after reading the manuscript discussed and debated with me about the many ideas contained within. Many of these people made invaluable suggestions. Their names are too numerous to mention here, but my thanks go out to each and every one of them. They know who they are.

I want to single out a few people for special thanks. I want to thank the stimulating students in my Yale University seminars. Between preparing the seminars and being prodded by the students, I am sure that I ended up learning more than anyone else from those weekly get-togethers. Yang Lie of MJ Whitman Advisers worked very hard on the various drafts of this book. So did Charles C. Walden, CFA, Senior Vice President of the Knights of Columbus and Director of Third Avenue Trust. Professor Stanley J. Garstka, Deputy Dean at the Yale School of Management, was also extremely helpful.

I also want to thank my wife Lois who was quite understanding these past few years as I vacillated between thinking that this book might make a significant contribution to investments and corporate finance and worrying that perhaps this might not be even close to true. She has been very patient in seeing me through the highs and lows involved in writing a book that has become so important to me personally.

Introduction

This book is an outgrowth of courses I taught for many years at the Yale University School of Management. Most of the courses had the word *investment* in their titles, but some involved such topics as restructuring troubled companies and investment banking. In this book, all three subjects are discussed because the three subjects are related.

In an important sense, the primary audience for this book are intelligent, passive investors who acquire common stocks because they want to own an interest in a company on a permanent or semipermanent basis. This book is not directed toward the investor speculator who acquires common stocks for the purpose of selling them to somebody else sooner or later—usually sooner.

Part of the process of becoming an intelligent passive investor is to understand not only the general financial environment but also who the other participants in the investment process are: Why do they do what they do? What are their problems? What are their potential profits? Most of these other participants probably are active, rather than passive, in the investment process.

In Part I of the book, value investing is described and then is contrasted with other investment disciplines, academic finance, Graham and Dodd fundamentalism, and conventional research as it seems to be practiced by most sell-side analysts employed by broker/dealer research departments as well as most buy-side analysts who manage money.

In Part II of the book, the underlying precepts of value investing are expanded by the discussion of certain analytic topics: corporate valuation, the substantive characteristics of securities, capital structure, promoters' and professionals' compensations, uses and limitations of financial accounting, uses and limitations of narrative disclosure, and the importance of semantics.

Part III covers resource conversion. The first chapter in the section surveys the overall field of investment banking by taking a theoretical company through various resource conversion activities: a leveraged buyout, an initial public offering, insolvency, a hostile takeover, and a merger and acquisition in which the takeover currency is an overpriced common stock. The next chapter covers both the methods used by activists when acquiring securities in bulk and the factors they usually examine beforehand. The subsequent chapter reviews restructuring troubled companies, and the final chapter covers pricing, the economics of stockholder litigation and of statutory appraisals, initial public offerings, leveraged buyouts, management buyouts, and share repurchases by companies.

It will be easier to understand the messages of this book if a few general principles are kept in mind.

- Except for the risk arbitrage exception, this book has nothing to say about trading. Risk arbitrage exists, for the purposes of this book, only in situations in which there are relatively determinant workouts in relatively determinant periods of time.
- In value investing, the goal is to determine a business's worth and its possible or probable dynamics, all independent of the price at which the common stock issued by that business trades. By contrast, the goal in other passive investing disciplines is to estimate the prices at which a common stock might sell in a market populated by outside passive minority investors (OPMIs).
- In value investing, there is no substantive consolidation between a company and its shareholders. The company is a stand-alone constituency, separate and apart from its shareholders.
- All financial relationships, including those between and among companies, managements, and shareholders, combine communities of interest and conflicts of interest.
- Corporate valuation is a complex matter involving quality of resources, quantity of resources, and long-term wealth creation. In the other investment disciplines, valuation focuses on forecasted flows, whether earnings or cash, discounted to a present value.

- Control securities are essentially a different commodity than OPMI securities, traded in different markets by different people who use different valuation methods.
- All markets tend toward efficiency. Most markets, though, do not achieve instantaneous efficiency. It is probable that most participants in most markets persistently earn excess returns, based on their costs.

This is not a book directed specifically at average OPMIs. The insights here are useful also to corporate managements, investment bankers, economists, those involved with academic finance, accountants, and attorneys. Many may view this book as a direct attack on academic finance; there is something to this view. In the preface to the fourth edition of their book on academic finance, *Principles of Corporate Finance,* Richard Brealey and Stewart Myers state, "There are no ironclad prerequisites for reading this book except algebra and the English language. An elementary knowledge of accounting, statistics, and microeconomics is helpful, however." For reading *this* book, algebra is useless; however, a deep understanding of the accounting cycle is essential.

Martin J. Whitman

PART I

DIFFERENT APPROACHES TO THE INVESTMENT PROCESS

Chapter 1

What Is Value Investing?

The difficulty lies not in the new ideas but in escaping from the old ones which ramify, for those who have been brought up as most of us have been, into every corner of our minds.

—J. M. Keynes

Value investing is different from other kinds of investing. It is wholly unrelated to technical and chartist analyses. The underlying approaches to and goals of value investing differ quite materially from those used in academic finance under the rubrics of the *efficient market hypothesis* (EMH) and *efficient portfolio theory (EPT)*, from those that are part of fundamental analysis as described in the various editions of *Security Analysis* by Benjamin Graham, David Dodd, and Sidney Cottle, popularly known as Graham and Dodd, and from those that seem to be the lifeblood of security analysis as practiced by conventional money managers and by research analysts employed by brokers/dealers. These fundamental differences are based on seven characteristics:

• **Value investing uses a balanced approach to analysis so that there is no *a priori* primacy given to any one factor in an appraisal.** In accounting terms, value investing treats every accounting number as being as important as any other number, with each number being derived from, a function of, and modified by all other accounting numbers. Businesses are examined as integrated wholes. The quality and quantity of resources existing in a business and the long-term wealth-creation potentials of a business are each consequential factors in value investing, and each factor is related integrally to the other. If future wealth creation, in the forms of increased operating profits, increased cash flows, or enhanced underlying takeover values, cannot be created out of the present existence of high-quality assets and high-quantity assets, then either those assets never existed in the first place or what assets did exist were mismanaged. If future earnings or cash flows do not create wealth (i.e., resources for the company, its shareholders, or both), then those earnings were fictitious to begin with.

In contrast to value investing's three-pronged approach, the approaches used by academic finance, Graham and Dodd, and conventional money managers give primacy to forecasting future flows, whether those flows are cash flows, reported earnings, adjusted earnings, or all three in valuation. Other accounting figures, especially balance sheet data, are correspondingly downweighted as increased significance is placed on estimated future flows.

• **In value investing, the essential goal is to value a business or the workout potential for credits issued by troubled companies.** In the other disciplines, the goal is to forecast the prices at which a security will sell in markets populated by outside passive minority investors (OPMIs). Business value may be one factor to consider in forecasting market prices for securities, but it is rarely, if ever, the sole factor and is frequently an unimportant factor.

• **In value investing, equity holdings are viewed as permanent or semipermanent commitments, subject only to a risk arbitrage exception.** The risk arbitrage exception exists when there are relatively determinant workouts in relatively determinant periods of time, such as when there has been a publicly announced merger transaction. In the other disciplines, equity investments are viewed as trading vehicles because of the importance placed on near-term price performance in markets.

• **In value investing, macrofactors such as the level of stock averages (e.g., the Dow-Jones Industrials), forecasts of interest rates, or the gross domestic product (GDP) are ignored.** The emphasis is strictly on microfactors that specifically will affect a company over the long term. In the other disciplines, the first factors to be considered usually are macrofactors.

• **In value investing, as part of a balanced approach, businesses are viewed as both going concerns and as resource converters, deploying and redeploying their asset bases and liabilities into new areas including mergers and acquisitions, changes in control, massive refinancings, initial public offerings (IPOs), and leveraged buyouts (LBOs).** The tendency in other disciplines is to view companies as strict going concerns engaged wholly in day-to-day operations in specific industries financed as they have typically been financed and managed as they typically have been managed.

• **In value investing, corporate analysis is viewed as something separate and distinct from market analysis.** In other disciplines, corporate analysis and market analysis are almost always integrated with each other. In value investing, a price decline for a security in the absence of any corporate permanent impairment of capital is viewed as a temporary phenomenon. In the other disciplines, a price decline is viewed as a loss of value.

• **In value investing, the analyst is extremely price conscious in making judgments about the attractiveness of a security.** In other disciplines, the strong tendency is to be outlook conscious rather than price conscious. Conventional asset allocators make investments on the basis of views about general or specific outlooks. In value investing, asset allocations are driven by price as related to the three factors inherent in a company: quality of resources, quantity of resources, and long-term wealth-creation potential.

The tools of value investing seem commonplace and important throughout the industrialized world, used not only by deal makers in the financial community but also by most private businesses for the analysis and financing of enterprises; yet those tools are largely ignored or deemed unimportant when OPMIs invest in publicly traded common stocks. Virtually all investment literature—whether written about trading systems, written in an academic context, or written as fundamental analysis as propounded by Graham and Dodd and their followers—is directed toward OPMIs. It seems as if virtually all business television shows and newspaper articles are directed toward a special kind of OPMI—"the average investor." On Wall Street, value investing seems very much to be a minority approach restricted to investors trafficking in corporate control; but on Main Street, where most businesses are privately owned, it appears to be the majority approach.

Value investing entails buying what is safe and cheap. *What is* refers to the use of analytic techniques that concentrate on the known situation of a company—the quality and quantity of resources in a company, with little or no concentration on forecasts of relatively near term flows (say, over the next 12 months). *Safe* refers to the survivability of a business as a business without any reference whatsoever to price volatility of the securities issued by that business. Safety is measured mostly by strong financial positions; by the quality of resources, if the investor is interested in such junior securities as common stocks; by strong covenant protections; and by reasonable quantitative characteristics in terms of asset coverage or earnings coverage, or both, if the investor is interested in owning corporate debt. *Cheap* means an acquisition price for a common stock that appears to represent a substantial discount from what the common stock would be worth were the company a private business or a takeover candidate. *Cheap,* in the case of a debt instrument, means an estimated yield-to-maturity, or yield-to-workout, that is at least 500 basis points (a basis point, or bip, is $1/100$ of 1% or .0001) greater than could be obtained from a credit instrument bearing about the same level of ultimate credit risk.

In November 1998, Toyoda Automatic Loom Works, Ltd. common stock, listed on the Tokyo Stock Exchange, appeared to be a good example of a common stock that was safe and cheap based on "what is" because the company was well financed and represented a way of buying into the common stock of Toyota Motor, a blue-chip automotive manufacturer at a discount of perhaps 35% to 40%. Toyoda common was trading at about 2,300 yen per share, or about $16.5–$17 U.S. dollars. Its adjusted balance sheet, expressed in U.S. dollars, was as shown in Table 1-1.

In November and December 1955, Kmart senior debentures and trade claims seemed to be good examples of credit instruments that were safe and cheap based on "what is." The Kmart situation is discussed in detail in Chapter 14. On average, these senior issues traded in public and private markets at prices averaging around $74. These instruments had average yields-to-maturity of around 18% in a market in which BB industrial credits were trading at yields-to-maturity of around 9% and BBB

Table 1-1. Balance Sheet for Toyoda Automatic Loom Works Ltd. (Adjusted NAV in $000s)

		6.0×	8.0×	Per Toyoda Share*	
Operating Income	$251,570	$1,509,420	$2,012,560		
Less: nonconvertible funded debt		259,917	259,917		
		1,249,503	1,752,643	$3.97	$5.56
192,725 shares Toyota Motor Common @ $25/share		4,818,125	4,818,125	15.30	15.30
Remaining portfolio of marketable securities at market 11/13/98		1,990,129	1,990,129	6.32	6.32
NAV appraising Toyoda as a closed-end investment company		8,057,757	8,560,897	$25.58	$27.18
Discount from NAV at market price of $16.59 for Toyoda Common				35.1%	38.9%

*Adjusted shares outstanding, 315,000; Toyoda Auto Loom share price @ 11/13/98, $16.59; exchange rate, 122.65 yen to the dollar.

obligations were trading at yields to maturity of around 8%. BBB is the lowest grade credit which Standard & Poor's, as a rating agency, defines as Investment Grade. Standard & Poor's defines a BBB credit as follows: "An obligation rated BBB exhibits adequate protection parameters. However adverse economic conditions or charging circumstances are more likely to lead to a weakened capacity of the obligor to meet its financial commitment on the obligation (as compared with credits rated AAA, AA, or A). Obligations rated BB, B, CCC, CC, and C are regarded as having significant speculative characteristics." BB is the highest grade obligation to be characterized as speculative.

It was problematic at the time as to whether Kmart would have to seek relief under Chapter 11 of the U.S. Bankruptcy Code. If Kmart did seek Chapter 11 relief, all cash service on the Kmart debt would cease. I concluded, however, that the odds were overwhelmingly that if Kmart ever did enter Chapter 11, the workout values for these Kmart instruments in a reorganization would be at least $100 or more likely $100 plus accrued interest. This confidence in the ultimate workout was based, in great part, on the seniority enjoyed by these debentures and trade claims.

Although no two value investors will use precisely the same investment techniques among themselves, all value analysts focus on analytic variables quite different from those emphasized in all the current literature on security analysis or corporate finance that is directed toward OPMIs. This other body of literature encompasses academic writings about the efficient market hypothesis (EMH), efficient portfolio theory (EPT), Graham and Dodd fundamentalism, and newer offshoots of modern capital theory (MCT) such as new finance.[1] Furthermore, value investing is removed completely from all technical chartist literature, the outpouring of works purporting to predict and explain price levels for general markets or for specific securities traded in markets popular with OPMIs.

Value investing becomes increasingly useful for those who also understand academic theory, as expounded in the EMH and EPT, and for those who also understand traditional fundamental analysis, as described in the various writings of Graham and Dodd. For example, the EMH is useful for securities traders whose sole goal is to consistently maximize a total return on a risk-adjusted basis (i.e., all the time). Graham and Dodd note important caveats for those who do not know much about the companies whose securities they hold or are considering acquiring. Value investing, in comparison, revolves around obtaining a fairly deep understanding of either the business, the securities issued by that business, or both. Importantly, the value analyst, as part of the analytic process, tries to understand where other market participants are coming from, why these others do what they do, and why they say what they say.

---

[1] See the book *The New Finance: The Case Against Efficient Markets* by Robert A. Haugen (Prentice Hall, 1995).

Graham and Dodd, in their 1962 edition of *Security Analysis,* describe the difference in analytic approaches in OPMI markets compared with those in private business markets:

> Security analysts ... should reflect fully on the rather startling truth that as long as a business remains a *private* corporation or partnership the net asset value appearing on the balance sheet is likely to constitute the point of departure for determining what the enterprise is "worth." But once it makes its appearance as a "publicly held company"—even though the shares distributed to the public constitute only a small part of the total—the net-worth figure seems to lose virtually all its significance. "Value" then becomes dependent almost exclusively on the expected future earnings (p. 551).

Graham and Dodd are insightful in pointing to the strong tendency to use different variables, or to weight the same variables quite differently, when valuing a private business versus estimating prices at which OPMI common stocks might trade. Value investors who seek control of corporations (and corporate processes) actively arbitrage these differences between corporate values and OPMI market prices. The arbitrage tools they use are described in Part III of this book, in which there are brief discussions about restructuring troubled companies, mergers and acquisitions (M&As), contests for control, LBOs, management buyouts (MBOs), and IPOs.

A value investor who is a passive rather than an active control investor is conscious of the discrepancies in valuations between a private business value and an OPMI common stock price. In value investing, it is assumed that sooner or later there will be an arbitrage between OPMI prices and private business, or takeover, values and that an LBO or M&A will occur at some substantial premium over OPMI market prices. According to Graham and Dodd fundamentalism and the EMH, on the other hand, the underlying assumption seems to be that in the vast majority of cases, the company whose common stock is traded in the OPMI market will continue indefinitely to be a going concern, engaged in the operations in which it always has been engaged, managed the way it always has been managed, owned pretty much the way it has always been owned, and financed the way it always has been financed.

OPMIs were defined in 1979 in *The Aggressive Conservative Investor,* by Martin J. Whitman and Martin Shubik, as any participants in a securities market, whether individual or institutional, who can be distinguished from others in two respects:

First, individually they have no control or influence over the businesses whose securities they hold or contemplate holding. Second, they do not have access to information other than that which is generally available to the public.

It is logical—efficient—that net asset value be weighted more heavily in a private business analysis than in an OPMI analysis. Control people influence how corporate assets are used and financed. OPMIs have no influence; for them, there are no opportunities to influence how assets might be employed or redeployed. Also, in an OPMI market, near-term prices of solvent corporations are bound to be much more influenced by reported earnings than by changes in reported asset values.

The best of the value analysts—including Warren Buffett, Carl Icahn, Ted Forstmann, Henry Kravis, Ron Perelman, and Richard Rainwater— worry about business values and business dynamics. Admittedly, these superior investors are all basically control activists rather than OPMIs. Nonetheless, their basic approach seems significant for OPMIs. In their own investment commitments, these superior investors seem to care not one whit about predicting a security's price when they have no influence in determining that price. Markets are not something they predict; markets are something of which they take advantage. As such, they carry a lot less analytic baggage than most OPMIs and a lot less analytic baggage than all who write about the efficient market hypothesis, Graham and Dodd fundamentalism, and the new finance.

Understanding value investing approaches and techniques ought to be extremely helpful in enabling OPMI securities investors to be successful. Indeed, value investing seems to be one of the more promising approaches for OPMIs who, although they are passive, seek to earn excess returns both on average and over the long term.

Admittedly, the returns to be earned from being successful at control investing probably are larger than they normally could be from OPMI investing, even though both types follow a value investing approach. There are many inherent advantages to control investing; even so, there are quite a number of inherent advantages to OPMI investing. Obviously, most investors will never become control investors, but anyone with a few thousand dollars or a self-directed 401(k) plan can become an OPMI.

Advantages to Control Investing

At the risk of overgeneralizing, the inherent advantages of control investing, especially for those who actually achieve elements of control, might be summarized as follows:

- Control investing creates edges so that a control person can obtain additional rewards over and above those that attach directly to securities ownership. These edges have three components:
  1. Something off the top (SOTT), or salaries, perks options, fees, expense reimbursements, and luxurious travel and entertainment perks
  2. An ability to finance transactions and processes on a highly attractive basis (i.e., an ability to use other people's money [OPM])
  3. An ability to create advantageous tax situations (i.e., tax shelters [TSs])
- In exploring investment opportunities in which control situations exist, security buyers frequently have the ability, the resources, and the time to conduct in depth due-diligence investigations, which can be far more comprehensive than would be possible relying solely on public records. (A notable exception, though, tends to be hostile takeovers, in which potential acquirers may be stopped from using inside information.)
- Control investing allows investors to obtain influence, control, or both over corporate processes, operations, and investments. One of the things this gives the control investor is opportunities to create values by changing the way assets are used or owned and by recapitalizing businesses.
- Control investing allows investors to obtain control over timing on a long-term basis so that they decide when to take advantage of favorable OPMI market conditions, whether to consummate an IPO, a going private, a massive refinancing of debt, or a merger in which common stock is issued as all or part of the merger consideration.
- Control investing allows investors to obtain self-protection, almost always with the unfettered ability to finance that self-protection by using the corporate treasury.
- Control investing allows investors to obtain the power to reward other professionals (e.g., investment bankers, attorneys, accountants),

to withhold favors or advantageous treatment from people dealing with the corporation or seeking to deal with the corporation, or both.

Advantages of Investing as an Outside Passive Minority Investor

Despite the advantages to control investing, there are a number of inherent advantages for OPMIs who follow the same basic analytic precepts of value investing that are followed by control investors. Again, at the risk of overgeneralizing, OPMIs can experience the following advantages that promise not only a margin of safety on the downside but also the prospect of excess long-term returns on the upside.

- Outside passive minority investors can acquire securities at ultralow prices. Frequently, prices in OPMI markets are only small fractions of what corporations are worth as measured by business values. OPMI market prices tend to be much lower—and also much higher—than prices that would be arrived at in arm's-length negotiations between and among informed business people. For example, in September 1998, it was possible to acquire the common stocks of leading semiconductor equipment manufacturers at prices far cheaper than would be available for first-stage venture capitalists financing high-tech enterprises *de novo*. FSI International common, Silicon Valley Group common, and Speedfam common all had cash holdings equal to at least 95% of book liabilities and were selling at discounts from tangible net asset values and at no more than seven times the peak earnings that had been achieved in the recent past before the industry was hit by a severe depression in 1997.
- In acquiring equities, OPMIs can restrict investments to high-quality, well-financed companies, a luxury frequently unavailable for control investors. In acquiring credit instruments, OPMIs can restrict their investments to senior instruments containing strong protective covenants in which pricing reflects much above average yields-to-maturity, or yields-to-event.
- For OPMIs, finding attractive investment opportunities is much easier and a much less competitive activity using value investing techniques than is the case for typical OPMIs. The typical value investor is among the

small minority of OPMIs concentrating on a buy-and-hold strategy emphasizing quality and quantity of resources in a business as well as long-term outlooks. Most OPMIs are instead vitally interested in near-term outlooks, especially reported earnings per share, and predicting levels of securities prices. In September 1998, for example, an investor could acquire the common stocks of extremely well financed Japanese non–life insurance companies, such as Tokio Marine & Fire Insurance Company, Ltd., at prices representing 30% to 75% discounts from a net asset value that consisted almost solely of marketable securities and performing loans. Few OPMIs would have been interested in these securities, because the near-term outlooks for reported earnings were poor and, over the longer term, insurance operations were bound to face increasing competition.

• Although the protections available for OPMIs are nowhere near as valuable as control investors' ability to self-protect in many instances, OPMIs obtain regulatory protections from governments, self-regulatory organizations, and the private bar, which will propagate class-action and derivative lawsuits on behalf of OPMIs and the company itself, respectively. Informed OPMIs using value investing techniques obtain considerable ability to self-protect through regulator-required disclosures, fair trading markets, and a modicum of reasonable behavior by fiduciaries and quasifiduciaries.

• Outside passive minority investors obtain liquidity and marketability for their investments. This means, among other things, that it tends to be a lot easier for OPMIs than for control investors to undo mistakes.

• Analysis of given situations tends to be a lot easier for OPMIs than for control investors when both use value investing techniques. The OPMI need only identify attractive securities from a price-to-value point of view. The control investor has to identify not only attractive situations but also doable deals (i.e., situations where elements of control might be available). It tends to be a lot easier to identify attractive securities than to identify doable, attractive deals.

Another way of understanding value investing—whether undertaken to achieve elements of control, to be purely passive, or to be undecided about whether an ultimate objective is control or sale to an OPMI market—is to analyze each situation as if investors were to put up $100 million or more of their own funds that will remain committed to the security on a permanent or semipermanent basis. The reality, however, is that many using value investing techniques are not permanent or semipermanent investors even though they analyze as if they were. Shorter-term players who use value investing techniques include the following:

- **Risk arbitrageurs, who make investments on the basis of the prospect that there will be reasonably determinant workouts in reasonably determinant periods of time.** Risk arbitrages usually involve deals in which there has been a public announcement. One example of a risk arbitrage was the announced common stock for common stock merger between KLA Instruments Corporation and Tencor Instruments. Just prior to the January 1997 announcement of the one-for-one common stock exchange, KLA common was selling at $40\frac{7}{8}$ and Tencor common was selling at $30\frac{1}{2}$. The risk arbitrage subsequent to the announcement involved either acquiring Tencor common at a price reflecting a discount from the price of KLA common or a combination of buying Tencor common at the discount price and selling short KLA common at a premium price relative to the price of Tencor common. On consummation of the merger, the arbitrageur would deliver, say, 100,000 shares of Tencor common purchased at 35 to cover a short position in KLA common in which the arbitrageur had sold 100,000 shares at, say, 39. The 4-point spread between 35 and 39 would have resulted in the arbitrageur's realizing a $400,000 profit before transaction costs and taxes.
- **Creditors holding nonperforming loans.** The restructuring process here, whether out-of-court or in Chapter 11, tends to be much like risk arbitrage because the analysis usually involves ascertaining what reasonably determinant workouts will be in reasonably determinant periods of time.

The Basic Concepts of Value Investing

Modern value investing is based on a number of basic concepts that differ drastically from those underlying the EMH and the theories of Graham and Dodd:

- Information can be used in a superior manner.
- Constituencies in financial dealings always involve both communities of interest and conflicts of interest.
- No market participant is deemed crazy or stupid.
- Value is a dynamic concept.
- Market price is not something to predict but something of which to take advantage.
- There is no general risk—only specific risk.
- The devil is in the details, not in general laws.
- Understanding institutions and infrastructures is a necessity.
- Understanding the roles of governing bodies is key.
- Flexibility rules.
- Knowing the elements of attractive pricing is critical.
- Value investors know more than does the OPMI market about matters that count.
- Earning excess returns is the norm in an efficient market.
- Control securities are essentially a different commodity than noncontrol securities.
- Most of the time, capitalization is not determined by equity investors' needs or desires.
- Diversification is a nonstarter in most markets.
- Every investment has something wrong with it.

Use of Information

As is pointed out *ad finitum* in EMH literature, OPMIs do not, as a rule, have access to superior information. This lack of access is immaterial, however, in value investing. The key in value investing is for the passive investor to use the available information in a superior manner. The value analyst, for example, will, in analyzing an equity security, attach great weight to the strength of an issuer's financial position and/or the ability of the issuer to obtain access to capital markets on an attractive basis. By contrast, those focused on EMH considerations would pretty much ignore a corporation's financial position and would instead tend to find key information in the amount by which actual reported earnings for a quarterly period exceeded, equaled, or fell short of consensus forecasts. Value investing's focus on financial position may be a superior use of available information compared with EMH considerations, where the emphasis is on forecasting future flows—a primacy of the income account approach. Emphasizing flows seems a far cry from using available information in a superior manner most of the time. For example, it was possible to invest in Forest City Enterprises class A common stock in 1991 at around $20 per share, even though the company's annual report stated that the appraised value of this investment builder's income-producing properties alone, virtually all financed with nonrecourse debt, exceeded $80 per share. At the time, Forest City, operated in the ultradepressed real estate industry and was reporting accounting losses based on generally accepted accounting principles (GAAP). Charges for depreciation and amortization were being deducted from profits for accounting purposes while, for economic purposes, property values were probably increasing. Focusing on appraised values rather than accounting earnings for Forest City seemed a good example of using the available information in a superior manner.

In value investing, the quality of information is judged by an estimate of how that information might affect corporate values, corporate dynamics, or the rights and privileges attached to various securities. In other types of investing, especially EMH, the test of the value of information is strictly an estimate of how that information might affect immediate market prices in the OPMI market. This is logical for the EMH, which is based solely on studies of securities prices and essentially excludes any study of corporate values not strictly related to market prices.

The differences in information requirements for value investing compared with those for typical OPMI investing seem striking. They might be generally summarized as in Table 1-2.

In value investing, the importance of a particular item of information depends on context. For example, in the other disciplines, except Graham and Dodd, quarterly reported earnings per share are almost always highly important, but in value investing, they are almost never important. Quarterly earnings do become important in value investing, however, insofar as they become an indication of a permanent impairment of corporate value, something more likely to be the case when a company is not well financed, or the quarterly results are evidence that the company is losing competitive position, or both.

Table 1-2. Information Usage: Value Investing versus Typical Passive Investing

Important in Value Investing	Important to the Typical OPMI
Long-term outlook— over a business cycle	Industry identification
	Earnings per share versus consensus forecasts
Ability to finance a transaction	Current P : E ratios
Each element in the accounting cycle	Primacy of the income account
What the accounting numbers mean rather than what the accounting numbers are (except when seeking to use the OPMI market)	Historical P : E ratios
	Reported earnings, unadjusted
	Comparative analysis
	Dividends—shareholder distributions
Benefits of control	Long-term earnings record
Quality and quantity of resources in a business	Immediate macro-outlook
	Long-term macroconsiderations
Comparative analysis is a limited tool	Equilibrium price
Doability tends to be a key variable	Technical factors
No equilibrium price for all markets	Trend of earnings
Change of control factors	Sponsorship
Securities law and regulation	Return on equity and assets
Income tax code	

OPMI = outside passive minority investor; P : E = price-to-earnings.

Constituencies in Financial Dealings Always Involve Both Communities of Interest and Conflicts of Interest

The relationships between and among the various constituencies involved in financial dealings always involve both communities of interest and conflicts of interest. There are no *a priori* real-world reasons for assuming that any one group's interests take precedence over other groups' interests in all contexts. It seems utterly unrealistic to assume that managements work exclusively in the best interests of stockholders. Each constituency—the company *qua* the company, management, short-term traders, buy-and-hold investors, senior creditors, trade creditors, junior

creditors, landlords, control shareholders, OPMIs, labor unions, governments, communities, financial professionals (investment bankers, attorneys, accountants, etc.)—is separate and has its own agendas combining
communities of interest and conflicts of interest with each of the other
constituencies.

Since the 1970s, there has been a significant, seemingly inexorable
trend toward entrenching management in office that has become embodied in state law, the primary province for corporate governance. This gives
rise to conflicts of interest between managements and OPMIs, especially
OPMIs seeking to maximize the near-term price performance of their securities portfolios. Managements do not succumb to takeover bids just
because they represent an otherwise unobtainable premium over OPMI
market prices. (Take, for example, the April 1997 buyout offer for ITT by
Hilton Hotels.) Most managements (with minor exceptions), however,
feel a community of interest with OPMIs in terms of desiring reasonable
near-term performance in OPMI markets for the common stocks issued
by the companies they manage.

Sometimes there are partial consolidations among constituencies
where communities of interest predominate; for example, all classes of
creditors believe they will be harmed if cash distributions are made by
the company to equity holders. Sometimes the previously consolidated
group will be dominated by conflicts of interest, so each constituency in
this situation is best viewed as a nonconsolidated stand-alone; for example, the various creditors in the previous sentence may argue about reorganization plans for a troubled issuer and how assets are to be
distributed in a reorganization to different classes of creditors. (Take,
for example, the April 1998 contretemps between the secured lenders
and the junior lenders in connection with the Marvel Comics Chapter 11
case.)

In value investing, the company *qua* the company is almost always a
unique constituency. Each other constituency tends to benefit when the
company is feasible (i.e., healthy and strong). At the same time, each
other constituency tends to benefit when it obtains distributions from the
company that may detract from feasibility (e.g., management compensation or cash distributions to shareholders that do not enhance a company's future access to capital markets). Also, as a practical matter, in
certain situations, such as Chapter 11 reorganizations, the company is un-
represented by professionals in a confrontational process. Attorneys and

investment bankers retained by companies in Chapter 11 almost always have a first loyalty to the management or control group that hired them and not to the company per se. In Chapter 11 reorganizations, there are frequently important conflicts between a company's quest for feasibility on the one hand and management's quest for compensation and entrenchment and a creditor's quest for cash and secured cash-pay instruments on the other hand.

An important thing to realize in value investing is that despite frequent use of terms indicating otherwise, the company is not the management; management may not be the control stockholders; and neither the company, management, nor control stockholders are OPMIs.

No Market Participant Is Assumed to Be Crazy or Stupid

Although this book presents value investing as a preferred technique for many investors, this by no means implies that other investment approaches—technical chartist approaches, momentum investing, IPO investing, EMH approaches, and Graham and Dodd approaches—are invalid. These approaches are only invalid insofar as their proponents believe they have discovered the Holy Grail, the one universal explanation of Wall Street and investing. Many in academic finance seem inclined to believe that they are expounding eternal truths and universally acceptable general laws.

The successful promoter using value investing understands why others do what they do, then takes advantage of it. For example, if you want to be involved in promoting LBOs, it is important to understand why prices in OPMI markets are—and ought to be—different from what an LBO buyer can afford to pay for a business. The OPMI price is not crazy for participants in OPMI markets; it is just not an appropriate value for the LBO market, where prices tend to be considerably higher than they are in many sectors of the OPMI market. Similarly, the venture capitalist realizes that pricing for IPO market purposes is, as a rule, many times higher than prices that would be paid for private companies if they were to remain private companies. For value investing purposes, the basic assumption is that pricing in IPO markets and the very different pricing in private markets are both quite rational within their own contexts.

Value investing is an unsuitable approach in several contexts. It would be crazy or stupid to become a value investor who ignores rather completely day-to-day OPMI market prices:

- when a passive investor operates with borrowed money and the collateral value of the borrowings is determined by daily OPMI pricing (i.e., marks to market). Such an investor ought to focus in great part on market risks (i.e., possible day-to-day changes in market prices) rather than on investment risk (i.e., long-term underlying corporate values).
- where a money manager's job or compensation is determined by near-term performance in OPMI markets.
- when clients demand immediate OPMI performance.
- when the money manager or the investor is untrained in value investing analytic techniques and is unable to make meaningful judgments about corporate values independent of OPMI market prices.
- when the investor is in the OPMI market strictly to gamble, with the OPMI market satisfying the participant's needs to play in a casino.
- when the investor is a short-run trader not involved in risk arbitrage.

Value Is a Dynamic Concept

Corporate values are continually changing. In good businesses that do not make massive distributions to shareholders, values tend to increase on a reasonably regular basis. These increases in underlying business value may have no particular relationship to OPMI market prices but rather may reflect improvements in operations, financial strength, and basic earning power. Liberty Financial, a life insurance and asset management company, had $48 billion of assets under management (AUM) on December 31, 1996, up from a *pro forma* figure of around $40 billion 2 years earlier. There seems to be a ready market for AUM at 2% to 4% of AUM. Liberty Financial obviously created values between 1994 and 1996, even though these were not necessarily reflected in OPMI prices or GAAP-determined net asset values. At 2% of AUM, the $8 billion increase in AUM from $40 billion to $48 billion would have a sales value of $160 million; at 3% of AUM, the increase in sales value would have been $240 million.

Corporate values are also created by macromarket conditions even in situations in which the OPMI market consensus is strictly bearish. In April 1997, for example, there seemed to be an OPMI consensus that high interest rates and inflation were negative factors universally. As a matter of fact, a high interest rate and a modest-to-high inflation environment probably would accelerate the creation of corporate values for a number of companies.

Even though high interest rates would tend to reduce the value of a business to be acquired by the use of acquisition debt, it would very much tend to increase future earnings and value for businesses whose assets consist of material amounts of interest bearing obligations and whose liabilities are largely free of interest-bearing obligations. The future earnings benefits would be especially large for companies whose portfolios of performing loans are expanding in size. Financial Security Assurance Holdings, known generally as FSA—a financial insurer—is just such a company. At December 31, 1996, about two thirds of its assets were in bonds, on which it earned about 6.3%. Any increase in interest rates would result in increases in the company's future net investment income.

Inflation would tend to reduce the quality of earnings of a capital-intensive company such as Cummins Engine because depreciation charges against income tend to become inadequate as replacement reserves in an inflationary environment. On the other hand, inflation tends to make it more expensive for new entrants to come into an industry, giving existing entities, such as Cummins Engine, insulation against new competition. Further, a well-financed company may find itself in a position to make attractive acquisitions insofar as inflationary pressures result in restraints on the operations of poorly financed firms. Finally, inflation probably increases takeover prices and makes takeovers a more common occurrence, as aggressive companies conclude that it is cheaper to *buy* at premiums over OPMI market prices than to *make* by entering an industry *de novo*.

Market Price Is Not Something to Predict but Something of Which to Take Advantage

In value investing, OPMI market price tends to be a realization figure, not a valuation figure. As a realization figure, an OPMI market price serves as an indication of the prices at which you ought to be able to buy or sell a security, assuming you want to buy or sell. Market price, as a valuation figure, is never a universally accepted valuation figure (i.e., a value measurement valid for all, or even most, contexts—OPMI market, LBO market, or IPO market).

Value investing perceives the existence of a long-term arbitrage between OPMI market prices and business values. When OPMI market prices are low relative to business value, publicly traded shares tend to be acquired by activists in hostile takeovers, LBOs, and going-privates. (Take, for example, the 1997 acquisition of Destec Energy for cash at a 60% premium over OPMI market price for Destec common.) When OPMI market prices are high relative to business values, common stocks tend to be issued to the public in IPOs and M&As, where the currency used for the M&A is common stock, in whole or in part (e.g., the buoyant IPO market that existed from 1995 through 1997).

There Is No General Risk—Only Specific Risk

In value investing, the word *risk* is always modified by an adjective. There is no general risk. There is market risk, investment risk, interest rate risk, inflation risk, failure to match maturities risk, securities fraud risk, excessive promoters' compensation risk, and so on. In value analysis, the tendency is to guard against investment risk, the prospect that things will go wrong for the business in which the activist has invested. Market risk, the prospect for price fluctuations in OPMI markets, is usually ignored. Put otherwise, the value analyst, in examining the risks in an investment, worries about permanent impairments of capital but not about unrealized market losses or a reduction in the amount of unrealized market profits.

The analysis of Kmart Debentures and Kmart Trade Claims (together, Kmart Credits) at the end of 1995 serves as a good example of the difference between investment risk and market risk. In late 1995, it seemed impossible to predict whether Kmart would seek reorganization under Chapter 11 of the U.S. bankruptcy code. It seemed a certainty that if Chapter 11 relief were sought, interest payments would stop and there would be no 18% yield-to-maturity. Further, the probability seemed to be that Kmart Credits would sell in the OPMI market at dollar prices well below the existing prices of around $74, if for no other reason than that the holders of debentures relying on interest income, which would no longer be paid, would dump their holdings by immediate sale into the OPMI market. Thus, Kmart Credits seemed to carry a high degree of market risk.

Despite the existence of market risk, however, Kmart Credits seemed to carry little or no investment risk. If Kmart did not file in Chapter 11, Kmart Credits would continue to be performing loans, affording as yield-to-maturity 700 to 900 bips above comparable credits. Furthermore, it appeared that if Kmart were to file for Chapter 11 relief, the company would be readily reorganizeable, and since Kmart Credits were, in effect, the most senior issue of Kmart, the holders of Kmart Credits seemed bound to receive, in a Chapter 11 reorganization, a value in new Kmart securities of not less than 100—more likely 100-plus accrued post-Chapter 11 interest.

Investment risk for a security has three general components in value investing:

- Quality of the issuer
- Terms of the issue
- Price of the issue

When the focus is on quality of the issuer and terms of the issue only, as is a basic precept of academic finance, a risk-to-reward ratio comes into existence. For academic finance, the higher the quality of the issuer and the more senior the terms of the issue, the less risk of loss the investor is taking. Also, the higher the quality of the issuer and the more senior the terms of the issue, the less the rewards are likely to be for the investor, thus the risk-to-reward ratio.

For academic finance, the price of the issue as it trades in OPMI markets reflects a universal price equilibrium; that is, it is the correct price for all purposes and all participants. Insofar as the price of the issue is too high or too low, however, no risk-to-reward ratio exists; it cannot exist. Suppose the price is too low. That means that the issue carries a reduced risk of loss and an enhanced potential for reward. In value investing, there usually is no risk-to-reward ratio simply because price of the issue becomes so important that it outweighs the risk-to-reward equation that appears to be valid insofar as an analysis is based on an assumption of the existence of a price equilibrium, so that the only factors to weigh are quality of the issuer and the terms of the issue.

When equity securities and nonperforming credit instruments based on forecasted future flows are analyzed, the appropriate discount rate encompasses three elements:

- Time value of money
- The risk that actual flows will be less than forecast
- The potential that actual flows will be better than forecast

When performing loans that sell at or near their principal amounts are analyzed, the appropriate discount rate reflects only two factors: the time value of money and the risk that actual flows will be less than forecast. From a credit risk point of view there are no material rewards for the holders of performing loans selling at prices close to the principal amount if actual flows turn out to be better than forecast; at best, the bondholder will be entitled only to the principal amount plus possibly a small call premium.

The Devil Is in the Details, Not in General Laws

Value investing entails a bottom-up approach, and ultimate investment decisions are governed by specifics, not general rules. For example, it is well demonstrated that buying new-issue IPOs across the board is a tough way to earn excess returns. This does not mean that the value investor never buys new issues. It does mean that value investors must be highly selective in acquiring new issues in OPMI markets. It also means that the overpricing of new issues, in general, ought to be an attractive arena for investors who do not choose to be OPMIs but rather seek to earn excess returns as venture capitalists, new-issue underwriters, or securities salespeople. Securities salespeople benefit by marketing IPO products because these products are exclusive, tend to be easy sells, and provide much above average compensation, certainly as compared with competing with discount brokers in the purchase and sale of securities in secondary markets.

Understanding Institutions and Infrastructures Is a Necessity

If you are to be successful at value investing, it is imperative that you understand the environment within which investing takes place. For value investing in the United States, you ought to be knowledgeable enough in three specific areas to at least be an intelligent client of knowledgeable professionals:

- Securities law and regulation
- Financial accounting
- Corporate income taxes

Other institutional areas in which it is useful to be knowledgeable are:

- Methods of operation for financial institutions
- Factors and processes involved in corporate control

including tools for the entrenchment of incumbents:

- Promoters' and professionals' compensations
- Capital structures
- Substantive characteristics of securities

Understanding the Roles of Governing Bodies Is Key

The various governing bodies in the United States play important roles in most investment processes, including:

- Taxing agency
- Provider of attractive finance
- Provider of direct subsidies
- Provider of infrastructures
- Securities regulator
- Regulator in other areas
- Provider of judicial systems

- Customer
- Competitor
- Provider of freebies (e.g., certain broadcast licenses)

Flexibility Rules

In the bottoms-up approach characteristic of value investing, no one approach is the correct one for all contexts. Take financial accounting, for example. It is the one tool with which analysts can obtain objective benchmarks essential to helping them reach conclusions. Normally, what the numbers *mean* for analysts is infinitely more important than what the numbers are *reported* to be. Applied Materials, a supplier of equipment to the semiconductor industry, expenses all of its very large annual expenditures for research, development, and engineering as charges to net income; in 1996, such charges amounted to 11.6% of net sales. In an economic sense, it ought to be argued that a portion of such expenditures for research, development, and engineering ought to be capitalized because their purpose is to create future earning power rather than to contribute to the maintenance of current earnings; thus, they are more in the nature of capital expenditures than current expenses. Applied Materials seems to be accounting quite conservatively. Most of Applied Materials' buy-and-hold shareholders care about what the numbers mean, not what the numbers are. Since Applied Materials has considerable surplus cash, expensing all research, development, and engineering does no harm to Applied Materials as a corporation. Assume, however, that instead of having surplus cash Applied Materials needed to raise capital and was seeking access to capital markets, especially OPMI markets for an IPO. It probably would be beneficial for the company and its stockholders in this instance if Applied Materials reported larger earnings per share, which would be achievable were a portion of research and development expenditures capitalized rather than expensed. In an IPO market, what the numbers *are,* especially the earnings per share number, tends to become a lot more important than what the numbers *mean.*

Value investing recognizes that most businesses are both strict going concerns engaged in day-to-day operations and resource conversion companies engaged in asset and liability redeployments and changes in control. In going-concern analysis, the emphasis tends to be on the primacy of the income account—what future flows will be, whether cash flows or accounting earnings. In resource conversion analysis, the emphasis tends to be on the market value of the corporation's assets and the prospects that the corporation might have access to capital markets on a superattractive basis.

Flexibility, rather than general rules, are the order of the day in specific situations. Sometimes going-concern aspects should be emphasized. Sometimes resource conversion characteristics should be emphasized. It was pointed out above that if interest rates rise, future net investment income for FSA will be larger than otherwise would have been the case, a strong benefit in analyzing the company as a going concern. In contrast, if interest rates rise the current market value of the FSA portfolio of performing loans will decrease, a distinct negative in valuing the company and its common stock.

As part of flexibility, value investors recognize the trade-offs inherent in each situation, knowing that every number in financial accounting is derived from, modified by, and a function of other accounting numbers. For example, companies with strong financial positions in good times are sacrificing return on equity (ROE) compared with what ROE would be were assets employed more aggressively, were there more leverage in the capitalization, or were both situations the case. At the same time, increasing ROE probably means a trade-off with safety most of the time. Prediction of future earnings or cash flows in situations in which such futures are not contractually assured is subject to high degrees of error. Seeking to maximize ROE or economic value added (EVA) makes the consequences of overestimating future flows much more dire for companies, and probably their OPMI stockholders, than would be the case were maximizing ROE modified by reducing ROE through increasing the company's financial strength. Increasing financial strength means either financing with less debt and more equity, holding assets (e.g., cash) on which the returns might be modest, or both. Strong finances—and a resulting lower ROE than would otherwise be the case—also may mean that a management skilled in the acquisition arena has lots of "dry powder" with which to make attractive acquisitions in the future.

Knowing the Elements of Attractive
Pricing Is Critical

For passive investors using value investing techniques, it is critical to have pricing parameters to determine whether a security is attractive enough to buy. In value investing, these parameters can differ, just as company characteristics differ. It would be hard for the case to be otherwise, especially because analysts have to make judgments in appraising management capabilities and the status of the three legs of the balanced approach: quality of resources, quantity of resources, and long-term wealth-creation power. Reasonable pricing parameters for OPMI investors can be seen as follows in selected industries:

- High-tech small-cap issues: Pay up to a 60% premium over net asset value, on the theory that this simulates pricing by a first-stage venture capitalist (e.g., the pricing for Silicon Valley Group common stock in August 1998).
- Community banks: For a well-capitalized institution, pay no more than 80% of book value (e.g., the 1995 pricing for Carver Federal Bank common stock).
- Income-producing real estate: Ignore book net asset value altogether; concentrate on appraisal values (e.g., the 1992 pricing for Forest City Enterprises class A common stock).

In value investing, credence is given to a wide scope of possible exit strategies, ranging from sale to an OPMI market to M&As to corporate liquidations.

Financial accounting is not cost accounting. Analysis of profit margins, especially among different companies, may be of only limited usefulness. This is almost always the case for securities holders, who have no access whatsoever to cost-accounting data or even long-form financials.

It frequently is easier to predict future flows by examining the quality and quantity of resources in a business rather than by extrapolating from the past earnings record. Neither tool need be used to the exclusion of the other, however.

Deal pricing is more than a function of a security's price. How much control buyers ought to be willing to pay depends a lot on how they are able to finance, the amount of promoters' and professionals' compensations that might be in the deal, and whether workouts are reasonably determinant within reasonable periods of time.

For control investors, there are many things to consider besides the all-in dollar price when contemplating an M&A, an LBO, or a hostile takeover. To summarize any contemplated transaction involves at least 11 general considerations:

- Pricing issues
- Securities law and regulation issues
- Income tax—and other tax—issues
- Other regulatory issues, such as antitrust laws, or specific agencies, such as banking regulators or the Federal Communications Commission (FCC)
- Accounting issues
- Issues concerning availability of information
- Issues concerning amount of financial commitment
- Doability issues
- Issues concerning ability to finance
- Issues concerning rate of return
- Social issues, including making deals with managements of the involved companies

Value Investors Know More Than Does the Outside Passive Minority Investor Market about Matters That Count

An important underlying assumption for value investing practitioners who are also well-financed buy-and-hold investors (i.e., not subject to margin calls and not involved in short-term risk arbitrage) is that given their investment objectives, they know much, much more than does the OPMI market about the particular investment. Indeed, active investors would never acquire a security unless they believed it to be materially mispriced by the OPMI market.

There are a number of corollaries that grow out of knowing more than the OPMI market. First, value investors never lose a night's sleep because of OPMI market prices. They know that it is an extremely rare event when an OPMI market action is more a determinant of how an investment might fare than is the bottom-up fundamental analysis of the investment situation. OPMI general market conditions were highly important in 1929, 1933, 1937, and maybe—but probably not—in 1974. In any event, market prognostications are of no importance in value investing. In the investor's lifetime, market conditions in politically stable environments in which there is no violence in the streets will be important so rarely that these macrofactors can be safely ignored.

By contrast, when you assume that the market knows more than the investor, it seems logical to worry about the market outlook, if for no other reason than that the market is sending the investor messages about value and trading.

Can anyone predict the course of OPMI markets? That is doubtful. What are market strategists good for? Comforting naive investors, not making accurate forecasts.

Earning Excess Returns Is the Norm in an Efficient Market

A market is defined as an arena in which participants reach agreements as to price and as to other terms that each participant believes are the best reasonably achievable under the circumstances. The attempt to obtain the best reasonably obtainable results is the hallmark of an efficient market. There are myriad markets, including OPMI trading markets, OPMI buy-and-hold markets, markets for control of companies, new-issue underwriting markets, markets for top management compensation, markets for the compensation of brokers and financial advisers, markets for the settlement of stockholder suits, and markets for consensual plans for companies reorganizing under Chapter 11 of the U.S. Bankruptcy Code.

Unless outside forces are going to impose disciplines that prevent excess returns from being earned, excess returns always will be earned by certain market participants as long as it is granted that markets tend toward efficiency. Indeed, excess returns have to follow as long as each participant seeks results he or she believes to be the best reasonably achievable under the circumstances. In other words, if circumstances are such that excess returns can be earned, excess returns will be earned.

Outside forces that impose disciplines in market circumstances include competitive pricing from other market participants, boards of directors, government regulators, courts, labor unions, communities, creditors, trade vendors, landlords, taxing authorities, accountants, and attorneys. In certain markets, OPMI trading markets being a prime example, competitive forces impose a severe discipline. Here, excess returns are difficult to come by and earning them consistently may well be impossible. By contrast, in certain other markets, the market for top management compensation being a prime example, earning excess returns is the norm. Here, the external force primarily responsible for imposing discipline is the company's board of directors. Board control of top management compensation runs the gamut from very weak to nonexistent. This topic is more fully discussed in Chapter 8, Promoters and Professionals' Compensations.

Control Securities Are Essentially a Different Commodity Than Outside Passive Minority Investor Securities

The simple truth is that control common stocks tend to carry inherent rights, privileges, and obligations that do not exist for OPMI common stocks. Not only does pricing in control situations tend to be markedly different than pricing in OPMI situations, but pricing ought to be different simply because the control investor tends to focus on different variables than does the OPMI, and insofar as they both use the same variables, weights tend to be markedly different. Put otherwise, whereas control common stock is identical to OPMI common stock in form, control common stock tends to be a very different instrument than OPMI common stock in substance. This topic is discussed more fully in Chapter 6, The Substantive Characteristics of Securities.

Most of the Time, Capitalization Is Not Determined by Equity Investors' Needs or Desires

Academics, and to some extent Graham and Dodd, seem to believe that the appropriate capital structure of a company whose common stock is publicly traded is governed by considerations revolving around the maximization of shareholder value. Holding such a belief about most companies' capital structures seems akin to believing that the sun revolves around the earth. Rather, for most companies, capital structure is governed by the requirements imposed by creditors, regulators, rating agencies, and, in many instances, by conventional industry standards. This topic is discussed more fully in Chapter 7, Capital Structure.

Diversification Is Nonstarter in Most Markets

It is appropriate to diversify when you are investing under conditions where you lack control, knowledge of the fundamentals of the business in which a commitment is being made, and price consciousness. Diversification, in other words, is a surrogate—usually a poor one—for control, knowledge, and price sensitivity. Broad diversification is probably appropriate for OPMIs untrained in value investing precepts but most likely inappropriate for a control investor seeking to put together an LBO.

Every Investment Has Something Wrong With It

Graham and Dodd point out in credit analysis that bond selection is a negative art; the elimination from choice for investment of bonds that have something wrong with them. In value investing, equity selection is also a negative art. For each investment, virtually the first thing done in value investing is to figure out, as best as possible, what is wrong. Because every investment has something wrong, the trick is certainly not to find perfect investments but to arrive at judgments that not enough is wrong to dissuade investing.

Equity investing always involves trade-offs. Companies with very strong financial positions (i.e., the absence of debt and the presence of large amounts of liquid assets), tend to have, during prosperous times, considerably lower returns on assets and on equity than those of comparable companies that are more aggressive in financing their asset bases and employing those assets. On the other hand, those who finance aggressively and employ assets aggressively tend to lack a margin of safety, especially if, in bad times, they have difficulty gaining access to capital markets.

Simple businesses that do not require material investments in assets and that throw off huge amounts of cash (e.g., mutual fund management companies and mobile home manufacturers) are inherently attractive, given the nature of their operations. As a trade-off, though, these are businesses marked by unusual ease of entry, so there tends to be increasing competition in these industries. An example of this is that the number of mutual funds that have come into existence since 1990. In mid-1997, around 7,000 mutual funds existed. In 1990, there were only 3100 mutual funds in existence.

Complex businesses that require massive capital investments (e.g., integrated steel companies or oil refiners), although relatively insulated from new competition, frequently fare rather poorly in down business cycles.

Finally, if a business as a business has "nothing" wrong with it, the price of its common stock might be too high. In value investing, a security's price is always an important variable. There is never any assumption that OPMI market price determines corporate value.

In value investing, there are no more important tasks than to try to figure out what is wrong and to reach judgments about whether what seems to be wrong ought to be a showstopper, precluding investment in the particular situation. Things that are wrong can include the following:

- A company with an extremely liquid financial position. Such a company may be run by an entrenched deadhead management that will never translate high-quality resources into wealth creation.
- A large ROE. Most of the time, this means a relatively small net asset value (NAV).
- A low ROE and a high NAV. This situation may mean that asset values are overstated.
- A large NAV. This can translate into a large earnings potential, large overheads, or both.

Chapter 2

Academic Finance: Efficient Market Hypothesis and Efficient Portfolio Theory

Many shall be restored that now have fallen and many shall fall that now are in honor.

—Homer

In Chapter 1, Toyoda Automatic Loom Works common stock was described, at a time when it was selling around U.S. $17 in April 1998, as safe and cheap for value investing purposes on the basis of "what is" rather than forecasts. This valuation was founded on two factors: going-concern operations were valued at 6 to 8 times latest fiscal year's operating income, and Toyoda's vast portfolio of marketable securities was valued at market prices as they existed on the Tokyo Stock Exchange. The conclusion in Chapter 1 was that Toyoda common was selling at around a 35% and 39% discount from workout values before accounting for possible taxes on unrealized appreciation.

Believers in modern capital theory (MCT) as embodied in the efficient market hypothesis (EMH) and efficient portfolio theory (EPT) never would have valued Toyoda operations and the Toyoda portfolio of marketable securities in the first place. That is not what they do. EMH and EPT analysis would have been restricted to studying historical market prices for Toyoda common and perhaps historical ratios of price to earnings or cash flow. If the discount of market price for Toyoda common relative to Toyoda net asset value (NAV), which was based largely on the market value of securities held in Toyoda's portfolio, were to be explained, the explanation would probably revolve around investor expectations. Furthermore, the discount would probably be viewed as irrelevant, not related at all to either Toyoda cash flows or the outlook for the Tokyo Stock Market. These two factors would be deemed much more likely to influence the near-term price performance of Toyoda common than would be the existence of a large discount from work-out value.

EMH and EPT probably would not be involved at all in the specific analysis of Kmart Debt—or other issues of distressed debt—in terms of details about covenants and reorganization processes. The EMH analysis would revolve around studies of the markets for distressed debt and macrostatistics about overall rates of money defaults.

As is pointed out in Chapter 1, in value investing, securities are examined from multiple points of view, including the company itself and control shareholders. By contrast, EMH looks at securities analysis solely from the point of view of outside passive minority investors (OPMIs). The key question in value investing in common stocks is: What is a business worth long term? The key question in MCT, however, is: At what price will a security trade today and tomorrow in an OPMI market?

In corporate finance, OPMIs and OPMI interests are merely the tip of a huge iceberg. To study financial phenomena by focusing on the day-to-day trading environment strictly from an OPMI point of view is akin in marine biology to studying the entire marine food chain by restricting the examination to the reactions of kelp and plankton floating on the ocean's surface. Kelp and plankton merely react; beneath the surface, there exist myriad actors, such as shark, tuna, cod, and whales. These beneath-the-surface actors in the marine food chain are similar to the groups in the financial community described in Chapter 8, Promoters' and Professionals' Compensations.

The EMH appears to be useful in describing a special case with two components:

1. The sole object of the investor is to maximize a (market) risk-adjusted total return consistently (i.e., all the time) realizable in cash by sale to the OPMI market.
2. The need to examine only a relatively few variables in analyzing a security or commodity. In the securities arena, issues analyzable by reference to only a few computer-programmable variables seem restricted to the following:
    *   Credit instruments without credit risk (e.g., U.S. treasuries)
    *   Derivative securities such as convertibles, options, and warrants. (The values for derivatives are determined by prices of other securities rather than by any analysis of the underlying values attributable to a security, such as a common stock.)
    *   Risk arbitrage securities where the workouts are short run (i.e., there are relatively determinant workouts within relatively determinant periods of time)

The basic problem with MCT is that it tries to make a general law out of what is really a very narrow special case. MCT teachings are not very helpful for value investing, where the analysis becomes relatively complicated regardless of whether the object of the analysis involves corporate control factors or buy-and-hold passive investing. Indeed, the underlying assumptions governing the EMH and EPT are either downright wrong or just plain misleading for value investing purposes. Such basic assumptions of MCT focus on 18 different beliefs:

*   Substantive consolidation is of prime importance.
*   Structural subordination is a significant factor.
*   Equilibrium pricing is universally applicable.
*   The OPMI market is the only relevant market.
*   Diversification is a necessary protection against unsystematic risk.
*   Systematic risk exists.
*   Value is determined by forecasts of discounted cash flow (DCF).
*   Companies are analyzed basically as going concerns; investors in marketable securities are analyzed as investment companies.
*   Investors are monolithic: their unitary goal is risk-adjusted total return, earned consistently.
*   Market efficiency means an absence of market participants who earn excess returns consistently or persistently.

- General laws are important.
- Risk is defined as market risk.
- Macroconsiderations are important.
- Creditor control is a nonissue.
- Transaction costs are a nonissue.
- Free markets are better than regulated markets.
- The OPMI market is better informed than any individual investor.
- Markets are efficient or at least tend toward an instantaneous efficiency.

Substantive Consolidation Is of Prime Importance

The ideas of substantive consolidation, in which the interests of the company and its stockholders are combined, and structural subordination, in which the company's *raison d'être* is to serve the best interests of its stockholders, especially its noncontrol OPMI stockholders, are central assumptions of the EMH. The substantive consolidation and structural subordination theories so important to MCT are relative rarities in the real world, though they do exist in special cases. (For example, see the 1997 annual report of Georgia-Pacific Corporation, which explains at length that company policy is to forgo returns on corporate investments if it is deemed that stockholders can use that cash more productively than can the company itself.) In MCT, though, the underlying assumption seems to be that substantive consolidation and structural subordination are universal, not special cases. These assumptions seem based, at best, on nothing more than anecdotal evidence. In any event, MCT approaches to substantive consolidation and structural subordination are not helpful concepts at all for value investing.

The terms *substantive consolidation* and *structural subordination* originated in reorganizations under Chapter 11 of the U.S. Bankruptcy Code. Substantive consolidation occurs when, for purposes of a reorganization, two separate entities are combined into one; say, for example, a solvent parent company is merged with and into an insolvent subsidiary as part of a reorganization plan. Structural subordination occurs when a senior class of claimants is made junior to a lower class of claimants even though, on the strict basis of stated creditors' rights, the senior class would normally enjoy priority over other creditors; say, for example, that because of findings of previous domination and control, secured bank debt is made the lowest class of claimant in a Chapter 11 reorganization plan.

Substantive consolidation seems to occur only occasionally in the real world, and contrary to the teachings of EMH, financial managers working for companies rarely make decisions on how to employ and redeploy corporate assets on the basis of the risk profile of the company's OPMI shareholders. The idea of net present value (NPV) revolved around discounting future cash flows estimated for a project at what Richard A. Brealey and Stewart C. Myers in *Principles of Corporate Finance* call "the opportunity cost of capital—that is, at the expected rate of return offered by securities having the same degree of risk as the project." To determine this expected rate of return, "you look at prices quoted in capital markets, where claims to future cash flows are traded…" According to MCT, if the present value of future cash flows from a project are greater than the opportunity cost of capital for OPMIs, the project ought to go ahead; if it is not, the project ought to be scuttled.

To begin with, few—if any—financial managers are in a position to figure out an opportunity cost of capital for OPMIs on the basis of factors that are fundamental to the business employing the financial manager. Efficient market theorists suggest a technical chartist approach to determining an opportunity cost of capital. Do not study a business; instead, study the relative historical volatility of OPMI stock prices and ascertain an appropriate discount rate taking into account that volatility. (This is known as the beta.)

A project's attractiveness for a company and its financial managers will be determined by factors particular to the company and its financial managers. Substantive consolidation based on looking at OPMI market price data is unlikely to enter into corporate decision making. Corporate investment decision making is instead likely to revolve around the answers to the following questions:

- Does existing management have the requisite know-how and "know-who" for the particular investment opportunities?
- Can the investment be financed attractively? With senior debt? With mezzanine junk? With common stock?
- Might the investment give the company more attractive future access to capital markets, especially equity markets?

- Does the investment help or hinder existing management in maintaining control?
- What are transaction costs, and who pays them?
- Given limited choices, might an alternative project be more attractive?
- How bad can a reasonable worst case be for the management? The company?

Net present value is a valid, extremely useful concept insofar as it compares the cost of a project with expected returns. It seems useless, however, when cost and returns are measured in a substantive consolidation context. Brealey and Myers explain on pages 73 and 74 of *Principles of Corporate Finance* that the goal of the business ought to be to make the shares "as valuable as possible" and that the company attitude ought to be that "instead of accepting a project, the firm can always give the cash to shareholders and let them invest it in financial assets." Almost no financial manager, however, will believe that watching stock prices, as is implicit in beta, is a way of making shares as valuable as possible for long-term OPMI shareholders and control shareholders. Financial managers, too, have agendas both for themselves and their companies that prevent them from just giving the cash to shareholders. For example, for most companies—even forgetting about restrictions on shareholder distributions that would be contained in loan agreements—to just give the cash to shareholders would have a negative effect on the company's continuing relationships with trade creditors and bank lenders.

As an aside, modern capital theorists seem to measure attractive finance solely by interest rates, deeming, say, a 6% margin borrowing by an OPMI stockholder as more attractive in a substantive consolidation context than a corporate issuance of 12% subordinated debentures. The real world is a lot more complex. Attractive finance includes many factors other than interest rates. In fact, you cannot analyze without looking at all the terms and conditions attaching to a borrowing. A 12% 12-year subordinated debenture with a bullet maturity may be (and probably is) much cheaper money than a margin loan bearing a current interest cost of 6%. The margin loan may, in effect, be a demand loan, with the possible negative cash flow consequences being draconian, when compared with the 12-year nonamortizing bullet loan.

Under MCT, the fruits of attractive investments by a company will be reflected immediately in an increase in OPMI market prices, if it is assumed that the market is efficient and the information is announced. As stated in *Corporation Finance,* by Stephen A. Ross, Randolph W. Westerfield, and Jeffrey E. Jaffe:

> Because information is reflected in prices immediately, investors should only expect to obtain a normal rate of return. Awareness of information when it is released does an investor no good. The price adjusts before the investor has time to trade on it (p. 363).

Although their statements seem to have validity from a minute-to-minute or day-to-day trading point of view, there is no evidence whatsoever that new information immediately effects common stock valuations from the point of view of value investing. The academic evidence is grounded in the statistical proof that no OPMI or groups of OPMIs outperform a market consistently (i.e., all the time). From a value investing point of view, this observation proves nothing outside of an immediate trading environment. No long-term fundamentalist ever tries to outperform an OPMI market consistently. Consistent outperformance is strictly the domain of short-run speculators. An underlying credo of value investing is that no one not engaged full-time in risk arbitrage can be expected to outperform a market over the short run by conscious effort.

Structural Subordination Is a Significant Factor

Value investors reject structural subordination as utterly unrealistic. As was discussed in Chapter 1, value investing holds that each constituency—short-term stockholders, long-term stockholders, control stockholders, the company itself, management, creditors, vendors, employees, customers, financial professionals, governments, communities, and so on—has both communities of interest and conflicts of interest both within itself and in conjunction with other constituencies. No one constituency is necessarily senior to others in all contexts, and no one constituency is necessarily junior to others. Myriad groups have relationships combining communities and conflicts; for example:

- Companies and management
- Management and control shareholders

- Management and OPMIs (The universality of "shark repellents" entrenching management in office is evidence of conflict.)
- Company and OPMIs (e.g., OPMIs might want dividends or share repurchase programs even though these shareholder distributions may diminish corporate feasibility)
- Trading OPMIs and buy-and-hold OPMIs
- Creditors and company and shareholders
- Senior creditor and junior creditor and preferred stocks and landlords
- Government and company
- Labor unions and company
- Workforce and labor unions
- Community and company
- Corporate value at the expense of some stockholder constituencies (e.g., undertaking an initial public offering [IPO] at an ultrahigh price disadvantages new stockholders while giving new financial strength to the company)

Tom Copeland, Tim Koller, and Jack Murrin, in their 1996 text, *Valuation: Measuring and Managing the Value of Companies,* incorrectly observe that "…shareholders are the only stakeholders of a corporation who simultaneously maximize everyone's claim in seeking to maximize their own" (p. 22). Creditors of companies where there is pressure to increase common stock dividends payable in cash would undoubtedly be very surprised to hear that their claims against the corporation are being maximized by paying out corporate cash to equity owners. Equally surprised would be managements and long-term buy-and-hold shareholders who are pressured by OPMI shareholders who want the company to maximize short-run reported earnings per share, even when this entails forgoing attractive investments in projects with a long-term pay-off or results in income tax bills that are larger than would otherwise be the case. The Copeland, Koller, and Murrin view, though, is commonly held in academic circles justifying belief in the benefits of structural subordination. Suppositions that such benefits exist to any material extent where OPMIs are the stockholders in question are based strictly on anecdotal evidence.

The MCT idea of agency costs also is not helpful in value investing. The concept of agency costs arose as a modification of structural subordination, giving grudging recognition to the observation that a corporation bears costs of management at the expense of shareholders and that as a consequence, management interests may not be aligned completely with those of shareholders. The concept of agency costs is too deficient in scope to describe adequately the real-world norm of pervasive communities of interest combined with conflicts of interest.

Structural subordination, in and of itself, is a nonstarter for value investing. Ross, Westerfield, and Jaffe incorrectly observed, in arguing that management influence may be limited vis-à-vis stockholders, that "shareholders determine the membership of the board of directors by voting. Thus, shareholders control the directors, who in turn select the management team" (*Corporation Finance,* p. 22). In the real world, perhaps 99% of the time, membership of the board of directors is actually determined by those who control the nominating process, not by stockholders voting proxies. To suppose otherwise is to elevate form completely over substance. The director nominating process also is controlled by management in the vast majority of cases.

Insofar as markets are efficient, with *efficiency* defined as each market participant trying to do as well as reasonably possible, structural subordination would exist only in that special case in which the management was a sole practitioner who owned all the outstanding equity of the business. When separate managements and separate shareholder constituencies are introduced, especially control shareholders and noncontrol shareholders, structural subordination becomes impractical for value investing purposes. Value investing operates within the context of trying to understand the diverse agendas of the important constituencies—those constituencies with clout. Entrenchment is normally very important for managements. Managements have succeeded completely in achieving a favorable environment for management entrenchment: State antitakeover laws that insulate managements in office have become virtually universal since the 1970s.

Dividend policy for many corporations will be driven, in great part, by the tax positions and liquidity needs of control shareholders. The price of the company's common stock may be a matter of indifference to a corporate management from time to time and from situation to situation. At other times, the OPMI stock price may be crucially important insofar as the company itself or key stockholders want to access the capital market by selling common stock, either newly issued or held by existing shareholders, or by using common stock owned by a key stockholder as collateral for borrowing.

None of this is to deny that many—if not most—managements feel strong communities of interest with OPMIs focused on the immediate market price of the common stock. Many managements want buoyant OPMI prices simply because they would rather have their stockholder constituencies happy, even though shareholder unhappiness would carry no downside risks for management. In virtually every case, however, these communities of interest are modified by the universal existence of conflicts of interest.

Equilibrium Pricing Is Universally Applicable

William F. Sharpe, a Nobel laureate and a typical efficient-market believer, stated in the third edition of his book *Investments* that if you assume an efficient market, "every security's price equals its investment value at all times" (p. 67). This observation could not possibly be more incorrect or more misleading for value investing purposes. For value investing, an OPMI market price, especially for a common stock, does not necessarily have any relationship to the price that ought to prevail were the security to be analyzed as issued by a company that is to be involved in mergers and acquisitions (M&As), hostile takeovers, going-private transactions, or liquidations. Not only is there no necessary relationship between prices that prevail in OPMI markets and prices that prevail in other markets (e.g., leveraged buyout [LBO] markets), but there *ought* not to be any relationship because by and large, different factors (e.g., borrowing ability versus near-term reported earnings) are used to determine value in these discrete markets, and insofar as the same factors are used (e.g., availability of control versus dividend policy), they are weighted quite differently.

There are even differences in pricing within value investing itself. Appropriate prices will differ depending on whether the value investor is involved with passive value investing, risk arbitrage, or control investing. Within control investing, pricing parameters tend to vary depending on whether the control buyer is primarily a financial buyer or a strategic buyer. Strategic buyers generally can afford to pay more.

Value investing is an offshoot of control investing. In value investing, a passive investor makes use of the same variables and phenomena in making investment decisions as does the activist, except that the passive investor is not going to have any elements of control that would permit the creation of extra value for the investor in the forms of various edges described in Chapter 1: something off the top (SOTT), such as salaries and perks; an ability to finance personal positions on an attractive basis, as with other people's money (OPM); and an ability to undertake attractive income tax planning through tax shelters (TSs). The value investor therefore ought to be a lot more price conscious than the control investor, since the latter is often in a position of being able to create excess benefits and excess returns even when overpaying, by many standards, for particular assets. Put otherwise, as far as price is concerned, control investors and OPMIs operate in different markets with different price structures.

To assume equilibrium pricing for all purposes and all markets is to put yourself in a straitjacket precluding your undertaking any analysis of most of what goes on in the financial community—M&As, IPOs, LBOs, and contests for control.

To be involved with value investing, whether as a control person or a value investor, you had best obtain detailed knowledge about fundamental factors affecting companies, about securities, about capital markets, and about government regulations and laws. Moreover, in many situations, you should also obtain elements of control over companies, over the processes companies go through, or over both or else decline to make any investment at all. For example, getting some elements of control over the reorganization process, even if only a negative veto, can be almost essential for success in Chapter 11 investing. This is in contradistinction to MCT, in which the focus is on the behavior of securities prices and markets rather than on obtaining detailed knowledge (and maybe even influence) about the companies in which you might invest.

Risk arbitrage is an investment process involving workouts of securities that are expected to create relatively determinant values in relatively determinant periods of time. One feature that tends to distinguish risk arbitrage from value investing is that although both are passive, investors would be unable to participate in risk arbitrage markets in general unless they are willing to pay up. Risk arbitrage markets tend to have pricing much more attuned to MCT-type efficiencies than do value investing markets. In value investing, a buy-and-hold strategy without determinable workouts, investors desiring to earn excess returns persistently might not be willing to pay more than 50% of what they believe the present value of the security would be in a workout or takeover. By contrast, persistent excess returns might be available for risk arbitrageurs whose pricing is equal to 90% to 95% of an estimated near-term workout value.

In MCT, there is a belief that markets are efficient, or, more accurately, that markets tend toward an instantaneous efficiency. In value investing, there is also the belief that all markets tend toward efficiency. In numerous markets, though, that tendency toward efficiency may take a long time to become effective, and there are frictions that may preclude those efficiencies from ever becoming evident. For example, investors think there are long-term tendencies that ought to result in a material shrinkage in the discount at which Toyoda Automatic Loom Works common sells from its NAV, but they do not know about how long it will take for the discount to narrow, the form it will take (Could or would Toyoda spin off into an investment company its portfolio of marketable securities?), or if it will happen at all. Here, the long-term tendency toward efficiency is quite weak. As a matter of fact, in Toyoda-type situations, the security is deemed to be attractive not because of a prediction that the market price will become efficient (i.e., reflect underlying values) but rather because at the price paid, the probabilities that excess returns will be earned over the long term with relatively little investment risk ought to be pretty good.

In simple trading situations (e.g., risk arbitrage), the tendency toward efficiency is very strong and tends very much to be instantaneous. Concerning the statement that *certain* markets tend toward instantaneous efficiency, there is no argument between value investing and MCT, but about the MCT statement that *all or most* markets tend toward instantaneous efficiency, value investors disagree.

In the EMH, the descriptive adjective is *consistently;* in value investing, it is *persistently. Persistently* means a majority of the time and on average over a long period; *consistently* means all the time. In value investing, the participant deals in probabilities, never in certainties.

In academic finance, there seems to be just one right price for a security, but in value investing, the right price can cover a wide gamut. A fair price in value investing would be defined as that price, and other terms, that would be arrived at after arm's-length negotiations between a willing buyer and a willing seller, both with knowledge of the relevant facts and neither under any compulsion to act. The one *sine qua non* that causes an OPMI stockholder to become a willing seller is a premium above OPMI market price; the one thing that causes a control buyer to become a willing buyer is a value for the control of the company that is more than the all-in price the control buyer has to pay. Often the spread between a willing seller price and a willing buyer price can be—and ought to be—huge.

Trying to gauge timing, especially about general stock market levels, seems an important consideration in MCT. In value investing, the investor does not gauge timing but rather takes advantage of whatever the market situation happens to be at that time. For MCT, timing is crucial; investors must gauge when prices might change in OPMI markets. One of the great advantages of value investing, especially for control people involved with well-financed companies, is that as activists, they tend to obtain complete control of timing in terms of deciding when to go public or when to go private. For noncontrol investors holding a portfolio of securities selected using value analysis precepts, there seems to be a strong tendency toward being indifferent to timing. If the fundamental analysis is good enough, market performance will be okay, if not for individual issues, then for portfolios consisting of five or more different issues. Put otherwise, if market performance for the portfolio is unsatisfactory, it would not be because of poor market timing but rather because the specific analyses using value investing techniques were flawed.

Special problems exist for the EMH given the concentration on OPMI market price as a universal measure of true value:

- The EMH fails to distinguish between an unrealized market loss and a permanent impairment of capital. In EMH, they are one and the same.
- The EMH fails to distinguish between a paper profit and an inability to cash in on gains for many non-OPMI activists, such as managements of companies that have just gone public via an IPO.
- The EMH fails to understand the huge population of OPMI investors whose needs are met by a contractually assured cash income from interest payments rather than from total return. For example, the vast majority of investors in tax-free bonds have a primary interest in the income generated from holding those bonds rather than in market price. Indeed, most investors in tax-free bonds hold such instruments as lockups and tend to be oblivious to what market prices might be. Tax-frees, also known as munis, are a huge market. These are bonds issued by state and local governments and their agencies. As of Sep-

tember 1998, approximately 1 trillion 430 billion dollar principal amount of munis were outstanding.

- The EMH adopts unrealistic views in such matters as employee stock options. In value investing, and according to common sense, the value of a stock option benefit to a recipient of those options clearly has no necessary relationship to the cost to the company to issue the options.
- In the EMH, there is a failure to understand that market prices self-correct over time for performing loans with contractual maturity dates.

For value investing, a given price for a security can represent both a tendency toward inefficiency in one market and a simultaneous tendency toward efficiency in another market. For example, examine the price behavior for the 437 publicly traded closed-end investment companies registered under the Investment Company Act of 1940, as amended as of December 31, 1997. These 437 issuers' assets consist by and large of only marketable securities. Most have all common stock capitalizations, their expense ratios are limited because of regulation, and many, if not most, are managed by mutual fund managers. Prices for mutual fund shares are always at least equal to NAV (as measured by the OPMI market prices of assets) or at premiums of up to 9% above NAV because of sales loads. Over 80% of the closed-end investment-trust common stocks in contrast trade at a discount from NAV and have traded at discounts consistently. This strongly demonstrates a tendency toward inefficiency in the OPMI market. If the OPMI market were efficient in all contexts, the market prices of the closed-end common stocks would equal precisely the market value of the assets of the closed-end funds, since these assets consist wholly of marketable securities just as in the case for mutual funds. This is the case for no-load mutual funds, not because of any external market efficiencies but because the mutual funds offer and redeem common shares at NAV; there are no other markets for mutual fund shares. At almost no time, however, have any of these closed-end investment-trust common stocks sold at a discount of as much as 35% below NAV. This demonstrates a tendency toward efficiency in the hostile takeover market because if shares were available at much greater discounts, hostile takeovers might make sense, even granting that it appears that every closed-end fund currently in existence has adopted significant "shark repellents" (management entrenchment devices that insulate incumbent control people).

Academic theories that OPMI prices are right, or correct, prices in nonarbitrage markets and therefore good allocators of resources revolves in part around a view that if the OPMI price is wrong, sophisticated investors who know real value will come into the OPMI market and, through their buying, make the price right or correct. Such a view ignores the fact that many, if not most, sophisticated long-term investors and insiders view untrained OPMIs trying to outperform the market consistently as a population to be exploited in going-public or going-private transactions and in providing to insiders SOTT, such as huge executive compensation packages. Such a view also misconceives what sophisticated investors do and do not do. First, they do not necessarily buy in OPMI markets. Many acquire equity positions not by buying common stocks in OPMI markets but rather by receiving, for no monetary consideration, executive stock options exercisable at the OPMI market price existing at the date the options were granted. Insiders generally want OPMI market prices to be low on the date options are granted, but most would prefer to receive options when a company is private and the exercise price of the option might be book value, rather than after the company goes public in an IPO at a price that might be 5 to 10 times book value. Most sophisticated control investors probably would never be interested in purchasing any common stock in the OPMI market at any price if that common stock did not deliver elements of control over the business. Rather, these people, and institutions, engage in control-type transactions away from the OPMI market, which gets for them promoters' compensations in the context of:

- Mergers and acquisitions
- Hostile takeovers
- Going-public
- Going-private, LBOs, MBOs
- Restructuring troubled companies
- Compensation for passive money management

In contrast to the conventional other financial disciplines, an underlying tenet of value investing is that for most purposes most of the time, many common stock prices in OPMI markets are either going to be far above liberal estimates of what corporate values would be if no OPMI market existed and that many other common stock prices in OPMI markets are going to be far below conservative estimates of the corporate values that would exist for private businesses and takeover candidates. In an active world, control people and quasicontrol people arbitrage these differences between OPMI pricing and corporate values. When very high OPMI market prices can be realized, new issues are sold to OPMIs as IPOs and, say, real estate tax shelters. In 1996, it seemed as if medical device companies that had received preliminary Food and Drug Administration (FDA) approval might receive a pre-public offering value, based on the price at which the issuer was to go public, for their equity of as much as $100 million, even though the businesses had virtually no revenues and were reporting losses. When very low OPMI prices exist (probably in combination with corporations' being reasonably well financed), existing common stock issues are acquired from OPMIs in going-private, M&A, and hostile takeover transactions (e.g., the 1990 LBO of Big V Supermarkets).

For the vast majority of firms (electric utilities used to be a notable exception), the variables used to value a business are different from those used to evaluate a common stock trading in an OPMI market. When the same variables are examined—say, the near-term earnings outlook—their importance is weighted quite differently, so there is no basis for concluding that OPMI market price is the best or even a reasonable measure of corporate value.

The Outside Passive Minority Investor Is the Only Relevant Market

For MCT, there seems to be but one relevant market: the OPMI market. In value investing, there are myriad relevant markets, including the following:

- Outside passive minority investor traders market
- Outside passive minority investor investment markets
- Markets for control of companies
- Leveraged buyout markets

- Consensual plan markets in Chapter 11 reorganizations
- Credit markets
- Initial public offering markets
- Markets for settlement of litigation

Efficient pricing in one market—the OPMI market, for example—is per se inefficient pricing in another market—the takeover market in value investing, for example. Almost any control buyer seeking to obtain control of a company whose common stock is traded in an OPMI market will have to offer a premium over the OPMI market prices if he or she is to attempt to acquire control using a cash tender offer or exchange of securities. A premium, too, probably (but not necessarily) has to be paid by a control buyer acquiring large blocks of common stock for cash in the open market or private transactions, or by a buyer using corporate proxy machinery and acquiring control through a voting, rather than direct purchasing, mechanism.

The importance of market price varies with the situation in value investing. Although market price may be all important to the OPMI holder of common stock, it tends to be far less important to the holder of control common stock or to the unlevered holder of a performing loan.

Diversification Is a Necessary Protection against Unsystematic Risk

Diversification as a hedge against unsystematic risk is a central tenet of EPT. It is part and parcel of the capital asset pricing model (CAPM). For value investing, diversification is only a surrogate—usually a poor one—for detailed knowledge about the corporation and its securities, control, and price consciousness and also, in some cases, ability to obtain attractive financing for a transaction.

Whether a value investor ought to concentrate or diversify depends on how much knowledge, control, outside (preferably nonrecourse) finance, and bargain pricing the investor can obtain. Certainly, followers of the EMH ought to diversify. The EMH is addressed to those who study securities market prices and have no detailed knowledge about corporations, to noncontrol OPMIs, and to people who utterly lack price consciousness because they assume that the OPMI market price is an equilibrium price with universal applicability. That diversification seems particularly appropriate for MCT passivists, however, does not mean that diversification is also completely inappropriate for others. Below is an investor matrix describing, in general terms, groups and individuals that should concentrate (top) to those (bottom) that should diversify.

- Business school graduate using all his or her resources—personal and financial—to start up a new business he or she will head
- A company, now in one line of business, that is undergoing an M&A
- Leveraged buyout fund
- Venture capital fund
- Investors in high-grade performing loans seeking reasonable amounts of cash income
- Knowledgeable value investors
- Knowledgeable risk arbitrageurs
- Typical OPMIs
- Investors using the teachings of MCT

Systematic Risk Exists

Part of EPT is the belief that systematic risk—common factors that will affect all companies whose common stocks are publicly traded—exists. Such factors include the business cycle, changes in market indexes, interest rates, and inflation. Systematic risk also is a nonstarter for value investing. Each of the above factors has different effects on different companies and the securities issued by those companies. A severe industrywide depression helped rather than hurt Nabors Industries in the late 1980s. Nabors, which enjoyed strong finances, was able to acquire a huge fleet of oil and gas drilling rigs on a bargain-basement basis, in great part because virtually all its competitors had questionable financial strength. Reduced market prices in the 1970s, caused by weak general markets, permitted Crown Cork and Seal to repurchase its own common stock at much more attractive prices than would have otherwise been possible. As pointed out in the previous chapter, higher interest rates ought to mean that FSA Holdings, whose principal assets are performing loans, will enjoy higher investment income than would otherwise be the case. General inflation and the increased costs associated with it probably would prevent a lot of new competitors and even existing competitors from spending the huge amounts of money it would take to become a new entrant or an expanded entity in diesel engine manufacture in order to compete with Cummins Engine. It is simply a gross oversimplification to assert that there exist common factors that would affect all American businesses. This is the tenet underlying systematic risk.

Systematic risk may in fact exist in a nonfinancial context. All corporations and all investors might fare poorly if the areas in which they are located are rife with political instability and physical violence. These have been unrealistic scenarios for industrialized countries, especially the United States, which, it is hoped, will continue to be the case.

Value Is Determined by Forecasts
of Discounted Cash Flows

For MCT, the worth of a common stock is the present value of future dividends. For value investing, by contrast, the worth of a common stock is the present value of a future cash bailout, whatever the source of the bailouts. Cash bailouts can come from the benefits of control, sale to an OPMI market, distributions to shareholders, or various conversion events, including sale of control of the business or refinancing on attractive terms.

Brealey and Myers stated in *Principles of Corporate Finance,* that "only cash flow is relevant" (p. 96). They are wrong, certainly for value investing purposes. Copeland, Koller, and Murrin stated in *Valuation—Measuring and Managing the Value of Companies,* that "the manager who is interested in maximizing share value should use discounted cash flow (DCF) analysis, not earnings per share, to make decisions" (p. 72).

The vast majority of projects that make sense create positive cash flows for a corporate owner over the life of the projects viewed as stand-alones. Very few corporations operating as going concerns, however, ever create cash flows consistently. Indeed, most are relatively consistent cash consumers that have to finance the cash deficits they create by obtaining outside capital, usually borrowings, on a regular basis. In value investing, there are four approaches to corporate valuation, which are discussed in more detail in Chapter 5, Corporate Valuation.

In any event, value investing is founded on a balanced approach. Here there is no primacy of forecasted future flows, whether cash or earnings. Rather, the interrelated elements needed to ascertain value are quality of resources in the business, quantity of resources, and long-term wealth creation power. There are four general interrelated ways to create corporate wealth using a value investing approach:

- Free cash flow from operations
- Earnings, where earnings are defined as creating wealth while consuming cash
- Resource conversion, in which you redeploy assets, change ownership or control, and finance or refinance
- Access to capital markets on a superattractive basis either for borrowing or for the issuance of equity securities

Companies Are Analyzed Basically as Going Concerns; Investors in Marketable Securities Are Analyzed as Investment Companies

For modern capital theorists, businesses are to be analyzed as strict going concerns, engaged in continuing operations, managed pretty much as they always have been managed, financed pretty much the way they always have been financed. Valuations are based on determining the present value of estimated future flows, whether cash or earnings.

For value investing, though, businesses are to be analyzed both as going concerns and resource conversion vehicles engaged in deploying assets, in redeploying assets, and in refinancing activities, including M&As. Valuations are based not only on determining cash or earnings flows but also on examining the company's separable and salable assets and gauging the company's prospects for accessing capital markets at ultra-attractive pricing.

Corporate analysis is complicated by the assumptions that no universal price equilibrium exists; that most businesses are appropriately analyzed as both going concerns engaged in day-to-day operations and resource conversion companies employing and redeploying assets and financing and refinancing liabilities; and that most businesses are likely, over time, to engage (or be engaged) in such conversion activities as M&As, hostile takeovers, and goings-private.

Once a corporation is viewed as an resource conversion complex rather than a strict going concern, then estimating future flows, whether cash or earnings, tends not to remain the sole, or principal, factor in a valuation. Rather, measuring the quality and quantity of resources existing at a particular moment becomes important.

Once it is assumed that no universal price equilibrium exists, the form of consideration paid may become much more important than the nominal value of a transaction, as measured by OPMI market prices. Which would be more valuable to a control seller, $100 million cash or $180 million market value of restricted common stock of the acquiring corporation? Besides price, in any merger or LBO transaction, the following factors will almost always be important considerations:

- Tax impact on important parties to the transaction
- Acquirer's ability to finance the transaction
- Accounting treatment, especially if the surviving company is to remain public
- Representations and warranties of each side
- Other contract terms (e.g., bust-up fees)
- Control issues as they effect corporate executives
- Probability and timing of closing the transaction
- Transaction costs
- Feasibility of the surviving corporation
- Financial incentives to insiders
- Probable impacts on OPMI market prices
- Probable reactions of the risk arbitrage community
- Minority shareholder litigation
- Government approvals

In MCT, there seem to be two principal exceptions to viewing the firm as a strict going concern. The first exception is when the value of a corporation's assets (and sometimes liabilities) can be measured by reference to OPMI market prices. Thus, in the EMH, a portfolio of performing loans will be valued at market insofar as it is deemed to be "available for sale." In this case, the future interest income potential of the portfolio is ignored. Even though assets that trade in OPMI markets are almost always marked to market under the EMH, there are exceptions when OPMI market prices are not in sync, as is the case for closed-end investment companies, which almost always trade at discounts from the OPMI market values of their portfolios.

The second exception concerns M&A accounting: whether pooling of interests or purchase accounting is appropriate. From a going-concern point of view, pooling is the appropriate method of accounting because financial results reflect the historic incomes from operations of companies that have combined. Purchase accounting, on the other hand, is a resource conversion concept that blends into the financial picture not only results from operations but also results of the price paid to acquire another going concern. If that price is ultrahigh compared with the acquired company's NAV, future income accounts will be burdened by a noncash charge for up to 40 years, amortizing goodwill.

In MCT, there does not appear to be any recognition that analysis based on a going-concern approach results in different, and often opposite, conclusions than arise out of a resource conversion approach. In value investing, this dichotomy is recognized. Both going-concern analysis and resource conversion analysis are valid. Which should be weighed more highly depends on the security being analyzed and the position of the investor undertaking the analysis.

Although noninvestment companies are evaluated, under academic finance, mostly as going concerns striving only to create cash flows from operations, investors in the securities of those concerns are evaluated on the basis of total-return concepts—flows plus valuation of portfolio holdings at market. Under MCT, however, investors are treated as the equivalent of investment companies even though many investors may have as their principal objective the creation of income from interest and dividend payments, which, of course, for analytic purposes, makes them the equivalent of going concerns.

Investors Are Monolithic: Their Unitary Goal Is Risk-Adjusted Total Return, Earned Consistently

Investors are anything but monolithic in value investing. Most will have multiple—or at least a mixture of—investment objectives:

- Cash return versus total return
- Long-term OPMI versus trading OPMI
- Control versus OPMI
- Control total return, usually including benefits in the forms of SOTT and access to attractive financing

Successful value investors as part of their analysis, understand other relevant points of view: those of long-term buy-and-hold OPMIs, trading OPMIs, the corporation itself, managements, control shareholders, governments, vendors, lenders, employees, investment bankers, accountants, and local communities. They know it is important to figure out who has the clout and what has to be done to satisfy the clout as part of the process of earning excess returns.

Investors and investment advisers concentrating on asset allocation and diversification seem per se to be speculators who start out with the following assumptions:

- Outside passive minority investor price is an equilibrium price.
- Outside passive minority investor prices will change as conditions change; therefore, focus on buying what is popular, when it is popular or likely to get popular.
- Do not obtain much knowledge of the specific company or the securities it issues.
- Be nervous.

Asset allocaters who believe in academic finance allocate investments in equity portfolios by concentrating on outlooks for particular industries and on outlooks for specific geographic locations; the better the near-term outlook, the more funds are allocated in that direction. In value investing on the other hand, asset allocation is price driven rather than near-term outlook driven; the cheaper an equity appears to be, on the basis of the three-pronged balanced approach, the greater the proportion of funds invested there.

Market Efficiency Means an Absence of Market Participants Who Earn Excess Returns Consistently or Persistently

Modern capital theory's underlying assumption that market efficiency means no consistent or persistent returns for any one participant has no basis in reality, except for OPMIs who analyze and invest using MCT precepts. Indeed, control investing is about getting something out of being involved with securities over and above the rights and privileges that flow from being the passive owner of a common stock, a fee interest in real estate, a preferred stock, a loan, a trade receivable, or a leasehold interest. How that something extra is obtained in corporate America and in the financial community is a subject worthy of systematic study and is examined in Chapter 8, Promoters' and Professionals' Compensations.

The only rational definition of efficiency for markets in which little or no discipline is imposed by external forces is that excess returns have to be earned persistently and even consistently in that market and that abuses will surface.

It can be theorized that no excess returns are ever earned in any market in which an asset value is marked to market. Earnings here determine the market value, so anytime earnings increase, market value increases correspondingly. Thus, no excess returns are earned, at least as a percentage of the market value of the earnings attributable to those assets. This may not be a useful concept, however, when assets that give rise to the excess returns are not marketable (e.g., top management salaries arising out of management control of proxy machinery, plus charter and bylaws full of "shark repellents" entrenching management in office). For value investing, it is equally relevant to measure excess returns both by examining returns as a percentage of cost or by depreciated cost, and also by examining returns as a percentage of market value. Weighting assigned to cost or market is dictated by specific circumstances.

For MCT, efficiency means that all information affects an OPMI market price, so that no participant in an OPMI market earns excess returns consistently. For value investing, efficiency means that there are not only OPMI trading markets in which MCT-type efficiency exists but also myriad markets in which little or no external disciplines are imposed, so that excess returns are earned by participants in those markets persistently. Indeed, in these markets with little or no imposed external disciplines, if excess returns were not earned persistently, those markets, under value investing, would be inefficient.

Activists seeking to earn excess returns persistently ought to seek out those fields in which external disciplines are weak or absent. The following forces are supposed to impose disciplines that in turn impose curbs on market participants' earning excess returns:

- Competitive markets
- Boards of directors
- Customers
- Vendors
- Labor unions
- Communities
- Social and religious consciousness

The following markets seem to be the least disciplined areas in United States today:

- Top management compensations
- Plaintiffs attorneys
- Investment bankers
- Bankruptcy professionals
- Leveraged buyout packagers and promoters
- Mutual fund management companies
- Hedge fund operators
- Market makers on NASDAQ (National Association of Securities Dealers Automated Quotations)
- New York Stock Exchange (NYSE) specialists

There are problems with U.S. financial markets, albeit they appear to be far and away the best that have ever existed. Here are a few of the problem areas:

- Promoters' compensation seems far too high under the U.S. financial system.
- Debtors, especially debtor managements, get too much entrenchment, protection, and compensation when restructuring public companies either out of court or in a Chapter 11 case.
- Initial public offerings tend to be grossly overpriced for their actual business value.
- Overwhelming institutional pressures exist to give resources to issuers able to deliver large gross spreads to the financial community, the merits of a particular issue notwithstanding.
- Regulation of trading markets is onerous.
- Investment company regulation is particularly onerous.

- The tax code is a nightmare, albeit administratively highly efficient compared with other economies. The code's sheer complexity is a burdensome problem, but the Internal Revenue Service (IRS) code must be complex to produce one final result: what the tax bill will be. Other measurement systems, especially GAAP, do not have to be complex. GAAP do not give final results; rather, they are only objective benchmarks that analysts use as one tool to determine approximate values and aid in examining alternative courses of action. From a taxpayer's point of view, a taxable event has three elements: (1) What is the tax rate? (2) Does the taxpayer control timing as to when the tax might become payable? (3) Does the event that gives rise to the tax also create the cash with which to pay the tax?

General Laws Are Important

Modern Capital Theory and indeed economics in general place primary emphasis on promulgating general laws. Although other, more mature social sciences, such as law and psychology, admit to the importance of general laws, they focus instead on individual differences that exist on a case-by-case basis. Value investing does promulgate general laws, but they have important exceptions. A first example is this: As a general law in value investing, quarterly earnings reports are unimportant; however, reported earnings for a quarter may be paramount to companies seeking to issue common stock in a public offering or in a merger transaction. A second example concerns price: In value investing, the general law is to try to buy bargains; that is, do not pay more than 50% to 60% of what you believe the security would be worth were the business a private entity or a takeover candidate. The exception is that you ought to be prepared to pay up (i.e., have a different pricing standard) if you are involved with risk arbitrage. Here, the 50% to 60% guideline might become 90% to 95%.

To the user, the ultimate value of a value investing approach compared with the value of academic finance depends on how realistic and useful the various assumptions are. Depending on context—say, day trading compared with a passive buy-and-hold strategy—each approach has validity. For day trading, a MCT approach seems a lot more useful than a value investing approach; for a passive buy-and-hold strategy, value investing seems more useful than MCT. Obviously, this book is based on the belief that for most participants in most investment processes most of the time, value investing is more valid and useful than is academic finance. Furthermore, it strongly supports the belief that value investing ought to be the context of choice from a public policy point of view when promulgating securities law and regulation, when deciding lawsuits involving valuation and disclosure issues, and when promulgating accounting principles in accordance with GAAP.

In any specific value investing analysis, the individual differences become much more important than the general laws. Thus, this book refers to "most of the time," not "all of the time." For example, in the management of corporate affairs, it is most productive most of the time to take actions based on management's beliefs about the long-term consequences of those actions; in most cases, this would entail ignoring near-term considerations insofar as those factors detract from creating cash flows or long-term corporate values. If the corporation needs to finance by seeking outside equity capital, however near-term considerations might have to dominate. Specifically, most of the time, corporate managers ought to manage so as to increase cash flows and basic corporate wealth even if this means sacrificing current earnings per share as well as reported earnings per share for the quarterly periods immediately ahead. If the corporation or its insiders need to raise equity capital in the short term though—say, over the next 12 months—it might be better to manage to increase earnings per share and to do things Wall Street analysts like, such as having the company operate as a "pure play" in an industry rather than be diversified. The risk of not being short-run conscious here seems to be not so much the prices at which issues of equity securities might be marketed by corporations or insiders but whether such issues can be sold at all.

In addition, in value investing, what you think of underlying factors tends to be more important than what you think other people think most of the time. What other people think—the conventional OPMI market wisdom—does tend, however, to become of critical importance to such activists as issuers and promoters when they seek access to outside capital markets, especially equity markets. Seeking such access tends to be an irregular, occasional event for most companies, rather than a continuous process, except for certain types of issuers—which now seem to be a minority of issuers—such as electric utilities, growing finance companies, and many real estate investment trusts (REITs).

Trade-offs are tricky in the value investing scheme of things. In a simple world, it might be said that superpricing for IPOs results in a misallocation of resources because it results in overinvestment in growth companies in hot industries and underinvestment in other parts of the economy. Perhaps this is so, but it seems obvious that the superpricing available for IPOs has in effect created a rather dynamic venture capital industry in the United States. During recent years, such investments, possibly in combination with an increased supply of technically competent people freed up because of defense cutbacks, seem to have made this country the premier economy for innovation and start-ups associated with such high-tech areas as digital communications and biotechnology. Certainly, the IPO phenomenon has made many of these high-tech companies real businesses because as a result of the going-public process, they have become extremely well financed. Also, the popularity of IPOs has resulted in dedicated managements. Most IPOs raise money only for the company. For insiders to realize a cash bailout after an IPO, the business generally has to prosper. Initially, all an IPO at $10 per share does for insiders who acquired common stock at 2¢ a share is give them cocktail party points in discussing their net worth. To convert that paper net worth to a meaningful realization probably requires in most cases that the underlying business actually prosper.

For most existing public companies, the sale of new issues of common stock has tended to be a marginal undertaking in terms of amounts of funds raised as compared with seeking other sources of outside capital in various credit markets, ranging from bank loans to other institutional borrowings to public debt offerings. Selling new issues of common stock is quite important, however, in that equity funds provide a borrowing base permitting more senior borrowings on more favorable terms for an issuer than would otherwise be the case. Probably most important, most activist managers properly believe that OPMI markets are capricious in terms of (1) pricing at any given time versus business value and (2) the availability of OPMI markets as a source of new equity capital on a reliable basis. Most of the new equity capital for businesses is therefore derived from retained earnings rather than the sale of newly issued common stock. In doing so, most active managers focus properly first on the needs of the business, both aggressive and defensive, and only second on the needs or desires of OPMIs. There is no substantive consolidation.

Risk Is Defined as Market Risk

For MCT, *risk* means market risk—what will happen to the price of a security—but for value investing, *risk* means investment risk most of the time—what will happen within the business and to the terms of the securities it has issued without regard to the market price of those securities. Value investors basically calculate risk by measuring what can go wrong with the business against the price paid for a buy-and-hold security. For passive investors acquiring securities using value investing precepts, there are four steps in the analysis of a security, shown below in descending order of importance:

1. Compare price with private business or takeover value.
2. Consider what can reasonably be expected to go wrong with the business from an investment—as distinct from a market—point of view.
3. Speculate on what reasonable exit strategies might exist 3, 5, or 7 years in the future.
4. Factor in general stock market considerations.

For most analysts most of the time, steps 1, 2, and 3 will be so important that step 4 can be ignored completely.

Macroconsiderations Are Important

Given the political stability that prevails in the United States and most of the industrial world, it is rare indeed in value investing that macroconsiderations become important in analyzing and investing in the deal. Macroconsiderations were probably important in 1929, 1933, 1937, and perhaps 1974. Draconian macroevents are so infrequent that the value investing disciple can safely ignore them. Another reason to ignore them is because no one seems to be able to forecast them.

In academic finance, it is believed that such macrofactors as the level of interest rates, the level of various stock indices, gross domestic product (GDP), employment data, and inflation, indices are virtually always extremely important inputs into most valuation processes. For value investing, individual business performance has always been more important in determining securities price performance on either a buy-and-hold or a control basis than have been macrofactors, except in maybe the aforementioned specific years.

In considering general conditions in value investing, it is apparent that since World War II, industrywide depressions have occurred with amazing persistency. The difference between now and the 1930s, though, is that now there is little or no domino effect from these depressions. Between 1973 and 1998, almost every U.S. industry went through depressions as severe as anything experienced by the particular industry during the 1930s, even though the U.S. economy was generally prosperous. These severe depressions affected, among others, the automobile industry, aluminum, steel, machine tools, energy, banking, real estate, savings and loans, row crops, airlines, water transportation, retail trade, and nuclear-dependent electric utilities. When this book was written in mid-1998, equipment suppliers to the semiconductor industry were in as bad a depression as they have ever experienced. Typically, many of the publicly traded common stocks of companies in depressed industries become ultracheap, as measured by both the quality and quantity of business resources, even as they appear quite expensive measured by price to current earnings and price to earnings forecast for the period just ahead.

Creditor Control Is a Nonissue

In MCT, the appropriate capitalization seems to be driven by OPMI needs and desires, whereas in value investing, it is driven by needs of the company, bailout of the clout, or both. Capitalization is discussed more fully in Chapter 7, Capital Structure.

Most corporations borrow money. They will be governed very much in what they do about shareholder distributions because of what their contractual agreements are with lenders as well as their probable sensitivity to lenders' needs and desires. Such lenders are both financial institutions and providers of trade credit. Also increasingly affecting shareholder distributions in recent years has been the emergence of mutual funds and individuals holding high-yield junior corporate debt and preferred stock.

Transaction Costs Are a Nonissue

In academic finance, transaction costs seem to be all but ignored except for bankruptcy costs. For value investing, there are virtually no financial transactions in any arena with which Wall Street is involved—except maybe discount brokerage (and that is doubtful)—that do not involve huge transaction costs. For certain participants in financial processes, huge transaction costs mean huge transaction incomes, even after overhead.

Free Markets Are Better than Regulated Markets

Lots of people—maybe most—would deny that resource allocation is the primary justification for the existence of the investment processes. Most would probably say that the primary purpose for the existence of the financial community is to provide investor protection, especially for holders of OPMI common stock. They seem to reason that if such investor protection were provided, it would, *a priori*, result in efficient resource allocation. This book does not agree with this view. It cannot be assumed that efficient asset allocation will result if investment decisions are made by the investing equivalent of kelp and plankton of the marine food chain—uneducated passive reactors whose goal in investing is to outperform a market consistently.

The most important things to realize about any financial system in any economy is that it is going to be replete with elements of inefficiency, misallocation of resources, frictions, and basic unfairness and that there will always be trade-offs. For example, it is a *summum bonum* for an economy to operate in an environment with high levels of integrity for securities trading markets, but overwhelming evidence indicates such integrity cannot be attained without onerous regulation, which obviously has counterproductive elements. The high degree of regulation of trading on the floor of the NYSE is but one example of this. As far as can be seen, the U.S. financial system's allocation of resources is good enough, even if it is acknowledged that from a long-term company-oriented point of view, OPMI markets grossly misprice a very large number—probably a majority—of common stocks.

Nonetheless, a historical focus on investor protection has had tremendous secondary benefits for all U.S. capital markets:

- The integrity of U.S. trading markets is superb.
- The U.S. public disclosure system is superb.
- Oversight of fiduciaries and quasifiduciaries is pretty good.
- Senior credit markets, both public and private, tend to be pretty efficient, partly because corporate disclosures, especially audits, have become so good.

Conversely, the focus on investor protection (i.e., OPMI protection) has also had unfortunate consequences in the United States:

- Generally accepted accounting principles have been bastardized. They are used to seek truth in reported earnings rather than to provide knowledgeable investors with objective benchmarks to be used as essential tools of analysis.
- Crazy legal theories, have proliferated, exemplified by fraud-on-the-market lawsuits, which postulate that plunges in OPMI market prices are evidence of insider fraud because the common stock never would have achieved high prices in efficient markets in the first place if insiders had made full disclosures.
- Stockholder litigation, driven by attorneys' fees rather than merits, has become commonplace.
- Many corporate managements and activists have become far more oriented toward short-run results than is really productive for the economy.
- For issuers that need access to capital markets, there tends to be a primacy of reported earnings; that is, what the numbers *are* becomes more important than what the numbers *mean*, especially short term.

Efficient-market theories, based on a view that the constituency to be served is the short-run–conscious, unsophisticated OPMI, have caused numerous problems. They were the proximate cause of the derivatives debacle of 1987 because of the failure to distinguish between credit risk and other risks. Also, they fostered an environment in which OPMIs do not believe they have to know anything.

There are three principal roles of the Securities and Exchange Commission (SEC) and these involve some conflicts with free markets. If the Securities and Exchange Commission did not foster regulation in these areas, the climate for OPMI investment might be as poor as it seems to be in most emerging markets. These roles are:

- To provide fair and orderly trading markets
- To provide disclosures to investors
- To exercise oversight over fiduciaries and quasifiduciaries

The Outside Passive Minority Investor Market Is Better Informed than Any Individual Investor

Value investing is useless unless practitioners assume that for their purposes, they are better informed than the OPMI market. This is not an unrealistic assumption, since most passive value investors are long-term buy-and-hold investors. Short-run market considerations, the lifeblood of the EMH, are unimportant in value investing. It is not that the value analyst has access to superior information vis-à-vis the OPMI market but rather that the value analyst uses the available information in a superior manner.

Markets Are Efficient or at Least Tend Toward an Instantaneous Efficiency

Efficient markets are a fundamental precept of the EMH. In value investing, all markets tend toward efficiency. Occasionally, there are markets, like the OPMI trading market, that tend strongly toward instantaneous efficiency. Insofar as a market is characterized by instantaneous efficiency, there is no argument between value investing and academic finance, but most markets do not seem close to obtaining instantaneous efficiency most of the time. Because this is so, there is actually a wide chasm between MCT and value investing even granting a universal tendency toward efficiency in all markets. In many markets (e.g., mutual fund management fees or top management compensation in many public companies), the tendency toward efficiency seems so weak that it might be realistic to ignore it.

Chapter 3

Graham and Dodd Fundamentalism

The race is not always to the swiftest nor the battle to the strong—but that is the way to lay your dough.

—Damon Runyan

Benjamin Graham and David Dodd would have appreciated and understood Toyoda Automatic Loom Works common. It would be one of their recommended net-nets, a security trading at prices below the market value of Toyoda's current assets, including marketable securities, after deducting all liabilities. Unlike value investors, though, Graham and Dodd would have thought of Toyoda common as an aberration in an international market in which the vast majority of concerns have to be appraised as strict going concerns rather than businesses with realistic resource conversion prospects. Further, Graham and Dodd, in assessing Toyoda common, probably would have had important concerns about the outlook for the Japanese economy and prices on the Tokyo Stock Exchange (TSE), factors ignored in value investing.

Graham and Dodd's credit analyses would not cover any appraisal of Kmart debt, or the debt of other distressed issuers. A Graham and Dodd analysis of fixed-income securities is by and large limited to appraisals of the probabilities of money defaults on instruments that trade at or close to their principal amounts.

Graham and Dodd were prolific writers. The first edition of *Security Analyis, Principles and Technique* was published in 1934. The fourth edition was published in 1962. Graham authored *The Intelligent Investor,* the fifth edition of which was published in 1973. New authors, somewhat enamored of the efficient market hypothesis (EMH) put together *Graham and Dodd's Security Analysis* in 1988.

A few other current authors, such as Seth Klarman in *Margin of Safety,* published in 1991, have adopted Graham and Dodd principles, but over 90% of the financial literature published since the 1970s focuses strictly on modern capital theory (MCT) in general and the EMH in particular. Nonetheless, Graham and Dodd are widely seen as having produced the bible of fundamental analysis. The funny thing about Graham and Dodd literature, though, is that very few people seem to have actually read it.

The Graham and Dodd approach has a number of things in common with value investing. Both disciplines focus on long-term fundamentals and reject all technical chartist approaches, whether promulgated by practitioners or academics involved with efficient markets and efficient portfolios. Both Graham and Dodd and value investing have long-term investment strategies and ignore trading strategies. Both approaches reject heavy emphasis on short-run operating results in analyzing companies; when it comes to financial accounting, both believe that what the numbers mean tends to be far more important than what the numbers are reported to be most of the time. Perhaps most important, Graham and Dodd and value investing are both highly price conscious. In both, if you buy at a low enough price, the probabilities for long-term success favor the investor. Graham and Dodd theory calls this consciousness of a low price the margin of safety. Value investing adopts price consciousness, too, but adds an emphasis on the quality of resources existing in a company.

Despite these similarities, value investing is quite different from Graham and Dodd's fundamental analysis. Graham and Dodd, purely and simply, are analyzing from the point of view of a minority holder of marketable securities seeking high dividends, capital appreciation, and an exit strategy that visualizes sales only to other minority investors in the open market. Value investing essentially conducts analyses from multiple points of view, including not only outside passive minority investors (OPMIs) but also the company itself, senior creditors, and control shareholders, present and potential. Value investing posits a variety of possible exits: sales in the open market to other minority investors, and resource conversion activities, including mergers and acquisitions (M&As), liquidations, massive refinancings, and spin-offs. The four basic areas of difference between the Graham and Dodd approach and value investing are as follows:

- The Graham and Dodd objective is to estimate prices at which securities will sell in markets populated by OPMIs, whereas value investing focuses on what a business could be worth as a private entity or takeover candidate. Graham and Dodd attempts to guard against market risk. Modern value analysis attempts to guard against investment risk and ignores market risk rather completely.

- A Graham and Dodd credit analysis of debt instruments is involved solely with estimating the probabilities of money defaults, whereas a value investing credit analysis of debt instruments is based on estimating what values are likely to be realized by a creditor in a reorganization or liquidation, assuming that a money default does occur.

- Graham and Dodd view macrofactors (e.g., economic forecasts, earnings estimates for Standard & Poor's 500 [S&P 500] or other broad indices, sector and industry earnings forecasts) as crucial to the analysis of a corporate security. Value investors, however, believe that such macrofactors are irrelevant.

- In common stock analysis, Graham and Dodd subscribe to a primacy of the income account theory: Analysis starts with an examination of the past earnings record, and future returns to stockholders will be measured in part by future operating performance and in part (at least in the older editions of *Security Analysis*) by having acquired a security at a price below "central value," where central value is essentially a function of general stock market statistics. For value investing, there is no primacy of anything as a general rule. The balanced approach of using value investing with common stocks requires that consideration be given to the quality and quantity of resources existing in a business at the time of analysis, and also that future returns to stockholders be measured in part by any number of possible scenarios, including future operating performance, M&As, refinancings on ultra-attractive terms, spin-offs, divestitures, and going-privates, and in part by having acquired a security at a price below a private business or takeover value.

Market Risk versus Investment Risk

On pages 440 and 441 of the 1988 edition of *Graham and Dodds Security Analysis* there is this remarkable statement:

> Clearly, the bond contract is inherently unattractive. In exchange for limited rights to share in future earning power, the bondholder obtains a prior claim on cash generated by the borrower and a definite promise of repayment at a stated date. Profitable growth will bring confidence to the investor but no material increase in return. The deterioration of profitability, however, will bring both anxiety and a downward market valuation of the issue.

Why would a downward deterioration in profitability not bring even greater anxiety and even greater downward market valuation to the holders of that company's common stock issue? As a matter of fact, if the bond is adequately secured or otherwise well covenanted, no money defaults might occur, and bondholders would feel no anxiety about holding regardless of market price. Sophisticated bondholders would probably conclude that they were incapable of predicting bond prices in OPMI markets for lower-rated issues to begin with; most people involved with value investing would certainly so conclude.

Graham and Dodd were probably right that there is a large amount of OPMI market risk in holding the bonds of debtors experiencing deteriorating profitability. It seems obvious, however, that great investment opportunities are created when market risk is ignored and investment risk is examined and guarded against. Assuming good covenant protections, is the bond form not inherently attractive when purchases occur after a downward market valuation caused by anxiety and a deterioration in profitability? Were investors unwilling to ignore market risk, they would miss opportunities to acquire debt instruments that seem utterly devoid of investment risk (e.g., the Kmart Debentures opportunity in 1995, disussed in Chapter 14, Restructuring Troubled Companies). The investment analysis of Kmart Debentures revolved around the fact that it would have been utterly unreasonable to conclude that these issues were being acquired at prices that represented a market bottom or even anything close to a market bottom, because the OPMI consensus, which could have proved right, was that the near-term outlooks were horrible and that Kmart, as an operation, was in deep trouble.

Credit Analysis

Graham and Dodd stated, on page 310 of the 1962 edition of *Security Analysis*, that "safety is measured not by specific lien or other contractual rights, but by the ability of the issuer to meet all its obligations," a valid statement if one is focused on market risk rather than investment risk. On page 313, they went on to say that "the theoretically correct procedure for bond investment, therefore, is first to select a company meeting every test of strength and soundness, and then to purchase its highest-yielding obligation, which would usually mean its junior rather than its first-lien bonds." In value investing, there might be some merit to buying the junior issue only if the analyst were in a position to determine that a creditworthy company would continue to remain creditworthy until after the bond owned matured. Almost no one is that good at predicting future corporate outlooks. Moreover, many—if not most—companies issue junior debt and preferred obligations (i.e., mezzanine securities) because of senior lender requirements that the businesses have expanded borrowing bases. Put otherwise, if these companies were so creditworthy to begin with, they might never have issued mezzanine securities in the first place.

Value investors involved in credit analysis are covenant driven, the exact opposite of Graham and Dodd investors. From 1992 to 1997, Eljer Industries Secured Bank Debt represented a good example of the importance of covenants. Eljer Bank Debt was a performing loan secured by virtually all the assets of Eljer and its subsidiaries. A principal subsidiary of Eljer, U.S. Brass, had filed for Chapter 11 relief, however, and it remained theoretically possible that a huge amount of product liability claims would be perfected against Eljer. If so, those claims would become unsecured obligations, junior to Eljer Bank Debt. Overall coverage for Eljer obligations could have become quite weak; furthermore, there might even have been some market risk in holding Eljer Bank Debt. Given its senior secured position, however, it was hard to figure out how the Eljer Bank Debt would not be made whole, no matter what course the subsidiary's Chapter 11 took.

Macrofactors

Benjamin Graham was very involved with macrofactors. In *The Intelligent Investor*, he wrote:

Prudence suggests that he [the investor] have an adequate idea of stock market history, in terms particularly of the major fluctuations in its price level and the varying relationships between stock prices as a whole and their earnings and dividends. With this background he may be in a position to form some worthwhile judgment of the attractiveness or dangers of the level of the market as it presents itself at different times (p. 26).

To some extent, it appears that Graham and Dodd believed that general market considerations deserved more weight than bottom-up fundamental analysis, a view that is anathema for value investing in part because bargain prices for well-financed companies seem to make them M&A or going-private candidates, a possibility that Graham and Dodd tended to ignore.

We shall conclude with a practical observation that is based on experience rather than theory. When the general market is high there are always a number of individual issues that appear definitely undervalued by objective standards and consequently even more attractive in contrast to the inflated level of other stocks. The analyst may be tempted to recommend these as unusual opportunities. Not only may the "neglected security" continue neglected for the remainder of the bull market, but when the downturn comes it is likely to decline in price along with the general market and to fully as great an extent. In a word, beware of "bargains" when most stocks seem very high (*Security Analysis, Principles and Technique,* 1962, p. 44).

This view makes sense when the purpose of an analysis is to estimate what OPMI market prices will be in the period just ahead. It makes no sense, though, when the purpose is to estimate what the underlying values of that business might be and what the corporate dynamics might be for that business going forward.

Value investors believe that at least for the U.S. economy, spending a lot of time on macrofactors, whether for the overall economy or for securities markets (e.g., the S&P 500), is not only a waste of time but also a refuge for incompetents who are uniformed about any aspects of corporate analysis but can sound intelligent by making predictions about unpredictable things.

One reason—but far from the only one—that value investors do not factor into their investment decisions any views about general economic outlooks, stock market outlooks, or about interest rate outlooks is that almost no one is any good at making such predictions. Furthermore, buy-and-hold value investors should be prepared to average down as long as the company invested in continues to appear solid. The appearance of solidity is a function of corporate analysis, not market prices; it entails an examination of the quality and quantity of resources in a business. Since investors are likely to hold the securities of good companies over their business cycles and will rarely if ever buy at or near a market low, why should they be hung up today on attempting to gauge for the next 2 years' levels of inflation, the S&P 500, the outlook for Asia and Russia, and interest rates?

From a value investing point of view, securities bargains are created much more by past corporate prosperity than by bear markets. Value is a dynamic concept, ever changing and, if you are putting the right issues in a common stock portfolio, ever increasing. For example, Capital South-west, Zygo, Raymond James Financial, St. Jude Medical, and MBIA, Inc. became far more valuable properties in 1998 because of their corporate achievements than they were in the early 1990s. Assuming that each of those companies had very disappointing operations in 1999 and 2000, each would still remain far more valuable than it was in earlier years.

Value investing is based in part on the fact that there has been a fundamental change in the business cycle since the end of World War II, as was pointed out in Chapter 2 under the heading Macroconsiderations. The best stance for OPMIs following value investing precepts is that because investors will do okay as long as the United States (or wherever investing is done) enjoys political stability and an absence of physical violence in the streets, doing okay means putting the probabilities on your side despite the fact that a number of investments will be losers.

At the time this book was written the Dow Jones Industrial Average™ is hovering at an all-time record high of 9,000. Are there common stocks of well-financed companies selling at bargain-basement prices? Most likely. Two areas in which common stocks seem depressed are Japanese companies (the TSE average has plummeted to around 14,000 from 40,000 in the early 1990s) and U.S. based semiconductor equipment manufacturers, a cyclically depressed industry.

Microfactors

The underlying Graham and Dodd assumption about microfactors is that a company ought to be viewed as a stand-alone going concern that will continue to operate in the future in the same industry as it has in the past. The rewards to the holders of common stock will come from the sale in a public marketplace of the common shares of a business that has increased its earning power and distributable income. When the common stock is acquired at prices below a "central" value, a greater profit is realized. Against this stand-alone going-concern background, it is thoroughly understandable that Graham and Dodd adopted the position that the past earnings record is the starting point for the analysis of an equity security.

> The concept of earning power has a definite and important place in investment theory. It combines a history of actual earnings performance over a period of years with a reasonable expectation that the past level or trend will be approximated unless extraordinary conditions supervene. This performance may be measured in terms of either (1) the earnings per share of common stock or (2) the rate of return earned on the common stock equity (*Security Analysis, Principles and Technique,* 1962, p. 468).

The purpose of a Graham and Dodd fundamental analysis is to judge what future prices are likely to be in an OPMI trading market. At any time, and for most issues, Graham and Dodd correctly observed that for the stand-alone going concern, the market price of its common stock is likely to be influenced much more by current earnings than by current book value. For Graham and Dodd, earnings were far more important than book values for publicly traded common stocks.

> The basic fact is that—except in certain limited parts of the common stock universe—asset values are virtually ignored in the stock market. Not only that; there is a sense in which tangible asset values are a negative factor in the company's exhibit. For, given any amount of earnings, the larger the net worth, the lower the profitability or percent earned on capital; hence the less favorable the showing. There is a temptation to accept this verdict of the market place and to confine our treatment of the asset factor to the exceptional cases or the special areas in which the net worth can be clearly shown to exert an influence on average price.... Analysts ... should understand all the implications of this widespread ignoring of the asset factor. Most of all they should reflect fully on the rather startling truth that as long as a business remains a private corporation or partnership the net asset value appearing on the balance sheet is likely to constitute the point of departure for determining what the enterprise is

"worth." But once it makes its appearance as a "publicly held company" ... the net-worth figure seems to lose virtually all its significance. "Value" then becomes dependent almost exclusively on expected earnings.... Viewing the picture broadly, we shall find that in the majority of companies taken at any one time the net-worth figure properly plays so small a part as to warrant our excluding it in the process of valuation (*Security Analysis, Principles and Technique*, 1962, pp. 551–552).

The value investing approach turns Graham and Dodd on its head. Value investors do not think of the companies in which they invest as merely stand-alone going concerns. Given any 3- to 5-year period, it seems likely that for most companies, to use Graham and Dodd language, "extraordinary conditions are bound to supervene" (*Security Analysis, Principles and Technique*, 1962, p. 468). These extraordinary conditions, or conversion events, encompass M&As, hostile takeovers, massive refinancings, divestitures, spin-offs, accessing public or private markets at ultra-attractive prices, and going-privates. The evidence indicates that few if any companies remain stand-alone going concerns for protracted periods; electric utilities used to be able to do so, but such no longer appears to be the case.

Against this background, it is understandable that many practioners of value investing would focus at least as much attention on the quality and quantity of resources in a business (a balance sheet approach) as they do on the earnings record (an income account approach). In value investing, it is assumed that all businesses ought to be appraised not only as going-concerns but also as private business or takeover candidates, or as companies bound to engage in other resource conversion activities when balance sheet considerations become important. Historically, this seems to have been the case for most companies. The Graham and Dodd approach appraises managements as operators of going concerns; the value investing approach appraises managements not only as operators of going concerns but also as investors engaged in employing and redeploying assets and financing and in refinancing these activities.

For forecasting earnings and cash flows in general, the past earnings record is far from the best or only tool for such forecasts. In value investing, the quality and quantity of resources existing in a business is also an essential forecasting tool. Both the past earnings record and present resources are used in value investing to forecast future operating results.

In value investing, there are always multiple exit strategies, not just sale to OPMI markets for bailouts of common stock investments: There are premium prices from such future conversion events as mergers, spin-offs, divestitures, recapitalizations, and share repurchases, including leveraged buyouts (LBOs) accomplished through cash tender offers, exchange offers, or merger transactions. If such resource conversion events are to be considered a long-term norm, it seems logical that value investing should, again, emphasize at least equally the quality and quantity of resources in a business rather than focus on the primacy of the income account.

Graham and Dodd theory does not ignore asset values, and value investing does not ignore earnings or the earnings record. The relative weights assigned to earnings and assets in an analysis, however, are usually quite different between Graham and Dodd theory and value investing. In practical terms, the microfactors Graham and Dodd concentrates on in most security analyses are:

- Earnings
- Trend of earnings
- Dividends
- Industry identification
- Return on equity
- Comparative analysis versus other industry participants

The microfactors to concentrate on in value investing seem similar to those on which LBO promoters concentrate:

- Ability to finance
- Long-term outlook
- Exit strategies:
    1. Future sale to OPMI market
    2. Refinancing
    3. Acquisition by another entity

Value investing OPMIs are of course in a different position than LBO buyers, who can use corporate assets to help finance their purchase of control. OPMIs get no control benefits from their passive investments and really cannot precipitate changes in returns on corporate assets by causing them to be used smarter or more aggressively. Good value investing OPMIs try to compensate for this by buying much more safely and cheaply than would be the case for an LBO. In virtually every case, the common stocks of companies in which value investing OPMIs invest ought to have extremely strong financial positions, and OPMIs should, at the time of purchase, try to pay no more than 50% to 60% of the price they think would be paid for the common stock were the company in the immediate future to become an LBO or merger candidate.

On pages 165 to 170 of *The Intelligent Investor,* there is an excellent discussion by Benjamin Graham of the reported earnings for 1970 by Aluminum Company of America (Alcoa). The discussion starts with two pieces of extremely sound advice: "The first is: Don't take a single year's earnings seriously. The second is: If you do pay attention to short-term earnings, look out for booby traps in the per-share figures" (p. 165).

The Alcoa discussion, covering the distinction between recurring earnings and nonrecurring earnings from 1970 Alcoa operations, is part of a chapter entitled "Things to Consider About Per-Share Earnings." Everything in that chapter is consistent with the value investing concepts regarding the analysis of income accounts. The significant difference, though, between Graham and value investing is that for the latter approach, drawing investment conclusions is somewhat more complex. Graham concluded that Alcoa common was in 1971 attractively priced, on the basis of (1) the company's past growth rate in earnings compared with those for Sears Roebuck and with the Dow-Jones Industrial Average™ and (2) the low price-to-earnings ratio based on average earnings compared with the price-to-earnings ratios then existing for Sears Roebuck and the Dow-Jones. For value investors, though, the attractiveness of Alcoa common would also have been a function of two balance sheet considerations: the financial strength of Alcoa and the quantity of assets available to create future earnings.

It ought to be noted, too, that many control buyers are at times not divorced from Graham and Dodd microstandards. When a control person is looking at exit strategies that entail going public by way of an initial public offering (IPO), the Graham and Dodd emphasis on earnings tends to be a lot more important than the value investing balance sheet considerations both in getting better pricing for the IPO and in getting the IPO off at all.

Value investing methodology has a few advantages over Graham and Dodd methodology. Two advantages are particularly salient: First, value investing is a lot less competitive than Graham and Dodd; there are a great number of smart analysts focused on earnings—not too many seem to care about balance sheets. Second, value investors who focus on the quality of resources in a business seem to be subject to a lot fewer truly unpleasant surprises than are those whose primary emphases are elsewhere.

A Few Final Words

In terms of common stock analysis, Graham and Dodd came up with a large number of terrific caveats for minority investors to live by if they were not in a position to know much about the companies in whose securities they were investing. The Graham and Dodd caveats are still valid for relatively uninformed investors, having stood the test of time even though the principles were based on conditions existing from 1934 to 1962. Since 1962, however, there seems to have been a disclosure revolution that started with the federal Securities Act Amendments of 1964. Disclosures are now so good that a diligent buy-and-hold fundamentalist can know an awful lot about a great many companies just by carefully reading the public record. This quality and quantity of disclosures just was not there in 1962 or in prior periods when Graham and Dodd were writing.

On page 54 of *The Intelligent Investor,* Benjamin Graham described the four characteristics that ought to exist for a portfolio of "high-grade common stocks":

1. There should be adequate though not excessive diversification...
2. Each company selected should be large, prominent and conservatively financed. Indefinite as these adjectives must be, their general sense is clear...
3. Each company should have a long record of continuous dividend payments...
4. The investor should impose some limit on the price he will pay for an issue in relation to its average earnings over, say, the past seven years...

The four factors that define high-grade common stocks for value investing are quite different, however:

- There should be a superstrong financial position for any common stock that goes into the portfolio. The Graham diversification principles for minority investors are valid.
- The company should be reasonably well managed with not too much overreaching on the part of entrenched management vis-à-vis minority shareholders.
- The business should be understandable, which restricts investment to companies that make full and candid disclosures to securityholders.
- The price of an equity security should reflect a substantial discount from what the equity would realize in the event the company were private or a takeover candidate.

As to the last point above, Graham says in *The Intelligent Investor,* in discussing secondary-quality common stocks, that "financial history says clearly that the investor may expect satisfactory results, on the average, from secondary common stocks only if he buys them for less than their value to a private owner, that is, on a bargain basis" (p. 92). Although financial history in recent years probably has not demonstrated Graham's 1973 observation, it remains, for passive value investing purposes, an excellent standard to use in acquiring common stocks, whether or not the companies that issue those common stocks would have been deemed to be primary or secondary by Graham.

Chapter 4

Broker-Dealer Research Departments and Conventional Money Managers

A bargain that stays a bargain is not a bargain.

—trader's credo

Research department analysts and conventional money managers probably would have had no interest in Toyoda Automatic Loom Works common stock in November 1998 unless they had some evidence that would have led them to believe (1) that there would be a dramatic improvement in reported earnings for Toyoda in the current fiscal year; (2) that some action might have been imminent, such as an acquisition of Toyoda by Toyota Motor, which would result in a workout value for Toyoda common at a substantial premium over November 1998 market prices; or (3) that the outlook for common stock prices on the Tokyo Stock Exchange (TSE) was quite bullish.

In December 1995, research department analysts and conventional money managers probably would have concentrated on having an opinion as to the probability that Kmart would seek Chapter 11 relief. Analysts who thought Kmart was likely to seek Chapter 11 relief would have avoided acquiring Kmart debt even if they believed that the ultimate workout in a reorganization would be not less than 100. They would have focused on the belief that if Kmart did file for Chapter 11 relief, the market price of Kmart debt would decline, probably dramatically; for those analysts, the time to acquire Kmart debt would have been after a Chapter 11 filing, not before.

Previous chapters have discussed the characteristics and limitations of the recommended approach of value investing, the characteristics and limitations inherent in the efficient market hypothesis (EMH) and all other academic approaches, and the characteristics and limitations of fundamental analysis as promulgated in the works of Benjamin Graham and David Dodd and their predecessors. In view of the endless reports put out by Wall Street research departments and the countless presentations, both written and oral, made by conventional money managers, it is instructive to look at the analytic approach that most research departments and conventional money managers follow. This chapter serves two purposes: First, it describes the analytic techniques that are followed by research departments at most broker/dealers—the sell side—and also by most money managers responsible for the noncontrol passive investing of funds entrusted to their care—the buy side. Second, it discusses the limitations—problems—inherent in usual research department–conventional money manager approaches.

How Research Departments and Conventional Money Managers Think

Research departments and conventional money managers seem to follow a strict going-concern approach. A firm is analyzed only as a going concern to be operated in the future pretty much as it has been in the past, in the same industry it has always been in, and financed as it has been financed traditionally. The market value of common stocks is deemed to be determined by future reported earnings, cash flows, or both, appropriately capitalized. A weight of almost 100% is given to this going-concern approach, one that is forward looking because it impinges on financial statement analysis. It emphasizes a primacy of the income account un-modified by considerations of the current quality of either a corporation's financial position or the net assets the company employs. Indeed, both high-quality assets and large net assets, or book values, tend to have neg-ative connotations for valuation purposes for many research depart-ment/money manager analysts. A strong financial position indicates to these analysts that management has not employed assets as aggressively as it might. A high book value, too, tends to be a negative because such numbers, *a priori,* spell lower returns on equity (ROEs) and returns on assets (ROAs) than would otherwise be the case. Put otherwise, the going-concern approach of research department analysts and conven-tional money managers seems to view financial factors that are thought of as positives in a resource conversion approach or value investing approach (i.e., strong financial positions and high asset values) as either a negative or unimportant.

Research department analysts and conventional money managers tend to believe that their objective is to estimate prices at which a security might sell in a future outside passive minority investor (OPMI) market. When consideration is given to underlying corporate values, it is not these corporate values, per se that count but rather how much, if at all, the un-derlying corporate values ought to fit into the estimate of future prices in OPMI markets. Other considerations in the estimation of market prices include dividend policies; technical chartist market considerations, includ-ing supply and demand for securities; industry outlooks; opinions about general market levels, interest rates, and gross domestic product (GDP); insider buying and selling; and Wall Street sponsorship.

Research department analysts and conventional money managers tend to be tremendously influenced by short-run corporate revenue and earnings reports. As part of estimating market prices, they tend very much to be trend players, especially on the buy side, refusing to acquire securities if they believe near-term outlooks for prices are unfavorable. As part of being short-run conscious, research departments and conven-tional money managers tend to place much greater weight on the prospects that the development of a catalyst might result in common stock price appreciation than on the acquisition of securities solely be-cause the price appears, on the basis of statistical considerations, to be cheap. They see a trade-off between catalysts and low prices in OPMI markets. The more likely that a catalyst will come into existence, other things being equal, the higher the price at which the common stock will sell. After all, OPMI markets, like all markets, do tend toward efficiency even though those efficiencies can be quite weak at times. For many research departments and conventional money managers, low price alone is not a sufficient condition for making a securities purchase. Rather, the essential condition for the purchase is the perception of a relatively near term catalyst that will result in price appreciation, whether that catalyst is embodied in prospects for improved earnings, for earnings in excess of consensus forecasts, or for such a transaction as a merger and acquisition (M&A), a major refinancing, or a liquidation.

For research departments and conventional money managers, a common stock tends to be deemed to be cheap statistically if price-to-earnings (P : E) ratios (or price-to-cash flow ratios) seem modest relative to comparables. The earnings (or cash flow) figures used for these P : E ratio calculations are the most recent reported earnings, the earnings forecast for the period just ahead, or both, with the period just ahead being either the next quarter or the next 12 months. Rarely are other measures of being statistically cheap used; when they are, the tendency is to not give them much weight. Other measures of being statistically cheap might include price-to–net asset value (NAV) ratios, in which NAV is determined by reference to either book value or appraised value, and price-to–average annual earnings ratios for the last 3 or 5 years.

Research department analysts and conventional money managers tend to be very conscious of comparative analyses. They give great weight to a comparison between quarterly earnings as actually reported and consensus estimates of quarterly earnings and consider intra-industry comparative revenue and earnings performance to be important. Many also attach material significance to growth trends compared to P : E ratios. For example, assuming a company's earnings per share are forecasted to grow at 30% compounded, a P : E ratio of 30 times is justified; 25% growth would justify a P : E ratio of 25 times. This is called growth at a reasonable price (GARP).

In using analytic techniques, research departments and conventional money managers rely much more heavily on field work (e.g., management interviews) than they do on intensive document reviews (e.g., in-depth analysis of audited financial statements or of court records).

Of the vast majority of research department reports in recent years, only a very few seem to provide excellent underlying analyses that are helpful for value investing. The thrusts of virtually all the reports, both the excellent and the not so excellent, are as follows:

- Estimate future earnings per share (EPS), EBITDA (earnings before interest, income taxes, depreciation, and amortization), or both. At the end of 1998, such estimates would be done by years for, say, 1999, 2000, and 2001.
- Apply to those EPS and/or EBITDA estimates of an appropriate P : E ratio based on the following:
  1. Industry identification
  2. Growth trend
  3. Other factors, such as management appraisal, sponsorship, return on equity, or economic value added (EVA)

Almost 100% weight tends to be given to this approach—estimating future flows, whether cash or earnings, and applying an appropriate capitalization rate to these estimated flows to arrive at a target price for a common stock. A change in quarterly earnings estimates is deemed to be very important news and very frequently results in a change in the target price.

Research department analysts almost never recommend outright sales or selling short. Many conventional money managers sell frequently— when they believe that a security does not have short-run appreciation prospects or that an alternative commitment has better short-run appreciation possibilities.

Problems Faced by Research Departments and Conventional Money Managers

The Difficulty of Forecasting Earnings

For most companies in most industries, it is very difficult to predict future revenues and earnings and cash flow results. Future events have always resulted in large numbers of such forecasts' being plain wrong. Traditionally, there have been industries in which such forecasts could be made with reasonable accuracy (e.g., integrated electric utilities or real estate properties benefiting from long-term leases to creditworthy tenants). For most other companies, though, predictions frequently will be in error by relatively wide margins whether those companies are automobile assemblers, aluminum producers, semiconductor equipment manufacturers, health-care providers, bank lenders, pharmaceutical firms, retailers, building product suppliers, or, as a matter of fact, just about any kind of U.S. corporation.

When research department forecasts prove to be overly optimistic, as many do, the analyst often has no anchor to windward, as would exist were the shares recommended on some other basis than merely estimates of future flows. One such other basis, rarely relied on by research departments and conventional money managers, is the acquisition of common stocks when those issues are selling at prices representing some sort of reasonable relationship to NAV. Another such basis is the restriction of common stock investments to businesses that enjoy strong financial positions so that the company will have staying power, possible comeback ability, and no likelihood of defaults on corporate debt obligations, in the event that future results are much worse than the analyst's forecast.

Ameliorating to some extent this lack of an anchor is the fact that research department analysts and conventional money managers tend to be traders, not investors. Losses can be cut by early sales, especially if securities holdings are confined to relatively marketable issues. Trading, though, does tend to limit prospects for super long term profits, whether realized or unrealized, available to those following a buy-and-hold strategy.

The Competitiveness of Conventional Analysis

Attempting to forecast future flows and applying an appropriate multiplier thereto is an extremely competitive activity within the financial community. There are probably thousands of analysts, on both the sell side and the buy side, trying to do pretty much the same thing, and many are very bright and diligent.

The Likelihood that It Is Impossible to Do Top-Down Analysis Rationally

Although predicting EPS and EBITDA for companies may be difficult, predicting the P : E ratios that might be assigned to that EPS or EBITDA in a future OPMI market may well nigh be impossible. Making forecasts about future general OPMI market levels probably is much more in the realm of abnormal psychology than of finance. There is no evidence that the general market and large sectors within it are governed by any price behavior other than a random walk. Put otherwise, no one really predicts market levels accurately. Indeed, it is probable that no one really can identify those macrofactors likely to influence OPMI market prices, and the weights that might be assigned to each factor.

For many analysts, too, predicting future earnings for a company starts with top-down estimates of the outlook for the general economy, for interest rates, and for inflation. Historically, making accurate estimates about these macrofactors has been hard to do.

Being unable to predict the levels or direction of general markets is ameliorated to a considerable extent, for conventional money managers with a modicum of intelligence, through diversification. Thus, if forecasts of EPS or EBITDA come through for a good percentage of the companies in a portfolio of common stocks, that portfolio ought to perform satisfactorily (certainly in comparison with other portfolios) regardless of what happens in the general market. All bets about ability to withstand market drops are off, however, for those money managers who operate with borrowed money.

With highly leveraged portfolios, money managers had better be right, or close to right, about future market prices a good deal of the time. Fortunately, in the field of institutional equity investment, most portfolios are not highly leveraged, whether they are the assets of investment companies (e.g., mutual funds), of defined benefit pension plans, or of insurance companies.

Fighting for the Heavyweight Championship with One Hand Tied behind Your Back: Predicting Future Earnings while Ignoring the Existing Balance Sheet

Analysts who focus on trends tend to think linearly: The past is prologue; therefore, past growth trends of EPS or EBITDA will continue into the future or even accelerate. The truth, however, is that the corporate world is rarely linear.

The fact is that for many—if not most—companies, analysis of the amount and quality of resources that a management has to work with is as good as or an even better tool for predicting future EPS or EBITDA than is the past earnings record. It appears most research department analysts and money managers ignore this tool, especially when it indicates a strong financial position. This is true even though theoretically, no analyst interested in ROE and ROA can safely ignore equity or assets, both of which are balance sheet items. Improved returns, if applied to larger equities and assets, will give securities investors a much bigger bang. The elementary fact is that both the past earnings record and the present balance sheet are good and frequently necessary tools for predicting future flows for many companies.

It is much easier for a management to improve returns if the company has a strong financial position with which to work. A prime example of this was Nabors Industries, an oil service company with which the author has been associated for many years. Nabors emerged from a prepackaged Chapter 11 reorganization in mid-1988 with an all-equity capitalization. At that time, Nabors was virtually the only contract driller not burdened by large amounts of debt incurred during the pre-1983 boom time in the oil drilling industry. Given its financial strength, Nabors was able to spend the next few years acquiring contract drillers and contract drilling assets at bargain prices; other industry participants did not have the financial wherewithal to bid against Nabors for these assets. In 1987, Nabors's cash loss from operations probably was in excess of $20 million; in 1997, Nabors's positive cash flow from operations was well in excess of $200 million.

The earnings record and the present balance sheet are both helpful tools for predicting future earnings, but one is not a substitute for the other. Which of the two ought to be more important in any given situation is a matter of analytic judgment. Giving blanket priority to income account considerations and thereby denigrating the importance of balance sheet items, however, seems to disadvantage many research department analysts and conventional money managers because they ignore qualitative and quantitative balance sheet data as sources for estimating future flows, whether cash or earnings.

Lack of Awareness of the Relationship between Income Account Numbers and Balance Sheet Numbers and of Analytic Conflicts between and among Related Numbers

When analysts focus only on forecasting future earnings and do not take into account balance sheet considerations, as is the case for many research departments and conventional money managers, there is no need to examine the relationship between income accounts and balance sheets. When they instead look at present balance sheets as either a helpful tool for predicting future earnings or as a margin of safety in case earnings forecasts do not work out, the relationships between income account numbers and balance sheet numbers become important—and sometimes result in analytic conflicts.

Assume, for example, that an analyst is seeking a margin of safety for a common stock holding by having the recommended stock sell at a price that is in a reasonable relationship to NAV. It will be impossible to obtain that margin of safety if the common stock in question sells at a high P : E ratio and the company enjoys a much above average ROE. Say that XYZ common sells at 30 times earnings and that XYZ's ROE is 20%. Then, *a fortiori,* XYZ common will trade at 6 times NAV. (XYZ earns $1 per share, making the price of XYZ common 30; an ROE of 20% on earnings of $1 results in an NAV of $5 per share; $5 NAV divided into 30 price equals a price to book ratio of 6 times.) Research department analysts and conventional money managers interested in companies that they perceive to be rapidly growing and also that earn high ROEs had better ignore the margin of safety that could be inherent in the price of a common stock being close to NAV if they are going to opt for growth and high ROEs. Furthermore rapidly growing earnings in past years mean that average earnings for those past years are less than they would have been had earnings grown less rapidly. Thus, growth investors tend not to look for any margin of safety that might be inherent in a common stock selling at a price that represents a relative modest P : E ratio based on average annual earnings for a past period.

The fact that the relationship also works the other way is not particularly relevant for most research department analysts and conventional money managers, it should be noted. The trade-off between high P : E ratios and high ROEs on the one hand and reasonable prices relative to NAV on the other hand functions in such a way that an analyst wanting to focus on common stocks selling close to NAV will not be able to invest in common stocks when the issue is selling at a high P : E ratio based on current earnings and the company enjoys an above-average ROE.

It is quite feasible to acquire common stocks at prices closely related to present NAV and at low P : E ratios based on what a corporation's earnings are likely to be when current difficulties, which are depressing current earnings and earnings forecast for the period just ahead, are overcome. The OPMI market, though, tends to be too efficient for there to be many opportunities to acquire securities when both prices are reasonable relative to present NAV and the P : E ratios are low relative to current earnings and immediate future earnings. Analysts and money managers focused on current earnings, forecasted earnings for the period ahead, and ROE must virtually ignore price as related to NAV. As a matter of fact, they do ignore NAV. Given the inaccuracy of most forecasts, however, they do so at their own peril.

Use of an Approach Antithetical to those Used by Private Businesspeople and Control Buyers Not Seeking Immediate Access to Equity Markets for New Capital

The basic objective of private business people and control buyers is to create wealth (and sometimes cash flows for themselves) in the most efficient manner, which usually involves following courses of action that minimize the present value of corporate income taxes payable. Research department analysts and conventional money managers have the opposite agenda: They want corporations whose common stocks they are holding or recommending to report maximum amounts of near-term earnings from operations, earnings that tend to be currently taxable at maximum tax rates.

They also desire companies whose common stocks they are recommending to be short-term oriented. In their view, managements ought to forgo projects with possible huge long-term payoffs if that entails sacrifices in creating near-term operating income. Given their druthers, most managements not seeking near-term access to equity markets probably would opt for the long-term view of wealth building.

Research department analysts and conventional money managers also tend to be more interested in what the numbers are, especially earnings per share, rather than what the numbers mean. If an otherwise attractive acquisition for a company using purchase accounting might result in large annual charges against reported net income to amortize purchase goodwill, analysts and money managers frequently will discourage managements from making such an acquisition even though, aside from the goodwill charge, the acquisition has promise of delivering a strongly positive net present value (NPV) to the company over the long term.

Furthermore, given the emphasis on a going-concern approach to analysis, analysts and money managers tend to want the companies whose common stocks they are recommending to have a single industry focus, at least in 1997 and 1998. They view those companies as operations rather than as converters of resources to other, and possibly higher, uses. If companies diversify into other industries, they no longer are seen as "pure plays"—they are harder to follow.

Many good managements, left to their own devices, would view the companies they control as both going concerns creating operating profits and resource conversion vehicles creating wealth by investing in different and sometimes even unrelated industries.

The current anathema of research department analysts and conventional money managers to corporate diversification does have considerable long-term merit. Too many companies have suffered because of diversification into industries not well understood by managements. Nonetheless, analysts' apparent distaste for diversification contrasts with what many managements would like to do provided that they do not find it necessary or desirable to placate Wall Street.

Analysts and money managers also tend to use different approaches to analysis than do control buyers of corporations. Rather than focus on a strict going-concern approach with an emphasis on near-term operating results, business buyers, such as leveraged buyout (LBO) specialists, tend to concentrate on three issues:

- How can a transaction be financed?
- What is the long-term outlook for the business?
- What are the various exit strategies that might be available?

The Lack of a Balanced Focus, Resulting in Common Stock Prices that are Much Too High or Much Too Low

By concentrating almost exclusively on earnings or cash flow forecasts and capitalization rates, analysts have no safety net when prices get way out of line. There is a strong tendency for prices in OPMI markets, both high and low, to have elements of irrationality that do not exist to anywhere near the same extent in negotiated transactions between reasonably knowledgeable buyers and sellers. In negotiated transactions, there is a

Table 4-1. The New Income Account

Variable	Value (000)
Net income	$13,000
Number of shares outstanding	10,800
Earnings per share	$1.20
Price-to-earnings ratio at price of 60	50.0x

tendency to consider and weight a whole gamut of factors in arriving at a transaction price, rather than just applying a capitalization rate to current earnings (or cash flow) and predictions of earnings (or cash flow) for the immediate future.

Given access to capital markets, though, an overpriced stock can be an important asset for a corporation run by a management with skills in M&As. The market price of a common stock can be enhanced by using the security in mergers, especially when analysts concentrate solely on P : E ratios, as in this sample scenario (Table 4-1):

1. XYZ common sells at 60, or 60 times earnings of $1 per share, or $10 million on 10 million shares outstanding.
2. ABC earns $3 million.
3. XYZ acquires ABC in a pooling of interest transaction by issuing 800,000 shares of XYZ common, which would have a market value of $48 million.

If the normative P : E ratio is 60, postmerger XYZ common should sell not at 60 but at 72.

Analyses That Focus on Base Case Forecasts Rather Than Alternative Scenarios

An investor putting $100 million or more of his or her own funds into an equity situation in which the funds will be tied up on a permanent or semi-permanent basis usually does not rely as heavily on base case forecasts as do research department analysts and conventional money managers. This is understandable because the latter groups enjoy marketability and can, at least theoretically, undo investments rapidly. One consequence of this, though, is that there is far less need and desire for research department analysts and conventional money managers to conduct in-depth investigations: Given high portfolio turnover, it becomes terribly unproductive to do in-depth investigations. Furthermore, it becomes impossible for even the largest organization to conduct in-depth investigations when the number of securities in a portfolio runs to hundreds of issues.

By contrast, large investors holding equities on a permanent or semipermanent basis tend to investigate relatively thoroughly on two bases: the base case and the reasonable worst case. Most also put the optimistic case into the investigations mix.

External Pressures That Can Compromise Analyses

Research departments of broker/dealers that also have an investment banking presence can face pressures to recommend the common stocks of investment banking department client companies, especially those whose public issues were underwritten by the firm. Sometimes, even if only in a small minority of instances, these recommendations are based more on the good of the firm rather than the good of the client. Money managers frequently are under pressure from their firm's marketing department to undertake portfolio window dressing. Probably the most common scenario is that good marketing may require that the portfolio consist largely of the most popular issues, instead of emphasizing issues that, although less popular, are more attractive fundamental values.

The Difficulty of Concentrating on Operating Ratios Based on Financial Accounting Statistics

Given their emphasis on viewing companies strictly as going concerns, research department analysts and conventional money managers tend to place great worth on the analysis of operating margins—gross profit margins and operating income margins. This type of analysis has limited usefulness in many industries because the data are derived from short-form (i.e., no detail by specific items) financial statements, rather than long-form corporate cost, or managerial, accounting data. For most companies, if analysts do not have access to cost-accounting data, it becomes extremely difficult to understand the nitty-gritty of operations. Profit-margin analysis based on financial accounting can be a helpful tool, but it is a limited one.

Also, comparative numbers can be tricky. Company ABC and company XYZ each have operating income of $1 million from conducting the exact same activities. ABC claims to have sales revenue of $50 million, and XYZ, for the same activities, books consulting revenues of $10 million. On the basis of these numbers, ABC's operating profit margin is 2% and XYZ's is 10%. Furthermore, ABC might treat, say, rent expense as a cost of goods sold, whereas XYZ might treat rent expense as an administrative or general expense, which would be a component of operating expense.

Heavy Reliance on Field Work to the Exclusion of Reading Documents

Reading the documents is no substitute for field work—interviewing managements, competitors, customers, government regulators, and others who can contribute information to an analysis. The reverse is also true: doing field work is not a substitute for carefully reading relevant documents—Securities and Exchange Commission(SEC) filings, stockholder mailings, court records, competitors' documents, and industry publications. Indeed, field work and document reading go hand in hand. Those who read and understand document contents tend to be much more skillful at field work than are analysts who ask questions before they have a good documentary background for asking those questions. Documents tend to be given short shrift, though, by many research department analysts and conventional money managers. In part, this is understandable: Much of what is in documents appears to have little relevance to predicting what near-term OPMI market prices will be, and reading documents is very time intensive, hardly worthwhile for those trading in and out of large numbers of securities in a portfolio. Finally, interpreting documents, especially financial statements, takes a fair amount of training; which many analysts seem to lack.

A principal problem for analysts who choose not to rely on documents they have intensely scrutinized, especially audited financial statements, is that many analysts involved in passive investing have been defrauded or otherwise victimized, by promoters selling stories with no hard-nosed backup. This was true for public holders of U.S. corporate bonds before the Trust Indenture Act, true in the 1960s when small companies went public, true in the 1970s and 1980s when tax-sheltered limited partnerships were all the rage, and true in the 1990s for analysts recommending common stocks of companies in emerging markets with virtually nonexistent document disclosure requirements.

Heavy Reliance on Perceptions of What Others Think

All rational analysts involved with passive noncontrol investing are probably influenced to some extent by what they perceive are the opinions of insiders or smart money. For example, if insiders and 10% shareholders are selling common stock, that is a factor to put into the mix of information. That information becomes far more meaningful, though, when it becomes a supplemental part of the buy-and-hold analyst's independent judgment about what the firm might be worth or what future dynamics for that firm might be. Depending on the individual situation, insider selling might mean on the one hand that a security is overpriced or, on the other hand, that the company is now a more attractive takeover candidate, in part because insider-owned blocks of stock can be purchased or otherwise tied up. The analyst is unlikely to be be able to make good judgments on this issue without having independent opinions about corporate values and dynamics.

A rationale for relying solely on perceived opinions of insiders and smart money is that the analyst's sole goal is to predict the prices at which a security will sell in the immediate future. If you are going to try to predict near-term prices, you had better focus on what you believe influential others think: buy and sell recommendations of major research departments, consensus forecasts of quarterly earnings, and insider trading. This in fact seems to be what a lot of research department analysts and conventional money managers do, especially those with no interest or little training in fundamental analysis. Relying heavily on the perceived opinions of others, to the exclusion of independent fundamental analysis, seems a tough way to make a living, though.

Conclusion

In summary, there are huge problems involved in obtaining satisfactory long-term performance by following what appear to be the basic precepts of research department analysts and conventional money managers. Both value investing and the teachings of Benjamin Graham and David Dodd also have problems. Nonetheless, it appears much easier and basically much more productive to adhere to value investing standards rather than research department and conventional money manager approaches. Still, it is obvious that some—though probably a substantial minority of—portfolios run by conventional money managers perform quite satisfactorily on average and over the long term. This can be attributed to the fact that many money managers are very smart. Even so, what even the best conventional money managers do seems to be the hard way to achieve satisfactory results compared with the results of analysts who lean more toward value investing.

PART II

REAL-WORLD CONSIDERATIONS

Chapter 5

Corporate Valuation

The truth is the only thing that nobody will believe.

—George Bernard Shaw

Concepts about corporate valuation are quite different in value invest-ing than in the other disciplines reviewed in prior chapters: modern capital theory (MCT), Graham and Dodd fundamentalism, or conven-tional money management. These others emphasize the primacy of the income account, or cash flows derived from income accounts. Value in-vesting, however, gives equal weight to the interrelated factors of the esti-mated quality and quantity of resources in a business. Indeed, if a value investor were forced to choose only one factor (which is never the case), most of the time that factor would be quality of resources rather than es-timates of future flows, whether cash or earnings. When the emphasis is on resources, the analysis revolves around measuring what is. When the emphasis is on flows, the analysis revolves around estimating what will be.

Going-concern analysis is the bedrock of business valuations in just about all literature about finance. The best analysts embracing the going-concern approach—for example, Benjamin Graham and David Dodd—do not ignore resource conversion. For Graham and Dodd, this meant being aware of liquidating values. They pointed to the attraction of acquiring common stocks at prices below liquidation value, especially prices below net net current assets. *Net net current assets* refer to current net asset value (NAV) after deducting all GAAP (generally accepted accounting principles) liabilities, both short term and long term. Graham also pointed out the importance of trying to acquire the common stocks of secondary companies at prices below their values as private business.

The least sophisticated analysts (i.e., followers of the efficient market hypothesis [EMH]) believe that resource conversion is the exclusive value determinant anytime values can be measured by trading prices in markets populated by outside passive minority investors (OPMIs). In all other cases, going-concern status is the value determinant. Thus, for academics, a resource conversion emphasis for corporate valuations manifests as a requirement that performing loans held in corporate portfolios be valued at market. In general, academic believers in the efficient market operate on the assumption that financial results for all corporations other than investment companies are to be measured strictly by going-concern standards, where as portfolio results for an investor in those corporations' marketable securities are measured strictly by resource conversion standards. This academic approach is not helpful at all in value investing, in which market prices for securities, when available, always deserve some weight. Rarely will they merit 100% weight or anything near it. In the case, say, of a portfolio of performing loans held by a pension plan with a goal of a steady flow of cash income and whose asset size is increasing regularly as new funds come into the plan, the weight placed on market prices by the portfolio would be minimal—and in important contexts, even negative.

The force driving academics, Graham and Dodd fundamentalists, and conventional money managers seems to be the strict going-concern assumption. Corporations are seen as devoted essentially to the same day-to-day operations they have always conducted within the same industries in which they have always operated, managed and controlled as they always have been managed and controlled and financed pretty much as they always have been financed. Until the early 1990s, this assumption accurately described the environment in the electric utility industry. It is likely that the going-concern assumption never accurately described most U.S. corporations with publicly traded securities. Today, the strict going-concern assumption no longer seems appropriate even for electric utilities.

Certain conclusions follow logically from the strict going-concern assumption. First, among buy-and-hold fundamentalists, there is a primacy of the income account and a consequent denigration of the balance sheet, or resource conversion, for corporate valuation purposes. (Furthermore, among traders not engaged in risk arbitrage, the income account is supreme; short-term movements in common stock prices, after all, are likely to be heavily influenced by changes in reported earnings and not influenced at all by changes in book values.) Second, as Graham and Dodd pointed out, the past earnings record of a corporation usually is the best tool for estimating earnings for the years just ahead over a business cycle or growth phase; they were absolutely right, granted the strict going concern assumption.

The strict going-concern approach seems unrealistic, however. Most companies whose securities are publicly traded will always combine elements of the going concern and elements revolving around the conversion of corporate resources to other uses, other ownership, other control, and other financing or refinancing. It seems likely that few U.S. corporations are going to go for as long as 5 years without being involved in resource conversion activities, such as mergers and acquisitions (M&As); changes of control; management buyouts (MBOs); massive share repurchases; major financings, refinancings, or reorganizations; sales of assets in bulk; spinoffs; investment in new ventures in other industries; and corporate liquidations.

Both going-concern considerations and resource conversion considerations are important in most corporate valuations. Indeed, in most situations, the two are related intimately to each other, derived from, modified by, and a function of each other. The current sales value of an asset is determined frequently by what it is believed that asset can be caused to earn. Much of the "what is" value for many—if not most—corporations probably was created by past going-concern prosperity. People who focus on the going concern tend to believe that value creation is strictly a function of future flows: estimated free cash flows appropriately capitalized for the EMH, or estimated earnings appropriately capitalized for Graham and Dodd and many money managers. In value investing, by contrast, corporate values are derived from one or more of four separate but often related factors:

- **Free cash flow from operations.** A minority of going concerns generate excess cash flows from operations that become available to service a company's capitalization. For example, companies engaged in money management are in an industry with a strong tendency to produce free cash flows. For this industry, all fees are received in cash and the companies' investments in infrastructure, research and development, inventories, receivables, and fixed plant are minimal. While no corporation would undertake a specific project unless it were believed that the project, as a stand-alone, would produce cash flows with a positive net present value, (NPV), it seems probable that most profitable going concerns actually do not create free cash flows but rather create earnings, because the nature of good going-concern operations is to expand by acquiring large amounts of assets that have to be financed by obtaining outside capital.

- **Earnings from operations.** Earnings are defined as the creation of wealth while consuming cash. This seems to be what the vast majority of prosperous going concerns, and all growing economies, do. In general, since earnings result in the consumption of cash, they cannot have any independent value unless they are also combined with access to capital markets, whether such access is to credit markets, equity markets, or both.

- **Conversion of assets to higher uses, other ownership or control, or both; the financing of asset acquisitions, the refinancing of liabilities, or both.** These activities sometimes take the form of mergers and acquisitions (M&As), contests for control, leveraged buyouts (LBOs), the restructuring of troubled companies, and acquiring securities in bulk through cash tender offers, exchange offers, and the use of corporate proxy machinery. The analyst who wants to acquire securities at prices that appear to represent large discounts from what they would fetch were there to be a future merger must be prepared for a few trade-offs. For example, it seems probable that the near-term earnings outlooks would be quite clouded in most situations where a company enjoys high quality resources and its common stock trades in OPM markets at prices that reflect a substantial discount from an adjusted NAV. In 1998, the long-term exit possibilities for such investments included multiple resource conversion and going-concern possibilities: redeployment of existing surplus assets to uses with higher returns than were being realized at the time of acquisition (for example, Tokio Marine & Fire ADRs, and Carver Federal Bank common stock); new ownership, which would pay substantial premiums over NAV to acquire these companies (e.g., depository institutions might acquire regional broker/dealers and financial insurance companies); use of the existing asset base to create large new NAVs (e.g., Forest City Enterprises, Tejon Ranch, and St. Joe); and use the existing asset base to realize markedly improved earnings and return on equity (ROE) during the next up cycle for a growth industry (e.g., U.S. semiconductor equipment common stocks, Cummins Engine common stock, or Tecumseh Products common stock).

• **Access to capital markets on a superattractive basis.** It seems probable that more corporate wealth, and certainly wealth for financiers, is created by this route than any other. Groups accessing capital markets on a superattractive basis include those financing many M&As as well as LBOs and those taking advantage of the pricing available relatively frequently in the market for initial public offerings (IPOs).

Any passive investment has something wrong with it, and good analysts spend a lot of time trying to figure out what is wrong and worrying about it. The value investor makes investment commitments when what is right seems to strongly outweigh what is wrong. One of the more important areas in which there are trade-offs between right and wrong is in the differences that arise when emphasizing resource conversion and de-emphasizing going-concern status. Frequently, what is right for resource conversion is wrong for a going concern, and vice versa. Here are a few examples:

• **Japanese nonlife insurers.** Viewed as investment companies whose principal assets are performing loans and passive investments in marketable common stocks, these well-financed issuers seemed inordinately attractive from a resource conversion point of view in the fall of 1997 when the common stocks were trading at discounts from an adjusted NAV of anywhere from 30% to 70% before deducting potential liability for income taxes on unrealized gains. Viewed from a going-concern point of view, however, these issues appeared hardly attractive at all, selling at 20 times or more reported earnings. The outlook for existing operations was very clouded, since for the first time, this sheltered industry was going to face real competition, especially price competition, concomitant with the big-bang reforms taking place as part of the deregulation of financial institutions in Japan.

• **Retailing industry.** From a resource conversion point of view, retail inventories are a current asset convertible into cash within 12 months. From a going-concern point of view, however, they are an illiquid fixed asset of the worst sort. If a retail business—Sears, for example—is to remain a going concern, it will have to keep its aggregate level of inventories relatively constant or even expanding. These assets are subject to fashion swings, markdowns, shrinkage, and obsolescence. Common sense here dictates that a going-concern analysis ought to take precedence over a resource conversion analysis, especially if the security to be owned is a common stock and not an adequately secured debt instrument. The Graham and Dodd approach favors companies that happen to be in retailing because these common stocks are trading at prices below GAAP net net current assets; most of the time, that type of pricing for retail equities is cheap but not safe. Retail inventories in a going concern have many more fixed-asset characteristics than current-asset characteristics, the form defining them as current assets for GAAP purposes notwithstanding.

- **Forest City common.** In a resource conversion situation, the company's huge portfolio of income-producing real estate properties, carried for GAAP purposes as a fixed asset, is very much a current asset, probably salable at close to appraisal values over the phone. A strict resource conversion analysis, though, is incomplete. As a practical matter, Forest City has many going-concern attributes, two of which are that the best properties are not for sale and that as a going concern, Forest City will dedicate cash flows from its successful properties to support cash drains from its poorer projects. Also, as a going-concern investment builder, Forest City has been supersuccessful in creating resource conversion values over the years.
- **Fixed-income portfolios of performing loans.** Assume, as is the case for most property and casualty insurance companies, that the company's principal balance sheet asset is a portfolio of performing loans and that this portfolio is growing in size. Assume further, as would be the case for most property and casualty insurance companies, that the company has little or no interest-bearing debt in its capitalization. Viewed as a resource conversion situation, the company's portfolio values are carried at market value, (i.e., marked to market). If interest rates rise, the market value of the portfolios go down. Viewed as a going concern, though, future investment income will increase, as rates go up, more than would otherwise be the case as new funds, as well as maturing funds, are invested at interest rates that provide increased returns. If interest rates rise, it seems likely that most insurance companies will benefit more from going-concern considerations than they will be harmed by resource conversion

considerations. (In the fall of 1998, among most OPMIs, there seemed to a knee-jerk reaction that higher interest rates were bearish—negative universally. That is just what that general sentiment is—a knee-jerk reaction. Some companies would be helped by higher interest rates, some harmed.)

In appraising managements, those using a strict going-concern approach evaluate managements strictly as operators. In resource conversion, however, managements are also evaluated as investors and financiers.

What is the value of surplus cash in a corporate balance sheet? In a liquidation analysis, cash can be worth only its principal amount: $1 million of surplus cash is worth $1 million. In the hands of a deadhead management, the surplus cash may have a present value of less than $1 million because it may earn lesser returns than if the funds had been invested in alternative investments and because it may not serve as a good insurance policy against adverse future developments. In the hands of a management skilled in employing surplus resources, though, surplus cash can be worth a substantial premium regardless of whether that cash is employed by the going concern or in resource conversion activities. Surplus cash's being worth a premium seemed to be the case for Intel Corporation and Toyota Motor Corporation in mid-1998. In 1998, Intel's huge surplus cash position gave it the financial wherewithal to enter any area of semiconductor manufacture that it desired. There were no practical restrictions on how much Intel could spend on research, development, and engineering. Also, because of its superstrong cash position, there appeared to be no practical constraints on the ability of Toyota Motor to diversify into new business areas. In early 1998, Toyota was in the process of diversifying into housing, telecommunications, and automobile finance.

For virtually all businesses or their control people, there are advantages to having the company financed comfortably. Taking companies private at premium prices over OPMI market prices by way of LBOs and MBOs requires that the companies have relatively strong financial positions. The essence of going private is that public shareholders are cashed out and their ownership interests in the business are terminated with the buyout of public shareholders financed in whole—or mostly—by having the acquired company borrow funds on a basis that will be nonrecourse to the new shareholders. Usually the only businesses for which this is possible are those with excess borrowing capacity, something created when companies have surplus resources in cash or assets convertible into cash. Put otherwise, surplus cash tends to be worth premiums to most players involved with LBOs and MBOs.

Although the passive investors involved with value investing do not ignore the going-concern aspect in the analysis of most securities, there is no question that most of the time, these investors place primary emphasis on resource conversion, which has certain advantages and disadvantages. The advantages in emphasizing resource conversion are as follows:

- Resource conversion is a relatively noncompetitive activity. Conventional money managers concentrate on forecasting earnings or cash flows.
- The businesses are easier to analyze. In value investing, analysts do not need to get involved in common stocks unless the businesses are extremely well financed and unless they can understand what the businesses do. Put otherwise, they can attempt to acquire for long-term holding what is safe and cheap. There are certain preliminary rules of thumb to ascertain cheapness when acquiring common stocks for passive investment:

  1.   Small-cap high-tech: Usually, pay no more than a 60% premium over book value, on the theory that this is the normative price first-stage venture capitalists would pay if they were financing the enterprise *de novo*. As compared with venture capitalists, passive value investors are creating positions in companies that are already public and cash rich. On the other hand, they have no elements of control over the companies in which they invest and research must be based more on the public record and less on due-diligence investigations involving insider information.

  2.   Financial institutions: Buy at a discount from adjusted book values (insurance companies), at a discount from stated book values (depository institutions), or at a discount from tangible book value plus 2% to 3% of assets under management (broker/dealers and other money managers).

  3.   Real estate companies: Buy at a discount from appraisal values.

- When long-term future earnings are to be forecast, estimating returns that might be earned on a realistic asset base is probably as good or better tool than is a corporation's past earnings record, although one is not a substitute for the other. Value investors ought to use both tools a good deal of the time.

•   Aside from those times when a corporation or its control shareholders are seeking access to equity markets, usually an occasional occurrence, American business seems to be run much more with a resource conversion emphasis than with a going-concern emphasis. This is certainly true for virtually all privately owned companies not seeking to go public, and it is probably true, also, for most of the better-run public companies. Most corporations whose managements do not have their eyes wholly on OPMI stock prices seek to create wealth in the most income-tax efficient manner. The most inefficient tax way to create wealth is to have reportable operating earnings, a going-concern emphasis; the most efficient tax way to create wealth is to have unrealized (and therefore mostly unreported) appreciation of asset values, a resource conversion emphasis.

•   There is a high level of comfort for a buy-and-hold OPMI following a value investing approach when investing in the equities of companies with strong financial positions. Not only does the cushion of a strong balance sheet make buy-and-hold investments feasible, but because if these strong financial positions are not dissipated, it is relatively easy for the value analyst to average down when common stock prices plummet.

•   Analysts concentrating on value investing are less likely to be victimized by securities frauds and securities promoters than are other investors. OPMIs will have a fair number of unsatisfactory investments because sometimes they misanalyze and because the future is mostly unpredictable. Losses because of management or control group malfeasance or outright fraud, though, are probably a lot less likely for value investing participants than for others, including institutional investors who rely on insider forecasts of the future and insider statements unsupported by public records as the principal weapons in their analytical arsenals.

The disadvantages to an emphasis on resource conversion are as follows:

•   When an analyst is trying to avoid investment risk, for any individual investment there usually exists a huge amount of market risk (i.e., the risk that common stock prices in OPMI markets will plunge). For most investments that seem cheap by resource conversion standards, it seems likely that the immediate earnings outlook will be anywhere from poor to uncertain (see the discussion of the Japanese nonlife insurers on

p. 103). Certainly the immediate earnings outlook is almost never good. The OPMI market tends enough toward efficiency that there exists a trade-off: Resource conversion investment criteria are met because the prospects are poor for those factors of the most immediate importance to participants in the OPMI market. Value-investing OPMIs are pretty much stuck with buying what is unpopular.

- The managements of companies with very strong financial positions tend to be very conservative, nonpromotional types, frequently indifferent to what Wall Street thinks or does. Frequently, these managers operate with no sense of urgency. There is a certain efficiency in this because these management groups, by and large, are not seeking near-term access to equity markets; the businesses they run are not in trouble.

- Value investors ignore factors that are important in the management of many portfolios, such as dividend payouts and marketability.

- Resource conversion seems to be largely unrelated to or the antithesis of certain short-term measures important to other analysts: return on assets (ROA), ROE, and economic value added (EVA). Indeed, the value analyst pretty much rejects as a tool of analysis any system that assumes that there exists a substantive consolidation between the interests of the corporation itself and the interests of those OPMIs who emphasize short-run prices in securities markets. EVA is based on an assumption of a substantive consolidation between the company and short-run OPMIs.

- With resource conversion, there seems to be a much more limited pool of eligible investments than exists under a going-concern approach.

- Resource conversion is unsuitable as an investing technique when the money manager is operating with borrowed money or is otherwise heavily influenced by daily marks to market. It is unsuitable also for traders who treat securities investing as one more casino game.

- To be successful at resource conversion investing, it seems to take not only a fair amount of training in fundamental corporate valuation but also a fair amount of knowledge about securities law and regulation, financial accounting, and income taxation—say, enough knowledge in these areas to be an intelligent client in dealing with full-time securities law, accounting, or income tax professionals.

- Resource conversion is not particularly relevant for portfolios—or portions of portfolios—investing in credit instruments without credit risk for the purposes of either obtaining assured streams of cash income or speculating on changes in interest rates.

Table 5-1. Statistics for Common Stock of Selected Semiconductor Equipment Manufacturers

Issuer (Recent Price)	Cash as Percentage of Total Book Liabilities (%)	Price-to-Book Ratios. Premium (or Discount) (%)	Price-to-Earning Ratio Based on Prior Past Peak Earns
ADE Corp. (9)	253	14.4	7.9×
Electroglas, Inc. (10)	552	16.2	5.2×
CP Clare Corp. (6)	124	(32.6)	7.0×
Silicon Valley Group, Inc. (9)	95	(46.4)	4.7×
Speedfam (12)	345	(30.9)	7.4×

Value Investing and Growth Stocks

When analysts either do not know much about the business being analyzed, or have no interest in examining the business from a qualitative point of view, forecasts of future growth have to be based on the past earnings record. Here, growth seems to be forecast by extrapolating past earnings trends linearly. Ignored are qualitative considerations such as a view (that the author holds) that despite 1997 and 1998 severe downtrends, the semiconductor industry will grow rapidly over the next 3 to 7 years as (1) the demand for chips grows and (2) technological innovation obsoletes old chips and old factories.

Because most analysts rely on past earnings trends rather than qualitative reasoning, many common stocks of semiconductor equipment manufacturers were available in September 1998 at bargain prices based on most measures other than current price-to-earnings (P : E) ratios and (P : E) ratios based on expected profitability for the next 9 to 12 months. Relevant statistics for a few issues of common stock were as shown in Table 5-1.

Value Investing and the Sell Side

Buy-and-hold investing is an integral part of value investing because value investors tend to be lethargic about selling securities. Part of the reason for that lethargy is that conventional macroconsiderations are not part of value investing. No attempt is made to predict the outlook for securities markets, for interest rates, or for the general economy. Much of the selling, switching, and reallocation of assets by conventional money managers revolves around their forecasts of trends in these macrofactors. Value investors do not worry about prospects for depreciation in market prices for the securities held.

In value investing, sales of junior securities (common stocks, preferred stocks, and subordinated debentures) ought to be made immediately if the analyst believes there has been a permanent impairment of capital for the company whose securities are in a portfolio. There should be an absence of lethargy here. Permanent impairment means that there has been a fundamental deterioration of the business: good finances have been dissipated, new products and new competitors are beating up the company, the industry is becoming obsolete, key management members are lost, and so on. In most passive investing using the value investing approach, though, it seems that permanent impairments occur infrequently simply because the selection process requires that companies be well financed. In general, this also means that they are managed conservatively and have staying power, an ability to live through tough periods without a permanent impairment of capital.

If value investing is going well, most exits from securities investments will take place because resource conversion events, such as takeovers, occur rather than because of sales of securities to OPMI markets. Value investing techniques are admittedly a lot more useful for identifying attractive values in OPMI markets than they are for identifying grossly overpriced common stocks. Obviously, any grossly overpriced common stocks should be sold. There are two very important reasons why it is difficult to identify grossly overvalued common stocks when there has been no permanent impairment of capital. First, what appears to be a gross overvaluation in an OPMI market may in fact be a very reasonable valuation in another market, say the M&A market. Second, in the hands of a management skilled in resource conversion activities, an apparently overpriced common stock for OPMI purposes becomes a highly valuable asset usable for access to capital markets or useful in M&As in the hands of skilled managements (e.g., the 1998 acquisition by Worldcom of MCI).

How aggressive sellers of portfolio securities ought to be depends a lot on the character of the portfolio. When the portfolio is generally expanding in size and its liability side does not require near-term service in cash, either to pay interest or dividends or to repay principal, then pressures to sell securities out of the portfolio become minimal. Most mutual fund portfolios, pension and profit-sharing plan portfolios, and common-stock components of insurance-company portfolios generate little pressure to sell. Assuming market price declines, such portfolios should emphasize averaging down existing positions rather than selling because of forecasts of market declines.

Of course, if the discipline being followed is MCT, Graham and Dodd fundamentalism, or conventional money management, portfolio turnover is bound to be much greater than under value investing. In these disciplines, the goal is to predict near-term market prices.

Finally, tax planning frequently makes sales of securities sensible. Realized capital gains in a portfolio, say from a takeover, frequently ought to be offset by realizing losses on other portfolio holdings to offset capital gains taxes that otherwise would be payable. The securities sold to realize capital losses cannot be repurchased for 30 days if the losses are to be tax deductible.

In the evaluation of future flows, whether cash or earnings, the appropriate discount rate, capitalization rate, or P : E ratio (they all are approximately the same thing) ought to reflect all relevant factors. Ascertaining an appropriate discount rate for credit instruments with minimal credit risk that trade at prices near their principal amounts entails two general considerations: (1) the time value of money and (2) the risk, subject to sensitivity analysis, that the actual future will be worse than forecast. Ascertaining an appropriate discount rate for equities or for credit instruments that sell at discounts from their principal amounts entails a third general consideration: the potential, subject to sensitivity analysis, that the actual future will be better than forecast.

Chapter 6

The Substantive
Characteristics of Securities

A hen is only an egg's way of making another egg.

—Samuel Butler

In his 1938 book, *The Theory of Investment Value,* John Burr Williams stated that "investment value [is] the present worth of the future dividends in the case of a common stock, or of the future coupons and principal in the case of a bond" (p. 6). Williams was right on the money in describing the investment value of a performing loan, whether a bond, a trade credit, or a lease. For that definition to be functional, however, the investment value of a common stock has to contain many more elements than the present worth of future dividends. Thus, Williams's definition ought to be restated: investment value is the present worth of future cash bailouts, whatever their source.

There are several forms of cash bailouts:

- Contractually assured payments by issuers to creditors in the forms of interest payments, principal repayments, and premiums for performing loans.

- Dividends to holders of equity securities.
- Sale of securities to a market, whether an outside passive minority investor (OPMI) market or a merger and acquisition (M&A) market.
- Other people's money (OPM), which allows borrowing without disposing of the underlying security.
- The present value of benefits from control or elements of control that might exist because of securities ownership.
- Favorable tax attributes that might be created out of ownership of certain flow-through securities (e.g., a limited partnership interest in a tax shelter [TS]).

For analytic purposes, there are five types of securities:

- Performing credit instruments, in which contracted-for cash payments are being made; most performing credits include loans, trade account payables, derivatives, leases, and many preferred stocks.
- Nonperforming credit instruments, or debt suffering present—or near-term prospects for—money defaults; these tend to have equity characteristics.
- Outside passive minority investor equity securities, which include many preferred stocks, common stocks, options, and warrants.
- Control securities, which consist principally of common stocks, nonperforming credit instruments, credit instruments likely to become nonperforming credit instruments, and general-partner interests in partnerships.
- Hybrid securities, including convertibles and units consisting of credit instruments with warrants attached; these securities are generally OPMI securities rather than control securities.

Probably the most important thing to understand in examining the substantive characteristics of securities is that control common stock is essentially a different commodity than OPMI common stock. Even though they are exactly the same in form most of the time and OPMI commons can be converted into control (or elements of control) common, and vice versa, the differences between control common and OPMI common are far more important than the similarities:

- They tend to trade in different markets at different prices.
- They tend to be analyzed differently.

- They tend to be bought and sold by different, largely unrelated constituencies.
- The different constituencies seek different returns on the investment. Most OPMIs seem to seek to maximize total return mostly by sale to an OPMI market in the relatively short run; they seem to be influenced by daily changes in market prices. Most control buyers seek something off the top (SOTT), TS, the use of OPM, entrenchment, and sale to another control market, or partial cash out in an initial public offering (IPO). Most control buyers are not heavily influenced by day-to-day price swings in OPMI markets unless they are actually attempting to buy, sell, or borrow against their securities positions.
- Corporate law—especially state law, court decisions in leading corporate states, and federal bankruptcy law—is designed to entrench control groups and managements in office at the expense of OPMI rights. In small part, securities laws, as embodied in the amended Securities Act of 1933 and the amended Securities and Exchange Act of 1934, also have the effect of delivering management entrenchment at the expense of OPMI shareholders. Three such regulatory areas entrenching management are securities' regulations governing cash-tender offers, exchange offers, and proxy solicitations.
- The bulk of U.S. securities laws, especially as embodied in the various acts administered by the Securities and Exchange Commission (SEC), are designed to and do protect OPMIs. One of the areas of protection is against several forms of overreaching by control people through provision of:
  1. Orderly trading markets
  2. Disclosures
  3. Oversight of fiduciaries and quasifiduciaries, including those who control public corporations

Much of the substantive differences between control pricing and OPMI pricing are resolved through long-term arbitrages, which are the very essence of the tendency toward efficiency that exists in all markets, specifically between and among disparate markets. There are times when OPMI market prices are superhigh compared with what businesses would be worth as private concerns. In that case, new shares are marketed publicly in IPOs and in secondary underwritings and M&As in which newly issued common shares, valued at or near OPMI market prices, are part or all of the consideration paid for an acquisition. At other times, OPMI market prices might be quite low compared with prevailing prices in control markets. Then, there is a tendency for cheap shares to be acquired for cash and debt, in M&A transactions, in hostile takeovers, and in the particular form of M&A called leveraged buyouts (LBOs), management buyouts (MBOs), or going-privates.

There are built-in limitations to this tendency toward long-term arbitrages. OPMI stock markets tend to be rather capricious, and certain sections of OPMI markets tend to be even more volatile than others. One extremely volatile section is the IPO market. The ability to sell IPOs can be vigorously proscribed at times (as was the case from 1991 to 1993 and in the fall of 1998), although as is pointed out in Chapter 8, Promoters' and Professionals' Compensations, the financial community has a vested interest in encouraging IPOs.

As for a control group's buying up common stocks from OPMIs, there are three key factors that often ameliorate this tendency toward efficiency. First, the businesses involved have to be reasonably well financed, have access to credit markets in order to whet the interest of most financial (nonstrategic control buyers), or both. Second, the entrenchment of incumbent management is frequently a showstopper preventing any real efficiencies from arising in the market for changes in control. Outsiders seeking control from entrenched managements usually have to incur huge up-front expenses and almost always are faced with uncertainty as to whether control will be attainable. Finally, any process involving changes of control entails considerable administration (i.e., deal) expenses for attorneys, investment bankers, accountants, tax advisers, and others.

In a very meaningful sense, nonperforming loans are much like common stock even though there probably are less dramatic price differences here between OPMI markets and control markets. In the case of nonperforming loans, obtaining elements of control usually refers to getting influence over the reorganization process for a troubled company rather than to getting control of a business. Control over reorganization is key for creditors, whether the company restructures out of court or in Chapter 11 bankruptcy.

As to control of operations, the tendency seems to be that there is almost as much management entrenchment in troubled public companies as in healthy companies. Corporate governance provisions are an important part of virtually all Chapter 11 plans of reorganization. Also, in dealing with nonperforming loans, loan governance provisions become crucially important, especially for out-of-court reorganizations. The key loan governance player for bank loans tends to be the agent bank. For publicly traded bonds, the indenture trustee—almost always the corporate trust department of a large commercial bank—is important.

In terms of corporate governance, management entrenchment provisions are now well-nigh universal. In general, though, it is far harder, with public companies, to remove a general partner of a limited partnership than to remove the management of a corporation. Usual management entrenchment devices, both corporate and limited partnership, include one or more of the following:

- Limited voting for OPMI common
- Staggered board
- Supermajorities
- Poison pills
- Parachutes
- Reincorporation in management-friendly states, such as Pennsylvania or Indiana
- Blank check preferred stocks
- A lack of stockholder rights to call special meetings

Outside passive minority investor market prices, whenever they exist, always deserve weight in any analysis. How much depends on the objectives of the investor and the characteristics of the investment; weight might range from as high as 100% to as low as 2%. Market price deserves 100% weight when an OPMI has as a solitary goal the risk-adjusted maximization of total return consistently (*consistently* means all the time). It may deserve 100% weight also when a money manager's job depends on stock-market performance, where the money manager/analyst knows little or nothing about the company in whose securities he or she is investing, or where the portfolio is fully financed with borrowed money. Finally, OPMI market prices probably deserve 100% weight or close to it in risk-arbitrage situations (i.e., such events as publicly announced mergers in which there will be relatively determinant workouts in relatively determinant periods of time). In all other instances, OPMI market prices deserve considerably less than 100% weight.

These 100% situations all involve trading by short-run–oriented speculators. When other conditions are introduced—for example, the investor, operating without borrowed funds, emphasizes contractually assured cash income rather than total return as an investment objective; the investor focuses on long-term buy-and-hold; or the analysis of a security involves great complexity (e.g., most common stocks)—weight to OPMI market prices in the analytic mix has to be reduced.

OPMI market prices are often a lot less important in the analysis of most performing loans than of nonarbitrage common stocks because:

- Holders of performing loans need look only to service on their loans for cash bailouts. Most common stockholders would instead look for a cash bailout by sale to a market.
- Performing loans are usually analyzed by reference to far fewer variables (e.g., current yield, yield-to-maturity, duration, and covenants) than are common stocks. Outside passive minority investor pricing for performing loans is most often much more realistic (i.e., close to corporate values) than is the case for common stocks. Thus, with performing loans, there is usually little arbitrage between OPMI prices and control prices.
- Time corrects many errors in holding performing loans. Such never has to happen for common stocks. Say a holder buys a 10-year 6% bond with a 10% yield-to-maturity. Assume the bond continues to sell at a 10% yield-to-maturity. The dollar price at the end of each year would be as shown in Table 6-1.

Table 6-1. Price by Year

Year to Maturity	Price (%)
10	75.42
9	76.90
8	78.66
7	80.53
6	82.58
5	84.84
4	87.32
3	90.05
2	93.06
1	96.36
0	100.00

For spread lenders OPMI market prices probably deserve considerable weight, though probably not as great as the spread between interest received and interest paid. Recent changes in generally accepted accounting principles (GAAP) requiring portfolios to be marked to market, however, elevate the importance of OPMI market prices because accounting data, as reported and unadjusted, become important for regulatory or credit-rating purposes. For those who carry performing loans on margin, OPMI market prices may deserve close to 100% weight.

Loans made at interest rates greater than the risk-free rate of money are substantively equivalent to credit insurance and put options. The extra interest rate is equal to insurance premiums paid to the lender for taking credit risks. The extra interest can also be viewed as having the lender sell a put option. The lender collects a premium for the right to put to the borrower, or require the borrower to buy, certain assets in certain events. For example, a mutual fund entered into a put agreement with Heller Financial in January 1996 for 1 year. The fund sold Heller the put for a 7% fee. The terms of the arrangement were that in the event Kmart filed for Chapter 11 relief in the next 12 months, Heller had the right to require the fund buy 100% of the principal amount of Kmart payables owned by Heller for 87%. This transaction actually went forward as a loan. The fund acquired from Heller for 80% cash a 1 year medium-term note bearing interest at Libor plus 10 basis points (bips). If K-mart filed for Chapter 11 within the year, Heller could satisfy the note at its option by delivering to the fund either 87% cash or 100% in Kmart payables. If Kmart did not file, the note would be satisfied by payment of 87% cash to the fund.

Yield-to-maturity is an artificial calculation except for zero-coupon bonds, in that it assumes cash received over the life of the loan will always be reinvested at the original rates of return. Yield-to-maturity is an essential tool, however, for comparative analysis, comparing the theoretical returns available between and among different credit issues. It is the annual return to be earned on a performing loan over its life. The yield has two components where a loan is priced at some price other than the payment to be made at maturity. The first component is the interest rate. The second component is either the amortization of discount if the bond was acquired at a discount from the amount to be paid at maturity or the amortization of premium if the price is in excess of the principal amount to be paid at maturity.

Any term of a security ought to be viewed as an option, or privilege, granted to an issuer or as an obligation imposed on an issuer or a holder. Here is a breakdown of the status of various securities terms:

- Call feature: An option to the issuer.
- Mandatory redemption: An obligation of the issuer.
- Cash dividend: Once it is declared, the recipient is obligated to receive it.
- Stock buyback: Any individual shareholder has the option of selling or not selling.
- Cash-tender offer or exchange offer: Individual securityholder has the option to accept or not accept it.
- Merger or use of proxy machinery: If the requisite vote is obtained, it is subject only to perfecting dissenter rights (which is hard to do); every securityholder is obligated to participate.
- Change of terms of a loan agreement regarding cash payments outside Chapter 11: Each individual debtholder has the option of going along.
- Change of any other term of a loan agreement outside of Chapter 11: If the requisite vote is obtained, all debtholders have to go along.

In reality, there are few rigid definitions of a security's classification; what a security is depends on where you sit. Subordinated debentures are a good example of a security that ought to have more than one definition. From the vantage point of the common stock, subordinated debentures are debt. From the vantage point of senior lenders, however, to whom the subordinates are expressly junior (that is what *subordination* means), the subordinates are part of the borrowing base, akin to equity. Another example would be preferred stock issued by a subsidiary where the parent company's sole asset is the common stock of the subsidiary. The parent company's principal source of cash would be dividends paid on the subsidiary's common stock. Payment of the subsidiary's common stock dividends requires prior dividend payments to the subsidiary preferred stock. The proceeds of payments on subsidiary common stock are used to service parent-company bank loans. Thus, absent any other covenants (such as the subsidiary's assets' being pledged to parent-company banks), the preferred stock of the subsidiary has a senior position vis-à-vis bank borrowings by the parent. In the consolidated financial statements of the company prepared in accordance with GAAP, however, the subsidiary's preferred stock appears to be junior to the parent company's bank debt.

This was the situation with Ambase, Inc. in 1990. Ambase's principal subsidiary was the Home Insurance Company. Ambase owned 100% of the outstanding common stock of Home Insurance Company, and it was dividends on Home Insurance common stock that gave Ambase most of its wherewithal to service Ambase bank debt. Home Insurance Company $14\frac{1}{4}\%$ preferred was, in all meaningful respects, senior to the borrowings from banks by parent company Ambase.

In certain academic circles, it has been argued that little justification exists for issuing preferred stocks rather than subordinated debentures. The reasoning is that interest payable by the corporation on subordinated debentures is tax deductible, but dividend payments on the preferred stock are not tax deductible. In the real world, there are myriad reasons justifying the issuance of and the existence of preferred stocks; here are a few:

- Qualified domestic corporations that receive dividends from less-than-80%-owned domestic corporations can exclude from income 70% of such dividends received under Section 243 of the Internal Revenue Code. As a practical matter, the combined tax bills of the two corporations may be smaller when the security issued is a preferred stock rather than a subordinated debenture.
- Many—if not most—corporations have "layer cake" capitalizations, and the issuance of preferred stock enables such corporations to issue considerably more senior debt than would otherwise be the case. For example, a typical finance company holding consumer receivables might have the capitalization, shown from the bottom up, in Table 6-2.

Table 6-2. Capitalization

Variable	Value (000,000)
Common and surplus	$100
Preferred stock	10
Junior borrowing base	110
Subordinated borrowings (equal to 100% of junior borrowing base)	110
Senior borrowing base	220
Senior debt (equal to 3–6 times senior borrowing base, of which about 66% would be short-term borrowings	660–1,320
Total capitalization	880–1,540

Assume the company can incur senior debt of 4 times its borrowing base. Without preferred stock being issued, such senior debt would amount to $800 million. With preferred stock outstanding, the senior debt issuable would amount to $880 million. In other words, the issuance of $10 million of preferred stock would allow the company to increase its senior borrowing by $80 million.

- Voting preferred stocks are an essential tool for tax-free exchanges in connection with mergers that qualify as reorganizations under Section 368(b) and (c) of the Internal Revenue Code. By use of preferred stocks and common stocks, it becomes feasible to satisfy the various needs and desires of disparate parties to the merger transaction:
  1. Those who desire to maximize long-term total return and control would receive common stock and/or super voting rights common stock.
  2. Those who desire cash income, relative seniority, or both, as well as something of an equity kicker, would receive convertible preferred stock.
  3. There frequently are regulatory and rating agency reasons for issuing preferrers rather than subordinates.

Preferred rights are spelled out in certificates of designation, which are part of a corporation's articles of incorporation. Privately negotiated terms of preferred stocks can have quite meaningful protections for holders, whereas protections for publicly traded preferreds tend to be sparse. The most meaningful protection for publicly issued preferred stock seems to be one requiring a two-thirds vote of the outstanding preferred class if the company is to issue a new preferred stock equal or senior to the existing issue as to dividends or liquidation. The right usually given to the preferred to elect two directors if six quarterly dividends are missed is normally not much of a right at all, since the typical preferred holder has no special access to the corporate proxy machinery or to the corporate treasury to finance a proxy solicitation. An important right for preferred stocks that usually does not exist is the right to vote separately as a class on all matters.

In the case of troubled companies, preferred stocks frequently are in better positions, *de facto*, than subordinates. Subordinates have rights to accelerate if an event of default occurs and is continuing. Given the subordinates' junior position in the capitalization, this right is often the right to commit suicide. The preferred, on the other hand, piles up dividend arrearages and might be in a better position to make reorganization deals.

In pricing convertible and other hybrid securities, there are a few simple computer-programmable variables resulting in a normal convertible curve:

- Yield
- Yield-to-maturity
- Percent premium over conversion parity
- Percent premium (discount) from call
- Beta of the underlying common stock

In a market tending toward instantaneous efficiency for new issues, convertibles might be offered at prices equal to 150 to 250 bip below comparable credits in terms of yield-to-maturity and at 25% to 45% premiums over conversion parity compared with the prices at which the underlying common stock trades.

There are trade-offs in comparing straight debt characteristics with convertibles. A shorter maturity and strong mandatory redemption requirements tend to be more valuable for a holder of straight debt, provided the debt does not trade at a premium over call price. Early maturity, early redemption, or the presence of both qualities diminishes the value of conversion privileges. For any convertible or option, long life tends to be a highly favorable characteristic. Any convertible feature is translatable into an option feature.

Alienability refers to factors that cause a security to have a fair value different from an OPMI market price. In general, there are four alienability factors:

- Contractual restrictions on the sale of securities to an OPMI market, or any other market.
- Securities laws restrictions on sale to an OPMI market.
- Blockage—the amount of shares held is inordinately large compared with trading volumes in the OPMI market. Restrictions on resale and blockage are mutually exclusive, since both cannot be operative at the same time. If there are contractual or securities laws restrictions preventing sale in an OPMI market, the existence of blockage becomes irrelevant while those restrictions are in place. In a valuation, the existence of restrictions or blockage results in discounts from OPMI market prices.

- Control—if a common stock is control common stock, it frequently results in valuations reflecting a premium above OPMI market prices.

Alienability discounts for restriction and blockage can run from 15% to 50% of OPMI market prices. It is hard to put a percentage number on control premiums, however, they will vary case by case.

Securities Act restrictions on resale can exist for securities not registered under the Securities Act of 1933. The restraint against public resale can be engendered by one of two conditions: the holder is an insider or the securities were never registered. Sales can be made in OPMI markets, however, pursuant to Rule 144 or a Section 4(a) exemption.

Securities Act restrictions on resale have become considerably less onerous over the years as Rule 144 has been liberalized. Presently, restricted shares held fully paid for at least 1 year can be "dribbled out" to the OPMI market by sale each week of the greater of 1% of the outstanding issue or 15% of the average trading volume over the prior 3 weeks. Once the restricted stock has been held for 2 years, holders are free to sell into OPMI markets without restriction. A holder of restricted stock may obtain rights of registration of the piggyback, the trigger variety, or both.

Many insiders have incentive to have low OPMI market prices and thus have inherent conflicts of interest with short-run OPMI speculators:

- Estate valuation purposes: The lower the OPMI market price, the less the value of the estate either at the date of death or 6 months thereafter.
- Going private: The lower the OPMI price, the less insiders will have to pay in a going-private transaction.

Control insiders have basic advantages over OPMIs in that the insiders control the timing of events. For example, those control people who seek to go private can wait for a bear market in OPMI prices. The fairness of going-private transactions will always be measured in part by premiums paid over current OPMI market prices.

The concept of dilution is never absolute. It is always relative to something: (1) OPMI price, (2) underlying values, or (3) percentage of capitalization owned.

In examining securities from the point of view of corporate feasibility, the central necessity is to be aware that a security issued by a company has to deliver one of two things to a holder: either the right to receive from the company cash payments sooner or later, or ownership interest in the company, present or potential.

The rights to receive cash payments from the company that attach to debt instruments and preferred stocks can constitute a cash drain on a business and thus detract from feasibility. Ownership interests—common stocks, warrants, and options—do not require cash service from the company, although such securities might not have much value to a holder unless they held promise of a cash bailout by prospects of sale to a market or of delivering control benefits to the holder.

Issuing ownership securities that do not require cash service (i.e., dividends) can detract from corporate feasibility insofar as the existence of nondividend paying equities detracts from a company's ability to access capital markets to sell new issues of equity. In the past, this had been a factor causing electric utilities and many finance companies to follow policies of paying out 60% to 80% of net income as dividends. For the vast majority of companies, though, dividend policy seems to have little or no impact on a their ability to obtain access to capital markets. Indeed, for high-tech companies perceived as growth vehicles, the payment of regular dividends may be looked at as a negative factor, detracting from growth, in OPMI markets.

The fact that any security has to deliver either cash pay or ownership can become quite important in the structuring of appropriate capitalizations in resource conversion contexts, as in both LBOs and the reorganization of troubled companies. The appropriate capitalization ought to be feasible—not too heavy on cash-payment instruments. Also, appropriate instruments have to be issued to participants in the capitalization. Banks and life insurance companies will desire cash-payment instruments with seniority and strong covenants. Control buyers could want ownership instruments because those instruments deliver elements of control, especially when these participants do not need cash-payment instruments to service the debt they may have incurred in their own entities. OPMIs and other noncontrol investors could want ownership instruments because those instruments have promise of delivering a cash bailout by sale to a market.

Chapter 7

Capital Structure

If it ain't broke don't fix it.

Modern financial theorists, and Graham and Dodd fundamentalists, for that matter, look at corporate capital structure exclusively from the point of view of what impact a capital structure is likely to have on the market price of a corporation's common stock. Value investors, like active investors, view capital structure as something that arises out of a process that involves meeting the needs and desires of a multiplicity of constituencies, including various creditors, regulators, rating agencies, managements and other control groups, outside passive minority investors (OPMIs), and the company itself. This chapter enumerates factors that ought to be weight in the determination of capital structure.

Adopting the modern capital theory (MCT) approach to appropriate capital structure, which theorizes about the probable impacts of capital structure on OPMI market prices, is akin to studying the solar system by assuming the sun revolves around the earth. In this analogy, the earth is an OPMI and it is given an importance in the solar system completely out of sync with readily observable reality. Although this perspective might be fine for an OPMI, it is inappropriate for an active investor, a value investor, or anyone wishing to take a corporate perspective on capital structure.

Capital Structure from the Corporate Perspective

An understanding of the specific factors affecting capital structure requires a knowledge of the several conceptual differences that arise from taking a corporate perspective rather than the traditional efficient-market or Graham and Dodd views.

Substantive Consolidation

An underlying assumption found in MCT and in Graham and Dodd is that there is a substantive consolidation between the interests of the OPMI and corporate feasibility. These theories hold that the exclusive way to determine the value of a corporation is to find the total market value of all its outstanding equity securities and add to this the amount of corporate obligations outstanding, either as measured by claim amount or market value.

From the value investing perspective, there is no substantive consolidation. Furthermore, OPMI desires frequently conflict with corporate feasibility. There are three obvious cases in which such conflicts are common: (1) the short-run OPMI desire for maximum reported earnings even if it means higher corporate income-tax bills than would otherwise exist; (2) the tendency of OPMIs to have very short run agendas, even though long-term expensive projects might enhance corporate values materially; (3) the OPMI desire for cash dividends or cash distributions in the form of common stock buybacks even when corporations might have much better uses for cash retained for corporate uses.

Accessing Equity Markets

Corporate feasibility and OPMI stock price are essentially equivalent when the corporation is seeking access to capital markets to raise funds through the sale of new issues of equity, especially common stock equity. Here, though, the close relationship is measured by whether the corporation can access capital markets at all, not by the per-share price the corporation will receive for the sale of a new issue of common stock that does not pay a cash dividend. In this instance, per-share price can have a more or less dilutive effect on common shares. The price has no real effect, however, on corporate feasibility.

Financing with Retained Earnings

For most corporations, accessing equity markets for new funds is a some-time thing, rather capricious in its doability and almost always very expensive in terms of overall underwriting costs. Consequently, the vast majority of public corporations fill their equity needs through retaining earnings. Only a small percentage of earnings, or none at all, are paid out to shareholders as cash dividends. The indicated percentage payout for Standard & Poor's (S&P) 425 Industrial Index in November 1998 was 43.6%.

There are important exceptions, though, to financing with retained earnings. The most notable one has been the electric utility industry. From 1945 through the late 1970s, most companies in the industry were experiencing average annual growth in the demand for electric kilowatts of about 7% per annum. Massive capital expenditures were needed to produce $1 of annual revenue (estimated at about $5 of capital expenditures for every $1 of annual revenue). Normal capitalization consisted of 50% to 60% long-term mortgage debt, 10% preferred stock, and 30% to 40% equity. Equity had to be increased relatively regularly and in relatively major doses. The industry ensured for itself access to equity markets by paying out as dividends 70% to 80% of earnings, which then made their securities attractive to income investors. Furthermore, per-share dividends were increased modestly as often as once a year. Every 18 to 24 months, however, the companies marketed new issues of common stock to obtain requisite funds to finance massive capital expenditures while keeping debt-to-stock ratios in line with mortgage debt covenants and with industry custom and usage. Thus, appeal to a constituency that wanted regular and increasing dividends ensured that utilities would have access to a capital source they needed.

There remain a number of companies in other industries that follow the electric utility model of paying out dividends representing a high percentage of their earnings and then periodically marketing new issues of common stocks. Real estate investment trusts (REITs) and many finance companies follow such policies. Indeed, REITs are required to pay out at least 95% of net income as dividends if they are to remain REITs and enjoy a flow-through income-tax status, where the REIT itself is not subject to income tax because otherwise taxable income is paid out to shareholders.

The concept of high dividends combined with frequent access to equity markets that is implicit in the efficient market hypothesis (EMH) and Graham and Dodd views of capital structures, however, is not common.

Dividend Policy

Benjamin Graham and David Dodd, in discussing dividend policy, focused on substantive consolidation. According to Graham and Dodd fundamentalism and the EMH, a company that enjoys a high return on equity (ROE) should retain earnings, and a company with a low ROE should pay out its earnings as dividends when its shareholders could earn more than the company could by reinvesting the net proceeds from dividend payments. For value investors, dividends are to be viewed as a residual use of cash, something to be paid to shareholders only after a company's needs to retain cash are met. The company's reasonable needs come first. The company's needs are of three types: to acquire assets, to pay or otherwise satisfy creditors, and to provide a margin of safety against an unpredictable future. Many high-ROE companies have little or no need to retain cash and can afford high dividend payouts (e.g., money-management companies). Many low-ROE companies had better retain most cash generated from operations if they are to survive (e.g., integrated aluminum producers, discount retailers, and meatpackers). ROE should not be a test for a firm's ability to pay dividends.

Constituency Stakes in Corporate Feasibility

There seems to be a view that the common stockholder community has a consuming interest in corporate feasibility but that other constituencies (notably creditors) do not. Creditors, it is postulated, just want to receive back principal plus interest even if it bankrupts the company, but such a view is unrealistic. The vast majority of creditors have continuing relationships with the companies to whom they lend, so they are interested in refinancing maturing debt and/or continuing to ship goods or rent properties. Everyone—not just common shareholders—has a stake in corporate feasibility.

Constituency Conflicts with Corporate Feasibility

Every constituency, including OPMI shareholders, also has conflicts with corporate feasibility. Each wants things from companies that detract from feasibility. Holders of common shares want dividends, creditors want cash payments and tough covenants, and managements want huge compensation packages.

As is stated in previous chapters, each constituency related to a corporation has objectives concerning the company that combine communities of interest and conflicts of interest. There is usually nothing special about OPMIs compared with other constituencies except that most OPMIs need not have a permanent or semipermanent stake in the company and that once an OPMI owns common stock, the OPMI has no further obligation to do things for the company. Thus, OPMIs are not smarter or better informed than other constituencies, and OPMIs do not have an exclusive interest in corporate feasibility. Two things, however, do distinguish many OPMIs from other constituencies: They have no particular need for a cash return and they have no need for elements of control. All other constituencies tend to be intelligent, their markets tend toward efficiency, and they each seek to maximize their financial interests. (These characteristics are not exclusive to OPMI shareholders; they are shared with creditors, regulators, rating agencies, managements, and control shareholders.)

Actually, other things being equal, OPMIs are often a lot less knowledgeable than others who have to rely exclusively on performance of the business for a cash bailout and who cannot, unlike OPMIs, look to a sale to a market for a cash bailout. Put simply, a life insurance company making a long-term private-placement unsecured loan to a company is probably a lot more knowledgeable about the company than are the OPMIs trading common stock on the New York Stock Exchange (NYSE). First, the insurance company can do due-diligence research beyond the public record. Second, the insurance company does not waste time and energy analyzing factors that probably have no relationship to specific corporate values (e.g., the level of interest rates or of the gross domestic product [GDP], dividend policy, or technical market considerations). Offsetting this somewhat is the likelihood that the insurance company knows that the more senior the issue and the shorter its maturity, the less the corporate analysis that needs or ought to be undertaken.

Market Efficiency

All markets tend toward efficiencies. Some markets tend toward instantaneous efficiency: trading markets for common stocks, risk-arbitrage markets, and derivative markets. Other markets take long times—say, 5 years or more—for efficiency tendencies to assert themselves: the merger and acquisition (M&A) market, the leveraged buyout (LBO) market, and the market for restructuring troubled companies.

Capitalization in Resource Conversion

Capitalization becomes extremely important in resource conversion activities. The resource conversion topics that are discussed in this book—M&As, LBOs or management buyouts (MBOs), initial public offerings (IPOs), and restructuring troubled companies—all involve major recapitalizations. For example, LBO analysis involves first a determination of an enterprise's value and dynamics and then an examination of the cost of money and an application of a new capitalization. Exactly the same economic procedures are followed when reorganizing troubled companies either out of court or in Chapter 11. In the case of LBOs, however, the capitalization is leveraged up, in that debt is substituted for equity. In the reorganization of troubled companies, the capitalization is leveraged down, in that equity, debt with soft terms or both are substituted for senior debt and other onerous obligations.

An easy way of remembering the above is to recall that in the reorganization of troubled companies, recapitalization tends to make sick companies healthy, whereas in LBOs, recapitalization tends to make healthy companies sick.

Factors Affecting Capital Structure

In all financial activities, there is a tendency toward efficiency: All participants in a process attempt to do as well as they reasonably can under the circumstances, given their agendas and the agendas of other participants. This certainly holds true for capitalization. Creditors comport, regarding this tendency toward efficiency, in the same way as do OPMIs, although the primary item on a creditor's agenda might be the avoidance of a money default whereas the primary item on an agenda of an OPMI involved in short-term trading would be the maximization of total return.

Efficient corporate capital structure, the financing layer cake of the corporation, takes into account myriad factors, including the following:

- The composition and characteristics of the assets that offset the capitalization
- The needs and desires of the several classes of creditors
- The needs and desires of regulators
- The needs and desires of rating agencies
- The needs, desires, and proclivities of management and control groups
- Custom and usage
- The professional advice of investment bankers, attorneys, and accountants
- The desires of OPMIs and OPMI representatives

The value investor should appreciate all of these.

The Composition and Characteristics of Assets

Asset management is mainly a function of liability management; by contrast, liability management is mainly a function of asset management.

What amount and types of liabilities that ought to be part of a corporate capitalization has to be very much a function of having assets employed in the business in ways that produce sufficient resources to service the liabilities. There are two sources from which liabilities can normally be serviced: internal cash flow obtained either from employment of assets or sale of assets, and access to capital markets for new financings (this is usually a function of the business's having earnings—the ability to create wealth).

The overall insurance industry provides a good case study of how the character and amount of liabilities influence—indeed, govern—the management of asset portfolios. Insurance companies' assets consist essentially of investments in debt instruments and other securities. Liabilities consist essentially of estimated obligations to policyholders in the form of policyholder reserves (life companies) and reserve for losses and unearned premiums (property and casualty companies).

In life companies, the policyholder reserve is a very long term, reasonably certain, and actuarially determined (on a year-to-year basis) liability. Given this type of liability, life companies' investment assets usually consist mainly of long-term privately placed loans. By contrast, property and casualty companies are subject to dramatic and relatively unpredictable (on a year-to-year basis) demands for cash payouts arising from, say, hurricanes or earthquakes. Thus, property and casualty companies' investment portfolios consist largely of marketable securities, salable to meet the businesses' sudden needs for cash to satisfy claims. Furthermore, property and casualty companies generally fund the dollar amount of their liabilities by investing in credit instruments (debt securities). Common stock investments are only a small portion of property and casualty company portfolios, limited to dollar amounts no greater than the firm's statutory surplus. Statutory surplus is net worth computed in accordance with insurance regulations, rather than GAAP. Each net worth figure, statutory or GAAP, is reconcilable with the other.

The analysis of capital structure is very much a function of where you sit. In some contexts, consolidated financial statements are useful, but in other, parent and subsidiary financial statements are key. From the perspective of common stockholders in a holding company, the consolidated financial statements present a useful indication of what the overall results and overall resources are for the company. From the point of view of a lender to the parent holding company, however, parent-company financials are crucial to determining credit worthiness. The parent company directly owns only the common stock of its subsidiaries, not the specific assets of the subsidiaries, even though these subsidiary assets are reflected in the consolidated financial statements.

To service their debts, most parent companies have to receive cash from their subsidiaries. There are essentially four ways in which this cash can be received: dividends, home-office charges, tax treaties, and sales by the parent of the common stock owned. Sales of common stock of the subsidiaries may be impractical. If the holding company is in a regulated industry (e.g., insurance or banking), cash payments by the subsidiaries to the parent may be vigorously proscribed. If the subsidiary—say, a finance company or department-store chain—borrows money, then the loan covenant may limit payments to the parent. Thus, a parent company that may appear, on a consolidated basis, to be quite solid really may not be creditworthy at all.

The Needs and Desires of the Several Classes of Creditors

Creditors as a group are probably the most important force determining what corporate capital structures will be. By and large, creditors are intelligent and many are relatively knowledgeable about the businesses they finance. Put otherwise, they operate in a market with strong tendencies toward efficiency.

Credit markets seem to be much bigger than equity markets and can be deemed to include all payables owed by businesses including accrued expenses, accounts payable, rents payable, taxes payable, and borrowing from banks, other institutions, and the public. Creditors are often a lot more knowledgeable about the business in which they invest than are OPMIs. They are much more serious analysts than are OPMIs. This is understandable because most creditors have to look to corporations for their bailouts. It is actual business performance that will generate cash to pay them principal and interest. It is quite understandable that creditors tend to have strong views about the amount of money they will let a company borrow. By contrast, most OPMIs look to a sale to a stock market for their bailout. Many, as for example those with a technical chartist approach, could not care less about the business. Their knowledge of it can be as restricted as knowing what the stock ticker symbol is.

Creditors of corporations, when financing their own businesses, often have far greater access to borrowings to finance their assets (portfolios of loans to corporations) than would be the case if their assets were common stocks. Portfolios consisting of performing loans generate contractually assured cash to service their obligations, but common stocks usually do not. Market price volatility is considerably less for performing loans than for common stocks.

Predictable cash return on an asset has an importance independent of total return. An asset holder cannot expect to service obligations existing in most capital structures with unrealized appreciation; service has to be made in cash.

Intelligent creditors usually base investment decisions much more on reasonable worst-case assumptions than on base-case assumptions. As knowledgeable and analysis oriented as creditors are about corporate values, though, they are not immune from making bad decisions. This is probably true because throughout U.S. history, forecasts of cash and earnings flows have been notoriously unreliable. Witness commercial bank lending to less-developed countries (LDCs) in the 1970s, energy lending before the oil bubble burst in the early 1980s, commercial real estate lending prior to 1986, and savings and loans' unacceptable interest rate risk and then credit risk in the 1980s. Still, their understanding of corporate values is much better than is that of the typical OPMI—bankers need to know how to read, but OPMIs do not!

The Needs and Desires of Regulators

Corporate capital structure is partially determined by well-informed analytic regulators who have as an agenda seeing that corporate capital structures are not too risky—that there is capital adequacy. These include bank regulators, insurance regulators, the Small Business Administration (SBA), and securities industries regulators, especially those working under the amended Investment Act of 1940.

The Needs and Desires of Rating Agencies

An investment grade imprimatur is essential for many companies operating in certain industries or seeking access to public markets for new issues of debt securities. Agencies providing investment ratings include Moody's Investors Service, Standard & Poor's Rating Services, Fitch Investors Service, Duff & Phelps Credit Rating Company, and A.M. Best Company. Corporate managements are very much aware of how capital structure affects the opinions of these agencies.

Creditors, regulators, and rating agencies tend to be efficient (and are probably smarter than most OPMIs). Most corporate loans are performing loans and most corporations remain solvent.

The Needs, Desires, and Proclivities of Managements and Control Groups

Once it is observed that managements and control groups have multiple agendas that combine communities of interest and conflicts of interests with various of their constituencies, disparate factors affect managements' and control groups' influence on what an appropriate capitalization will be. Few managements are likely to conclude that the appropriate capitalization is that structure which will maximize the trading price of the OPMI common stock.

Custom and Usage

Custom is one of the strongest determinants of capital structure. Industry capital structures tend toward uniformity as the various providers of capital adopt common standards or norms. For example, historically, electric utilities have often been financed 50% to 60% with publicly held mortgage debt, 10% with preferred stock, and 30% to 40% with common stock and surplus.

In the LBO arena, senior secured lenders will lend approximately four to five times operating income (minus the excess of capital expenditures over depreciation plus a working capital facility) to finance a deal. Sometimes subordinated debentures, preferred stock held by the sellers or others, or both are available, though nowadays, almost always some meaningful common stock investment is made by the purchasers. The purchase price for the business might be 7 to 12 times the above-mentioned operating income.

Similar custom-and-usage ratios exist for finance companies, hotels, banks, cable companies, insurance holding companies, airlines, and others. Good value investors become familiar with these ratios industry by industry.

Most custom-and-usage capitalizations are the most efficient way to capitalize companies, but this is not always true. Take department-store and discount-store capital structures. Despite the general economic prosperity of the 1990s, a plethora of department store and discount store chains (Federated Department Stores, Macy's, Caldor, Kmart, Wards, Bradlees, Zayre) have had to reorganize their capital structure either out of court or in Chapter 11. The main reason was too much credit granted from three sources—financial institutions, trade creditors, and landlords.

The Professional Advice of Investment Bankers, Attorneys, and Accountants

Such fee-based advisors as investment bankers, attorneys, and accountants are important influences in determining corporate capital structure. Investment bankers tend to have great expertise in structuring the terms of securities so as to sell the securities in private placement and OPMI markets. Attorneys are key in dealing with securities questions as they effect the terms to be included in securities issues. GAAP is the province of accountants while both attorneys and accountants deal with income tax issues.

The Needs and Desires of Outside Passive Minority Investors and Their Representatives

The OPMI market is the only constituency addressed by Graham and Dodd fundamentalism and proponents of the EMH in their discussions of capital structure and dividend policy. Indeed, the emphasis is even narrower because the focus is almost exclusively on estimated near-term impacts on OPMI market prices.

This emphasis seems misplaced. It has validity when the company itself and control shareholders are seeking access to capital markets to sell common stock to an OPMI market. This is an occasional occurrence, and the interests of the company itself revolve around being able to market common stock at all rather than around the price at which common can be marketed (an OPMI interest).

It is not that OPMI interests are ignored in determining a capital structure but that those needs are tempered by requirements of other constituencies. In terms of capitalization, it is a good rule of thumb that satisfying creditor requirements is a lot more important than meeting OPMI desires in structuring a capitalization.

Risk is a word that should not be used without an adjective in front of it. Just because a common stock might have a lot of market risk (i.e., a plunge in OPMI market price) and a company might have a lot of investment risk (i.e., the business is unlikely to survive as a going concern) does not mean that adequately secured lenders to the corporation are taking any credit risk at all. Creditors can be confident that the loan will remain a performing loan or that in a reorganization, they will receive a value of principal amount plus interest and interest on interest. General risk really does not exist.

Conservative Capital Structures

In practice, many corporations operate with conservative capitalizations that provide an insurance policy for holders of junior securities and the corporation itself. In addition, trade creditors and public bondholders are not made nervous. The cost of doing this is a lower ROE (and perhaps stock price) than would otherwise be the case in buoyant periods when the business is prospering. If you pay to insure your house, however, and it does not burn down, that does not mean the expenditure for insurance was wasted.

Conservatively capitalized and well-managed companies are also more likely candidates for hostile takeovers. Raiders must rely solely on publicly available information; therefore they see good management and a strong balance sheet as insurance against a bad purchase. Not surprisingly, increasing corporate leverage is a standard tactic used by corporation managements to thwart takeovers.

Should OPMIs acquire the common stocks of companies with conservative capitalizations? Presumably, such common stocks will sell at lower prices, have greater potential for appreciation if they are to become leveraged in the future, and are more likely targets for takeovers. In addition, such investments would be more conservative because if operations are not as profitable as expected, there should be less downside.

On the other hand, there are offsets to make an OPMI want more leverage. If the company is unleveraged, the OPMI, as an investor, is not as likely to capture as much of the upside. The OPMI might also be "in bed" with managements or control groups who do not need access to stock markets and who do not care about the stock price in the short run. Investors on margin might not be able to wait an indefinite period of time for a return; or if they change their mind and need to cash out in the short run, they may do so without appreciation. Professional money managers who are primarily asset allocators and are evaluated on the basis of short-run performance might not want to take this kind of risk.

There is no universal answer to the question of whether to buy the stocks of leveraged or unleveraged companies. It depends on who you are and what you know. If you are a conventional asset allocator who does not know too much about finance or companies, then you might be better off taking the more conventional approach to choosing your portfolio. On the other hand, if you read all the literature, understand individual companies and industries, and can appreciate the nuances of capital structure, then you might be better off going the underleveraged investment route. If you believe in the precepts of value investing, however, conservative capitalizations become highly desirable for OPMIs.

Chapter 8

Promoters' and Professionals' Compensations

Is this a game of chance? Not the way I play it.

—W. C. Fields

The highly regarded broker-dealer, Smith Barney & Co. (now Salomon Smith Barney) used to run advertisements on television, the punchline of which was "At Smith Barney, we make money the old fashioned way. We earn it." The guts of the message was that superior returns might be earned by outside passive minority investors (OPMIs) relying on Smith Barney research and Smith Barney stock selection.

Those advertisements might well have been right about the benefits to OPMIs of Smith Barney's research and stock selection. The old-fashioned way to obtain riches hardly involves being an OPMI or a superior stock picker. Rather, it involves being a promoter or a professional. The vast majority of Wall Street fortunes seem to have been obtained by those who had an edge—an ability to earn promoters' or professionals' compensations.

Most OPMIs never will have opportunities to obtain promoters' or professionals' compensations. Nonetheless, understanding how and why these others are remunerated ought to help many OPMIs become better investors than would otherwise be the case. Furthermore, no one can really understand Wall Street without also having some insights into what promoters and professionals do and how they are compensated. Incidentally, *professional* tends to be an overworked word in the financial community. Mostly, it does not refer to people with special qualifications, licenses, or credentials, such as attorneys and accountants, but to someone who works full time in the financial community and is compensated by receiving fees, commissions, a piece of the action, or all three.

Defining Markets for Value Investing Purposes

A market is any arena in which participants reach agreements as to price and other terms that the participants believe are the best they can reasonably obtain under the circumstances.

There are myriad markets, including capital markets. The efficient market hypothesis (EMH) seems to recognize the existence of only one market—that populated by OPMIs. The New York Stock Exchange (NYSE) and NASDAQ (National Association of Securities Dealers Automated Quotations) are well-known OPMI markets. For value investing, other markets are as important as or more important than the OPMI market in terms of having a functioning economy and establishing values. These other markets include the merger and acquisition (M&As) market, the leveraged buyout (LBO) market, and the contests for control market. Although these markets deal in the same instruments as does the OPMI market, common stocks, and senior obligations, the prices prevailing for common stocks and other equity interests in these other capital markets and the terms embodied in transactions tend to be strikingly different from OPMI prices and terms.

Other noncapital markets influencing value investors include markets for top management compensation, markets for consensual plans within a Chapter 11 plan of reorganization, private claims markets, insurance coverage markets, and settlement of stockholder litigation markets.

The Pervasiveness of Excess Returns in Many if Not Most Markets

Nothing happens in the financial community that does not entail huge transaction costs for clients, whether those clients are retail, institutional, or corporate. Huge transaction costs for clients means huge transaction incomes for certain Wall Street participants who incur relatively small costs to create those incomes (i.e., the earning, by these promoters and professionals, of excess returns).

Excess returns are far from the exclusive province of Wall Street. Excess returns also seem to be earned relatively persistently by top corporate executives. These executives include not only principal owners, or sole owners of businesses, but also professional managements that may not be significant corporate stockholders.

Finally, certain entrenched companies that are realistically monopolies and oligopolies, such as The Coca-Cola Company and The Gillette Company seem to persistently earn returns that are in excess on the basis of the companies' costs to create earnings. These companies probably do not create excess returns for their shareholders, however, in a substantive consolidation context, where corporate earnings results are measured as a percentage of the market value of the equity as it is traded in OPMI markets.

The Why of Excess Returns

Unless an external force imposes disciplines on a market, certain participants are bound to earn excess returns in that market. That is merely part of the definition of a market in which participants strive to do as well as they reasonably can. If no external force is going to limit a participant's earnings, then that participant has to earn excess returns as a percentage of the cost involved in creating those earnings. An underlying assumption of the EMH is that the OPMI market is efficient or at least tends toward an instantaneous efficiency. An efficient market here means that participants in those markets cannot earn superior returns consistently (i.e., all the time). According to the EMH, no market participants have an information edge, and when any participant in an efficient market earns excess returns, those returns can be only temporary and inconsistent. This is so because earning excess returns either will bring new entrants into that sector of the market or will produce increasing competitive pressures from existing participants, which will cause those excess returns to diminish and disappear. In other words, competition from other participants is the external force precluding OPMIs from earning excess returns consistently.

Value investors believe that the very definition of efficiency dictates that excess returns will be earned by many participants in certain markets. That is where all those rich people in the United States without inherited wealth come from. Further, the EMH stance that it is darn near impossible to earn excess returns in the OPMI market seems absolutely correct. Whether excess returns are earned is a function of disciplines imposed—or not imposed—by external forces, which influence specific markets. Corporate top-management compensations and mutual fund management fees are examples of markets in which excess returns seem to be earned persistently as a percentage of the costs incurred to create income. By contrast, OPMI markets, in which the goal of participants is to maximize risk-adjusted total returns consistently, are examples of markets in which excess returns seem almost never to be earned as a percentage of an investor's risk-adjusted total return.

Each participant in a market, striving to do as well as reasonably possible, is subject to the ground rules laid out for participants playing in that market. The participant, if he or she can, takes advantage of the specific ground rules.

The ground rules for the OPMI market, as laid out on the floor of the NYSE, is probably best viewed as a simulation of what economists call pure and perfect competition. Here, transactions take place at the prices at which demand curves intersect supply curves. At any time, there are hundreds or thousands of buyers and sellers in a market characterized by pure and perfect competition. None of the participants in the market has enough buying power or selling power to materially change market prices, and all participants are very short run conscious because they are attempting to achieve superior—or at least average—results consistently.

Given the reasonably good simulation of pure and perfect competition that exists on the NYSE, OPMIs interested in short-run trading are hard put to outperform any index, or market, consistently. Put otherwise, the external forces—competition among participants and regulation that maintains orderly markets and precludes market price manipulations—are highly effective. In addition, OPMIs tend to be subject to huge transaction costs based on what specialists and broker-dealers earn on trading activities by OPMIs, with such costs embodied in spreads between bid and asked prices, commissions charged, margin interest, and use by broker-dealers of credit balances that would otherwise earn interest income for OPMIs.

Interestingly enough, the U.S. OPMI market comes close to achieving a simulation of pure and perfect competition simply because regulation by government (particularly the Securities and Exchange Commission [SEC]) and by self-regulatory agencies seems diligent, pervasive, and reasonably intelligent. Were it not, excess returns (and less-than-average returns) would probably become available to many more people and institutions than is now the case.

What about other markets—those much less regulated and in which the ground rules and external forces differ from those existing for OPMIs in OPMI markets? Assume there is a market with a limited number of participants (a monopoly or oligopoly), in which participants can be highly knowledgeable and are not short-run conscious, and in which any existing competition does not tend to take the form of price competition. Given those ground rules, an efficient market—one where each participant is striving to do as well as he, she, or it reasonably can—would be one in which the participant earns excess returns, if not consistently, then certainly persistently and on average. In many markets, promoters do in fact earn excess or even infinite returns based on the cost of their initial investments: many money managers of mutual funds; LBO promoters, such as Kohlberg Kravis Roberts and Morgan Stanley; and many specialists and market makers.

What is the basis for the EMH view that OPMI prices determine a true universal equilibrium value? As far as can be determined, there exist only two legitimate reasons for this view, neither of which seem to deserve much weight: (1) usually, OPMI market price is the only precise price available continuously and instantaneously; and (2) in number, but probably not in amount of assets controlled, there are more OPMIs than any other type of investor. The EMH view that the OPMI market has to price efficiently seems to be hogwash because this view centers on a theory that if prices in OPMI markets become too cheap, knowledgeable insiders will come into OPMI markets and bid prices up. This just does not happen, because:

• **Corporate insiders can and do participate in OPMI market price fluctuations without putting up money and without risk.** They acquire stock options and stock appreciation rights at 100% of fair market value (i.e., the OPMI price). These securities are obtained directly from the company, not from the OPMI market. Why would anyone want to lay out money to buy common stock in the OPMI market when the insider can get virtually the same bang for bucks without any investment by having the company issue options? Indeed, the insider eligible for options wants a low OPMI price to be even lower at the time of the grant of options because income-tax law usually requires that the strike price be no less than 100% of OPMI market price at the time of issuance.

• **Potential control buyers are discouraged from acquiring OPMI common stock at ultra low prices because of the universal existence of "shark repellents" insulating existing managements in office.** A control buyer who does not believe a transaction to be doable is unlikely to be interested no matter how attractively priced he or she believes the security is priced from a passive investment point of view.

Even if the price of a common stock appears overpriced in the OPMI market, insiders may be very reluctant to sell into that market, especially when keeping control is high on the insider's agenda:

• Outside passive minority investor overpricing frequently is not overpricing at all in the control market, which is often governed by different valuation parameters.
• Insiders get benefits from common stock ownership over and above pure ownership, so they have less interest in sales to an OPMI market.
• In the hands of a skilled management, overpriced common stock in an OPMI market often becomes a corporate asset and is used in M&As to create additional corporate value per share.

Earning Excess Returns in the Financial Communities

There seem to be a number of institutional elements in the U.S. economy that can and do impose disciplines that prevent or limit the earning of excess returns. Value investors agree with the EMH stance that competitive forces entering a market are probably the most important single element imposing that external discipline. These competitive forces would prevent a participant from continuing to earn excess returns. Besides competitive markets, external disciplines can be imposed by the following elements or institutions:

- Boards of directors
- Laws and regulations
- Courts
- Lenders and other credit grantors
- Tax authorities
- Control security holders
- Labor unions
- Communities
- Rating agencies

Markets in Which External Disciplines Seem to Be Lacking

Merchant Bankers (Promoters of Leveraged Buyouts)

Normally, people who put their own money into deals are known as principals, and those people who put deals together for fees but who do not have their own money in the deal are known as brokers. Merchant bankers are often brokers masquerading as principals. They usually invest none—or very little—of their own money in the deal, but they both collect their fees for putting deals together and obtain an equity interest in deals without any—or any material—money investment. Merchant banking has become a main activity for such major Wall Street names as Kohlberg Kravis Roberts & Co.; Forstmann Little; Morgan Stanley–Dean Witter; Merrill Lynch & Co., Inc.; The Goldman Sachs Group, L.P.; and Citicorp Ventures.

Until the 1980s, principal broker-dealers, such as Goldman Sachs and Morgan Stanley, believed that their best use of capital—both human and financial—was to employ capital in their own broker-dealer activities rather than to become involved in owning non–broker-dealer equities on a permanent or semipermanent basis. This attitude is no longer pervasive, and much capital is now employed in structuring LBOs so that the merchant banker becomes a permanent or semipermanent investor in a corporation in which the merchant banker has meaningful elements of control.

Merchant banking has become increasingly competitive in recent years. This is to be expected, given the tendency toward efficiency that seems to exist in all markets. As far as can be determined, however, most of the better merchant bankers continue to earn excess returns as deal promoters, in part because there is so much outside money, run by passivists, such as pension funds that are eager to participate in LBOs. Merchant bankers structure fees for such investors so that they receive compensation as hedge-fund operators.

A typical setup for merchant banking activities is a limited partnership, a form also used for hedge funds engaged in venture capital investing, arbitrage, distress, and trading activities. Although terms may vary, a usual relationship is that the promoter—the general partner (GP)—receives an annual management fee of 1% to 2% of funds committed plus a profit participation of 20% of gains, sometimes accrued or paid only after the limited partners (LPs) receive a preferred return of 6% to 10%. For most limited partnerships, the final terms are arrived at after negotiations with a lead investor. In powerful limited partnerships (e.g., Kohlberg Kravis Roberts), the GP tends to dictate the GP–LP arrangements. Sometimes the GP gets to keeps for itself various benefits, such as deal fees, rather than turning them over to the partnership.

Hedge-Fund Operators

Normally, hedge-fund operators run limited partnerships as GPs. There cannot be more than 100 LPs if the business entity is to avoid becoming a registered investment company (RIC); also, the partnership cannot have more than 35 LPs if it is to avoid becoming a registered investment adviser (RIA). Compensation to GP usually follows the merchant banker model outlined above: an up-front continuous fee of 1% to 2% of assets managed per annum, plus a profit participation after the limited partnership has earned a "bogey" of, say, 6% to 10% per annum. Profit participation can range from 20% to 50%. Those who do such hedge-fund deals include:

- Merchant bankers–LBO promoters
- Risk arbitrageurs

- Vulture funds
- Venture capitalists
- Real estate syndicators
- Oil and gas syndicators
- Movie producers

There is probably some uniformity in the financial hedge-fund market revolving around 1 (a 1% annual management fee) and 20 (a 20% profit participation), but there seems to be little scholarly literature published on the subject. Promoters' compensations may be different in nonfinancial areas:

- Before 1986, real estate limited partnerships had more like 3% to 5% management fees and 50% participation in profits plus property management fees. It seems that since the real estate tax-shelter (TS) debacles between 1986 and the early 1990s, promoters' compensation has gravitated more to the economic equivalent of 1 and 20, whether the real estate promoters are being compensated as GPs or as managers of real estate investment trusts (REITs).
- Oil and Gas syndications used to have promoters' participations based on the concept of one third for one quarter: put up 25% of the money invested for a 33% interest, plus management and operators' fees.
- There probably are norms for promoters' compensations in show-business and movie deals, usually under the rubric of producer's compensation.

Governance of limited partnerships is almost always strictly in the hands of GPs. The norm is that LPs have fewer governance rights than exist for OPMI shareholders of corporations. This is especially true for publicly traded limited partnerships.

In raising funds, it is better from the promoter's point of view to raise funds for a blind pool: After funds are committed, the promoter can invest in whatever he or she chooses. This is not always possible, since many potential LPs want to invest only in specific deals.

The limited partnerships referred to here are privates exempt from SEC registration under Regulation D because each has fewer than 35 investors. In the 1980s, publicly registered limited partnerships were common, especially in real estate and in oil and gas. (See the excellent book *Serpent on the Rock,* which was published in 1995 and describes business practices at Prudential Bache Securities.) There is a saying that a limited partnership is defined as a business association in which in the beginning the GP brings to the association experience and the LP brings to the association money. At the termination of the association, the GP has the money and the LP has the experience.

Bailouts for LPs are varied. For example, the sales pitch for real estate tax shelters prior to the 1986 amendments to the Internal Revenue Code was that returns would be made up of tax losses, perhaps some cash income followed by sale at a terminal date, whereas for a venture-capital limited partnership, the bailout revolves around taking portfolio companies public at super prices in future initial public offerings (IPOs).

Investment Bankers

Investment bankers earn huge fees providing services in three areas:

- Advisory, including fairness opinions, other valuations, financial strategies, and litigation support
- Merger and acquisition activities (i.e., business brokerage)
- Distribution of securities through public underwritings and private placements

Securities Salespeople

Since the advent of competitive commission rates in 1975, an increasing emphasis of Wall Street sales forces has been to offer exclusive products with large gross spreads rather than to emphasize the purchase and sales of securities in secondary markets. For example, the fairly typical gross spread on the 1986 IPO of Boston Celtics, L.P. was $1.29 per unit, which would compare with a commission in the secondary market charged a customer of, say, anywhere from 2¢ a unit, where the customer obtained a discount to a maximum of 40¢ per unit for 1,000 units acquired from a full-service nondiscounting broker-dealer. Of the $1.29 gross spread, anywhere from one third to one half might have ended up as security salesperson's compensation. It seems that for some years, many security salespeople earned excess returns marketing exclusive products with large gross spreads, including real estate and oil and gas limited partnerships, load mutual funds, and IPOs. There are probably tremendous institutional pressures within the financial community to keep coming up with products that will continue to permit sales forces to earn excess returns. Not only are the commissions earned on IPOs large, but most IPOs are designed to be easy sells in that at the time of initial offering, demand exceeds supply.

Money Management

Control of funds for basically passive investments is an inordinately profitable business with very little price competition whether such control is through registered investment companies or registered investment advisers. There are three principal sources of excess returns when a firm has assets under management: sales load, management fees, and control of portfolio trading. In addition, those who control funds are in a position to deliver excess returns to other controllers, by, for example, appointing outside directors and choosing attorneys and accountants for funds.

There is a ready market for the sale of companies with funds under management at prices, which in 1998 ranged from 2% to 5% of funds managed. Table 8-1 shows funds under management for selected participants.

Table 8-1. Funds Under Management for Selected Companies (As of October 31, 1998)

Company	Billions of Dollars
Fidelity Investments	$621
Vanguard Group	$398
Dean Witter Intercapital, Inc.	$104
Dreyfus Corportation	$101
AIM Group	$94

Money Managers and Financial Advisers

Money management is a low-overhead, all-cash business with opportunities to capitalize cash flows and be acquired or go public at high multiples.

The problem with Forbes 400, a listing of the 400 richest people in America, is that the estimates of wealth are based on the quantity of net worth, not the quality. If quality of net worth were considered, perhaps the Forbes 400 list would consist of many more money managers and correspondingly fewer real estate people, oil and gas people, and entrepreneurs owning OPMI-traded common stocks in controlled corporations, shares that are unlikely to be salable at OPMI market prices.

Promoters in Trading Environments

A discussion of promoters in trading environments is more often the purview of those involved with academic finance and EMH rather than of value investors. Players earning excess returns persistently from trading activities include the following:

- Stock exchange specialists
- Market makers
- Users of free or almost free credit balances at broker-dealers
- Certain spread lenders

There is confusion in the academic literature on whether excess returns are earned on sunk costs or present values. As a practical matter, stock exchange specialists can earn excess returns forever, as can the owners of television stations, because once they have the franchise to earn excess returns, no one is in a position to enter the market and cause entrenched players to give up their returns.

Top Corporate Managements

If boards of directors do not impose discipline on top managements' compensation, no other entity will. The steepest slope in the industrial world seems to be in the United States between the earnings of managements and those of employees.

Controlling management compensation is the province of boards of directors, but discipline imposed on management compensations by boards of public companies seems virtually nonexistent. *De facto,* board appointments are made by managements that are unlikely to appoint either people who are not friends or who are troublemakers. Delaware is the leading corporate state. There are virtually no cases in Delaware involving allegations of excessive management compensation. There is an Internal Revenue Service (IRS) rule denying corporate tax deductions for certain management compensation in excess of $1 million per year per individual, but the rule is easily circumvented.

Top executive compensation has several components:

- Salaries
- Perks
- No-risk or low-risk equities, especially through stock options
- Certain transactions, including leasing properties to company or providing other services for compensation
- Participation in merchant banking activities, such as management buyouts (MBOs)
- The chance to employ friends and relatives
- The control of corporate governance, including management entrenchment

Other Professionals Who Tend To Enjoy Excess Returns

Other professionals can earn what seem to be excess returns:

- Defense attorneys
- Plaintiffs' attorneys (In the United States, the existence of class actions and absence of security for costs helps promote excess returns.)
- Management consultants
- Tax advisors
- Bankruptcy attorneys

Other professionals who are probably less well compensated than investment bankers and attorneys include the following:

- Business brokers
- Appraisers
- Providers of litigation support (expert witnesses)

Two groups of professionals that provide truly essential services, yet seem to be grossly undercompensated are auditors and indenture trustees. Auditing has been a notoriously unprofitable profession in this country, given the legal developments in accountants' liability. With the prerequisite of independence, auditors are held to far higher standards than are other professionals, especially investment bankers and attorneys. Such high standards are essential. Without reliable audit standards, the U.S. economy probably would cease to function because it would probably be impossible to grant commercial credit.

Corporate Monopolies and Oligopolies

Many corporations—The Coca-Cola Company, Microsoft Corporation, Intel—earn superior returns consistently, relatively insulated from competition and other external forces that could impose disciplines.

Effective Promoters Understand the Importance of Know-Who and Know-How

The elements of know-how include financial and legal considerations as well as factors that are industry specific and company specific. Elements of the former encompass the following:

- Generally accepted accounting principles (GAAP)
- Characteristics of securities
- Securities law and regulation

- The Internal Revenue Code
- The restructuring of troubled companies

There are limits on due diligence to obtain requisite know-how. In its economic as well as legal sense, *due diligence* means reasonable care under the circumstances. How much did the author really have to know about Kmart to become a senior creditor at a price of 74 in 1975? How much would he have wanted to know about Kmart if he had been considering acquiring control? A lot more than he did.

The Intellectual Problem with Excess Returns

If it is assumed that all assets are to be marked to market and be available for sale and that the market value of those assets will be what can be earned on those assets, then there never can be excess returns. When earnings increase, asset values also increase, so the return on assets (ROA)—that is, earnings as a percent of asset value—stays constant. Thus, the concept of no excess returns, as per the EMH, is valid but not helpful; underlying it is a concept of substantive consolidation, in which whatever earnings there are are reflected in a surrogate for corporate asset values—to wit, the OPMI market price of a common stock.

The common cliche used in the EMH that there is no free lunch is misleading. Rather, the more appropriate statement in terms of promoters' and professionals' compensations is that somebody has to pay for lunch. Those who do not get free lunches, and who in fact pay for promoters' lunches, are nonprofessional OPMIs whose returns are limited to what they earn directly from their holdings. This constituency is the major source of lunch money for all the other participants in the financial community. It is also the only constituency to which the EMH and Graham and Dodd fundamentalism seem to direct their message. Outside passive minority investors are at the tail end of the Wall Street daisy chain. The *raison d'être* of the financial community is to provide governments, industries, and commerce in general with access to capital markets. The main function of secondary markets (e.g., the NYSE) is to facilitate such access rather than to provide investor protection for OPMIs. Investor protection is very, very important not for itself but because it is an essential element in providing productive users of capital with access to capital. This it does by having a secondary market that gives securityholders liquidity. Another function of secondary markets is to provide prices. A fundamental tenet of this book is that the OPMI market for most equities does not provide—and should not be expected to provide—a pricing mechanism that is universally useful or even efficient in most contexts.

Chapter 9

Uses and Limitations of Financial Accounting

Manager to accountant: "How much is two plus two?"
Accountant (cautiously): "How much do you need it to be?"

Financial accounting, as embodied in the United States in generally ac-cepted accounting principles (GAAP), is the one essential tool for the analysis of commercial enterprises and the securities they issue especially for any analyst interested in assaying the quality of a business's resources. In value investing, GAAP reports serve three purposes:

- To provide analysts with objective benchmarks, essential tools of analysis that analysts use to determine one or more economic realities or truths
- To define reality for certain special purposes
- To provide a road map for analysts both in due-diligence investiga-tions and in less thorough investigations, in which analysts rely exclu-sively on public records

In value investing, in contrast with most mainstream security analyses, GAAP results are not usually supposed to be descriptions of economic reality. Furthermore, there are no top-down rules for the use of GAAP that have universal applicability, contrary to what seems to be the case with conventional approaches. Rather, each accounting item is evaluated from the bottom up in specific contexts. Rarely are results uniform. For example, in examining the property, plant, and equipment accounts of a hotel-motel chain, mainstream analysts likely would look at depreciation as a noncash charge against the income account. By contrast, although value investors would view depreciation attributable to buildings charged against the company's income account as being a noncash charge giving rise to cash flows from operations, they would likely view any depreciation charged against the company's income account attributable to furniture and fixtures as being the equivalent of a current cash expense or expenditure. Put simply, well-maintained, well-located bricks and mortar do not suffer much if any economic depreciation, but furniture and fixtures decline in value because they are used daily and have to be replaced with relative regularity.

In value investing, the role of financial accounting is to help analysts understand and value, from a long-term point of view, a business and the securities it issues. It is unimportant to use GAAP results, especially earnings results, as a tool to estimate the prices at which common stocks of operating companies will sell in near-term trading markets populated by outside passive minority investors (OPMIs). Indeed, in value investing involving the analysis of operating companies, the conclusion reached is that those focused on trading prices in OPMI markets are speculators, not investors—people who never will be able to make reasonable use of the many insights that an analyst can obtain through using GAAP judiciously.

In value investing, the use of financial accounting as an analytic tool for passive investing seems similar to the use of financial accounting as an analytic tool by those who acquire control of businesses; by those who make large-scale investments in common stocks—say, $100 million or more—in companies whose securities they anticipate holding on a permanent or semipermanent basis; and by those—mostly creditors—who seek to earn a return by looking only to the company's resources and expected performance rather than to a sale to a market of the security held. Rarely in these contexts is there deemed to be a primacy of the income account.

Rather, an analysis involves the entire accounting cycle: the income account and both the quality and quantity of a business's resources.

The Conventional Approaches

The conventional roles visualized for financial accounting appear to be quite different than the roles accounting has in value investing. Conventional approaches to financial accounting are those that seem to be followed by most broker-dealer research departments and most investment-company money managers. The conventional approach is endorsed also in the literature recommended in study guides for those seeking the designation chartered financial analyst (CFA). Three volumes make up the bulk of the CFA study guide literature covering financial statement analysis:

- *Fundamentals of Corporate Finance,* third edition, Stephen A. Ross, Randolph W. Westerfield, and Jeffrey F. Jaffe (Irwin, 1995)
- *Investment Analysis and Portfolio Management,* fifth edition, Frank K. Reilly and Keith C. Brown (Dryden Press, 1997)
- *The Analysis and Use of Financial Statements,* second edition, Gerald I. White, Ashwin Paul C. Sondi, and Dov Fried (John Wiley & Sons, 1997)

The roles of GAAP under conventional approaches appear to be as follows:

- Accounting data should reflect the truth, or economic reality, to the maximum extent possible. The important figure for which truth is to be ascertained is the firm's periodic net income from operations, or other measures of a firm's performance during a period.
- The reaction of OPMI trading markets to the dissemination of accounting information as measured by OPMI market prices is a matter of crucial importance. The only market that counts is the OPMI market.

White, Sondi, and Fried discuss, in Chapter 5 of their book, "Empirical Research: Implications for Financial Statement Analysis," the principal avenues followed in the conventional approach: the classical approach, market-based research, and positive accounting research.

They point out that the classical approach "attempts, using a theoretical perspective, to develop an optimal, or 'most correct' accounting representation of some true (but unobservable) reality" (p. 216).

In describing market-based research, they wrote that

> Its primary focus is the market reaction to (or association with) reported accounting data. Market based research uses observable relationships between reported earnings or other measures of firm performance) and market return to draw conclusions about the role of accounting information (p. 216).

The "positive" accounting theory approach, they wrote, adapts much from market-based research but recognizes further that accounting information as reported defines reality for a whole gamut of non-OPMI market contexts, including

> …management compensation plans, debt agreements with creditors, and the host of regulatory bodies interacting with the firm. More important, it recognizes that since financial statements impact these other environments, there are incentives for accounting systems to be used not only to measure the results of decisions but, in turn, to influence these decisions in the first place (pp. 216, 218).

The classical approach and market-based research seem based on the following underlying assumptions that have little or no validity from a value investing point of view:

- Firms are strict going concerns (except for assets—securities, which are traded in OPMI markets) and are to be appraised as such. Thus, there exists a primacy of the income account and a consequent denigration of other elements that make up the accounting cycle. This makes sense because if a company is a strict going concern, the past earnings record ought to be the best tool for predicting future earnings.
- Predicting prices for near-term OPMI trading markets is an analyst's primary or principal task. Thus, there exists a primacy of the income account. OPMI markets clearly seem to react more to current earnings per share reports than any other accounting number, especially balance sheet numbers for solvent corporations.

- Prices in OPMI markets are universal equilibrium prices that reflect all (or almost all) available present information. Prices will change as new information, both accounting information and nonaccounting information, becomes known.
- *Market* is defined as the OPMI market. Other markets (e.g., the leveraged buyout [LBO] market) are ignored.
- The presence or absence of price volatility in OPMI markets is deemed important for all investors, even buy-and-hold fundamentalists who do not finance their holdings using borrowed money.

In summary, the purposes and uses of accounting in value investing seem quite different from those in conventional approaches. Value investors view financial accounting as a tool to help analysts approximate (1) the performance of a business during a particular period and (2) the quality and quantity of resources existing in a company at any one moment. Over and above these factors, financial accounting is also a tool used in value investing to make judgments about many nonfinancial (i.e., non-numeric) factors, such as appraisals of management, and to find information about such material documents as leases, loan agreements, and pension plans. In conventional approaches, one key role of financial accounting, albeit not the only one, is to measure the true performance of a business during a period while emphasizing the reactions of traders to new accounting information as measured by changes in securities prices.

Financial Accounting Reports as Objective Benchmarks

Financial accounting—GAAP—is a system in which reports are made within a relatively rigid code whose descriptions of reality are limited because the underlying assumptions of the system frequently are unrealistic. Among the GAAP assumptions that are unrealistic in many contexts are that:

- Property, plant, equipment are to be carried at historical cost as depreciated.
- Constant price levels exist.

- Current assets and long-term assets are to be defined in a standard, inflexible manner.
- All accounts on the right-hand side of a balance sheet are either net worth or above-the-line equivalents of payables.
- Accrual concepts are to be used in most contexts in which costs and expenses are matched, even when such accruals are at odds with the cash experience of the company.
- Sometimes liabilities are burdened with a cost of money and sometimes they are not.
- There exist no liabilities (e.g., deferred income taxes) that may have a large equity component.

Furthermore, even given the limited number of choices available to corporate managements under GAAP, none of those choices need reflect economic reality:

- Inventory accounting
- Accounting for long-lived assets
- On–balance sheet and off–balance sheet liabilities
- Accounting for long-term employee benefits
- Accounting for income taxes
- Accounting for business combinations

Generally accepted accounting principles originally were designed as a system to report on the results and the position of a consolidated corporation as a stand-alone. In the late 1990s, there have been trends designed to consolidate substantively reports of the company with stock-market measures pertinent to others. This is exemplified by proposals to charge a company's income account with the estimated value of stock options issued to employees. This seems utterly unrealistic because it assumes that the value of a benefit received by an employee to that employee equals the cost to the company of granting that benefit. It is basic to value investing that the company is a stand-alone constituency. The value of a noncash benefit to an employee ought not to be equated to a cost to a company. In value investing, the corporation is a separate and distinct constituency from the corporation's stockholders in almost all contexts.

Because GAAP impose relatively rigid sets of rules and are overseen and reviewed by independent professionals who render opinions (public accountants), audited financial statements are often the only numeric reports available to security analysts that give them reliable, objective information prepared in a disciplined setting. Generally accepted accounting principles are not truth or reality, but a tool analysts use to determine their own versions of truth. By contrast with GAAP, other numeric reports (e.g., investment bankers' opinions and appraisers' reports) often lack objectivity and independence. These other reports tend to be derived in settings lacking professional standards or disciplines, and the other professionals rendering them usually are influenced, sometimes heavily, by who has hired them and who is paying their fees and expenses. This does not seem to be the case, however, for the vast majority of independent audits.

As has been pointed out, reality tends to be one thing when a company is examined as a going concern but quite another when the same set of numbers is used, for resource conversion valuations. Here is an example: For a going concern, retail inventories are anything but a current asset; a retail chain had better maintain or even increase its investment in inventory if it is going to remain in operation, because such inventory is a fixed, long-term asset. On the other hand, if the retail chain is to go out of business, inventory becomes a true current asset, convertible into cash over the next 12 months.

In the real world, why would anyone expect financial accounting to disclose truth or reality for most analyses? In fact, though, GAAP data seem to reflect economic reality in quite a number of special cases. For example, the balance sheets of investment companies registered under the amended Investment Act of 1940 reflect reality based on valuing portfolios at OPMI market prices in accordance with GAAP.

Furthermore, it seems likely that for most credit analysis, GAAP are realistic enough. Here, GAAP are not used to value, per se, but rather to give analysts enough information to gauge the probabilities that a debt instrument will be serviced in accordance with its terms. By contrast, and as is pointed by White, Sondhi, and Fried, "the ultimate objective of equity analysis is valuation" (p. 932). From a value investing point of view, when analysts are interested in the quality of resources existing in a business, especially if they are evaluating a senior credit, the one crucial disclosure to them would not necessarily be corporate valuation but rather the existence—or nonexistence—of liabilities that might be equal to or senior to the credit instrument being evaluated. This latter information is readily disclosed in most audits.

In value investing the focus is most often on *what the numbers mean* rather than *what the numbers are*. Value analysts do not expect GAAP numbers to reflect truth or reality; rather, they view GAAP numbers as raw materials to be used, so they adjust the numbers to approximate reality. Truth or reality are something to be determined by analysts, not by accountants who prepare financial statements in conformity with that relatively rigid set of limiting assumptions known as GAAP.

For conventional equity analysts, to repeat, there is a primacy of the income account; what is wanted most from GAAP is an accurate reflection of periodic results from operations. In Value Investing, by contrast, there is no *a priori* primacy of anything other than balance: the whole accounting cycle is the focus. In almost any analysis, the value analyst will be interested in not only periodic results from operations but also the quality and quantity of resources available to the company whose common stock is being analyzed. The value analyst realizes that every accounting number is derived from, is modified by, and is a function of all the other numbers that are part of the accounting cycle. Income-account numbers can be no more accurate or meaningful than balance-sheet numbers. Each group is derived from, is modified by, and is a function of the other. White, Sondi, and Fried's view that "the usefulness of the reported balance sheet for investment decisions is limited" (p. 933), seems to be in error from the point of view of value investing. A more appropriate statement might be that the reported balance sheet and the income account are intimately related to each other for investment decision purposes but that the usefulness of the reported balance sheet for day-to-day or hour-to-hour stock-market trading decisions is much more limited than is the status of current or forecast income accounts.

When analysts want to forecast future earnings for a business relying on GAAP results, they frequently conclude that the quality and quantity of a business's resources at the end of a recent period may represent a better tool for predicting future results than does the past earnings record—even the earnings record of the very recent past. More importantly, though, value analysts know that neither present resources nor past earnings are tools to be used exclusively to forecast future earnings; both can and most often should be used in concert.

Value analysts do not subscribe to a primacy-of-earnings approach to analysis, because they have observed that few if any businesses whose common stocks are widely held are in fact strict going concerns engaged in traditional day-to-day operations managed as they always have been and financed as they always have been financed. Value analysts assume that very few companies will go as long as 5 years without being involved in mergers and acquisitions (M&A), restructurings, massive refinancings, changes in control, and liquidations in whole or in part. When companies are not strict going concerns, management appraisals ought to assess managements not only as operators but also as investors employing and redeploying assets and also financing and refinancing businesses. These investor appraisals are not possible for analysts focused strictly on that part of GAAP concerned with reporting the results of operations, with emphasis only on recurring revenues and profits.

Although it is too much to expect GAAP to report truth or economic reality for purposes of equity valuations, GAAP are the basic tool needed for making judgments about the managements of most companies as either operators or investors. For many value analysts, the investment function tends to be much more important than the operating function even though operating skills are not usually divorced from investment skills. Nonetheless, one good investment deal can have more significance than 10 years of brilliant operations. Look at the histories of Berkshire Hathaway Inc. or Nabors Industries.

Market-based research is concerned exclusively with the trading environment in OPMI markets. In terms of GAAP, market-based research attempts to fathom how new accounting information is likely to affect OPMI prices. In following this approach, analysts miss much about the usefulness of financial accounting for equity evaluations in markets other than OPMI markets—say, LBO markets, or markets for venture capital investments, or markets for the senior debt of troubled issuers.

A numeric example of differential pricing for LBO markets compared with pricing in OPMI markets demonstrates that large amounts of real values tend to be missed by those who look to market-based research. Assume common stock XYZ is trading in the OPMI market at around 16, perhaps because XYZ's near-term earnings outlook is poor or because the market prices for companies in XYZ's industry sector are depressed. Assume further that a control buyer, relying in part on audited financials, believes that XYZ common is worth not less than 35 because (1) XYZ has a favorable long-term operating outlook based on both base case and reasonable worst case forecasts, (2) the control buyer gauges that a strong ability exists to finance a transaction attractively grounded largely on perceptions that XYZ enjoys strong finances and might have certain assets that could be sold without interfering with going-concern operations, and (3) the buyer believes that various benefits, such as management salaries and fees, can be obtained. The control buyer then either makes a cash-tender offer for XYZ common at 21 or else proposes a cash merger at 21 with a shell corporation set up for the express purpose of acquiring XYZ in a merger transaction. The control buyer group can consist of outsiders, incumbent management, or combinations thereof.

Market-based research focuses strictly on the arbitrage that would exist between the OPMI market price of 16 and the takeover price of 21 or perhaps slightly higher. The question asked in market based-research is how the OPMI market will react in terms of trading prices to the announcement (or leak) of a takeover at a price of 21. Market-based research would be completely oblivious to the use of accounting information by potential control investors and others to determine that XYZ common might have a takeover value of approximately 35. That analysis seems to be the province strictly of value investing. Indeed, the efficient market hypothesis (EMH), the father of market-based research, is concerned only with OPMI trading markets, ignoring completely long-term buy-and-hold fundamentalism.

The use of GAAP in value investing is similar to the use of the Internal Revenue Code by skilled tax practitioners. Both the value analyst and the tax practitioner are essentially translators. Both take relatively rigid reporting systems, GAAP and the revenue code, and using the rules embodied in those systems, convert them into something usable. For the value analyst, the goal is to translate GAAP into something reflecting the economic realities pertinent to the business being examined. For the tax practitioner, the goal is to translate the revenue code so that the present value of taxes payable by clients is minimized. For example, tax practitioners attempt to report as tax-deductible losses those items which have economic profits built into them; the well-maintained bricks and mortar owned by the hotel-motel chain cited previously may in fact appreciate in value over time, yet depreciation charges against the bricks and mortar are tax deductible. The skilled income tax practitioner does not seek economic truth but uses, to the extent permitted by the revenue code, accelerated depreciation methods, shortened lives, and minimal salvage values in charging the income account prepared for tax purposes with depreciation deductions for the buildings owned by the hotel-motel chain. The value analyst, on the other hand, takes the depreciation figures used for tax purposes and tries to translate those figures, overstated in terms of economic reality, into economic reality.

When an analyst is dealing with what the numbers mean, what is important is only that items be disclosed. There is no emphasis whatsoever on where and how items are disclosed. This is antithetical to all conventional approaches, in which the perceived primary goal of financial accounting is a statement of periodic income from operations that is as correct as possible. Subscribers to this conventional view of the role of GAAP include academic finance, Graham and Dodd fundamentalists, and accounting authorities ranging from the Financial Accounting Standards Board (FASB) to the Securities and Exchange Commission (SEC). Since the 1970s, however, accounting disclosures have improved so much, as is explained in the section of this chapter on GAAP as a road map (pp. 165–172), that it is hard to complain merely because accounting authorities give much time and attention to the form in which accounting data is disclosed rather than to substantive disclosures. The fact is that improvements since the 1970s in the quality and quantity of substantive accounting disclosures have also been dramatic.

Important goals in the conventional approach are that accounting statements exhibit comparability and consistency. More important than comparability and consistency, when financials are viewed as objective benchmarks, is reconcilability. Analysts ought to be given enough information so that they can make financial statements comparable and consistent for their analyses.

Generally Accepted Accounting Principles as Defining Reality for Certain Specific Purposes

For value analysts using GAAP as an objective benchmark, what the numbers *mean* is most often far more important than what the numbers *are*. For value analysts, GAAP numbers as reported more often than not do not reflect economic reality, but this is far from always the case. Good analysts are always aware of those instances in which the GAAP numbers actually do define certain realities—in which what the numbers *are* actually does become more important than what the numbers *mean*. This section of the chapter reviews those special circumstances when the reported accounting numbers define economic reality, legal reality, or both realities:

- **The OPMI trading environment.** Here, one reported number—earnings per share (EPS) quarter by quarter—seems to define reality, especially in relation to when that EPS number equals, exceeds, or falls short of consensus forecasts.
- **Those times when corporations or insiders are seeking access to capital markets to sell equity issues.** In these instances, and from the points of view of the corporation and insiders who might sell, reported EPS usually have a big influence not only on the price at which an equity issue might be marketed but also on whether the issue can be marketed at all.
- **Tests as to whether corporations are meeting loan covenants, requirements, or other contractual requirements.** These figures are usually based on reported GAAP results. Such results typically cover many things other than EPS, including minimum net worths, earnings coverage of interest, cash flow coverage of debt service, stock-to-debt ratios, and working capital ratios.
- **Capital adequacy tests for regulated financial institutions.** These usually deal in GAAP numbers as reported or in codified adjustments to GAAP numbers. This is the case for depository institutions, insurance companies, and broker-dealers.
- **Rating agencies.** These rely a great deal on reported GAAP financials.

Generally Accepted Accounting Principles as a Road Map for Due-Diligence and Less Thorough Investigations

Audited financials, interim financials, and the management discussion and analysis (MDA), available either in stockholder mailings or SEC filings, provide a comprehensive disclosure framework that enables a value analyst to understand much about most—but far from all—businesses and the securities, both credit and equity that they issue. Financial statements cover the accounting cycle through the balance sheet, the income account statement, the statement of cash flows, and the statement of stockholders' equity, all as supplemented, especially in annual audits by footnote disclosures and the independent accountant's opinion. The MDA, issued quarterly and unaudited, is required to discuss the following:

- Results of operations, including trends in sales and categories of expense
- Capital resources and liquidity, including cash flow trends
- Outlook based on known trends

A convenient way to get a handle on all of the types of information disclosed under GAAP is to examine the table of contents of the 1999 edition of the *Miller GAAP Guide: A Comprehensive Restatement of Current Promulgated Generally Accepted Accounting Principles,* by Jan R. Williams (Harcourt Brace):

Generally Accepted Accounting Principles
    Accounting Changes
    Accounting Policies
    Business Combinations
    Cash Flow Statement
    Changing Prices
    Consolidated Financial Statements
    Contingencies, Risks, and Uncertainties
    Convertible Debt and Debt with Warrants
    Current Assets and Current Liabilities
    Deferred Compensation Contracts
    Depreciable Assets and Depreciation
    Development Stage Enterprises
    Earnings per Share
    Equity Method
    Extinguishment of Debt
    Financial Instruments
    Foreign Operations and Exchange
    Futures Contracts
    Government Contracts
    Impairment of Loans and Long-Lived Assets
    Income Taxes
    Installment Sales Method of Accounting

Title Plant
Mortgage Banking Industry
Not-for-Profit Organizations
Oil and Gas–Producing Companies
Real Estate Transactions
Real Estate Costs and Initial Rental Operations
Real Estate: Recognition of Sales-Regulated Industries

These topics do not tell value analysts everything they want to know about a company, but for most companies, the GAAP-required disclosures provide a road map that not only tells analysts what is important to understanding a company and the securities it issues but also—and perhaps more importantly—gives them clues about important things they do not know. Admittedly, there probably will not be GAAP-related disclosures, at least early on, that a new product being developed by a competitor might negatively affect an issuer, as for example, when Microsoft's Internet Explorer won market share from Netscape. Nonetheless, the tendency toward making negative disclosures under GAAP is a strong one. Since the 1970s, independent auditors have been devastated by damage awards in securities lawsuits claiming accountants' liability. It can be taken for granted that large accounting firms are going to press managements, which are responsible for preparing the financial statements reviewed by auditors, to make any negative disclosures that are admissions against interest. Independent auditors of the statements of companies with publicly traded securities are usually very careful in comporting with not only GAAP rules, which cover what is to be disclosed in financial statements, but also generally accepted auditing standards (GAAS), which cover the procedures to be followed in preparing an audit. The climate fostered by developments in accountants' liability may not be overly productive for society as a whole. Nonetheless, the environment created is something that prudent value investors recognize and take advantage of.

How is the GAAP road map used by value analysts in general in most of their analyses?

- As a disciplined setting in which to understand the operations and the investment potentials of the business.
- As a huge aid in flagging contingencies, risks, and uncertainties of all sorts.

- As a good tool for appraising managements. For example, when managements have accounting choices (e.g., accounting for oil and gas exploration by using either full cost accounting or successful efforts accounting), analysts will look at the choices made by management to gauge whether management is basically conservative or promotional. A superstrong balance sheet may be evidence that a management is extremely conservative.
- As a good tool for ascertaining which documents are material and ought to be reviewed: long-term loan agreements, leases, pension plans, labor contracts. These will, to a greater or lesser extent, be described in financial statement footnotes.
- As a good tool for looking at the quality of a company and its survivability as gauged by the auditors' opinion. A "clean" certification is at least a small source of comfort; a qualification in the certificate about a company's ability to survive as a going concern should be a source of caution for holders of parent-company common stock and perhaps for other holders of junior securities—say, subordinated debentures.

For many types of analyses, GAAP are not all that helpful, although it is always an essential tool. When the quality of a corporation's resources is measured in part by the presence or absence of liabilities either on the balance sheet or in footnotes, GAAP are crucial. When a business's success is measured by new discoveries (e.g., oil wildcatting) or new inventions (e.g., an advanced computer chip not yet marketed), GAAP disclosures are far from central to an analysis from the point of view of an OPMI stockholder.

Generally accepted accounting principles have a number of basic shortcomings:

- Most GAAP are directed toward the interests of parent-company shareholders. For such constituents, consolidated financial statements are most meaningful. For creditors, there is often a need for consolidating—rather than consolidated—financial statements so that the creditors can assess how cash might flow from operating subsidiaries to parents as well as examine the balance sheets of material corporate entities.
- Generally accepted accounting principles based on accrual accounting frequently run into difficulties explaining corporate cash experiences. Cash accounting, by the way, has considerable problems in failing to

disclose corporate wealth creation and operating results, as measured by accrual principals.

- Generally accepted accounting principles are often not helpful when businesses create wealth through having unrealized—and therefore unreported—appreciation of assets for which there are no readily ascertainable market values. Companies with large holdings of undeveloped acreage are examples of these types of businesses.
- Generally accepted accounting principals are probably not very helpful for investors focused strictly on forecasting future growth trends in income or cash flow without looking to the leavening provided by non–income account GAAP disclosures.
- Generally accepted accounting principles are something of a vaccine against securities frauds. It seems logical that most people engaged in unscrupulous stock promotions or outright frauds would choose to promote as investment vehicles those entities where the false sizzle is a story unrelated to GAAP. Tax shelters, penny stocks, emerging market equities, trading systems, commodity plays, new discoveries, and new inventions are the raw materials used by most unscrupulous promoters. The factor these investment vehicles have in common is that GAAP do not weigh heavily as part of the investment story.

The road-map aspects of GAAP are crucial to making value investing decisions. Audited statements, including footnotes and the accountant's opinion letter, constitute comprehensive disclosures within a disciplined setting. Those responsible for preparing the statements have strong financial incentives to have those statements flag certain business problems—say, potential environmental liabilities.

In value investing by passive investors, there is frequently a primacy of the quality of resources in a company. A major factor in gauging the quality of resources is the presence or absence of liabilities, whether on the balance sheet, in the footnotes, or undisclosed altogether. Auditors will make great efforts to flag and describe these liabilities:

- Long-term debt
- Environmental contingencies
- Litigation contingencies
- Pension plans and other long-term employee obligations
- Material leases

Footnote topics include the basis of consolidation, fixed assets, inventories, income taxes, pension and other postemployment benefit plans, debt, lawsuits and other loss contingencies, marketable securities and other investments, significant customers, sales to related parties, and export sales.

Under GAAP, a corporation is required to accrue a loss on balance sheet when (1) it is probable that an impairment has occurred and (2) the amount of loss can be reasonably estimated. Moreover, footnote disclosure is required when a loss is reasonably possible. Having these loss disclosures is usually quite important to most value analysts.

Risks and uncertainties are also part of a GAAP audit. Under GAAP, a company is required to disclose the following:

- The firm's major business activities and markets
- The firm's use of estimates
- Certain significant estimates
- The firm's current vulnerabilities due to certain concentrations

Supplementary schedules are another tool providing important disclosures for value investing purposes:

- Estimates of the value of proved oil and gas reserves discounted to present value at a 10% discount rate (known as SEC PV 10)
- Schedule V of annual reports to the SEC giving data about developed real estate
- Impact of changing prices
- Disclosure of sales revenue, operating income, and assets employed for major business segments, by geographic areas; data about export sales
- Disclosures related to financial instruments and hedging activities

Management discussion and analysis of quarterly results and of financial position, liquidity, and capital resources is required to include a breakdown of significant effects of known trends, events, and uncertainties (e.g., decline in market share). There is also to be a discussion of discontinued operations and other nonrecurring items.

Although GAAP are always an essential tool, the importance of that tool in the information mix depends on what is analyzed. Generally accepted accounting principles are probably almost always key in credit analysis; they are also always key in the equity analysis of most strict going concerns; they are sometimes not helpful in analysis of tax shelter (TS) investments; and they are least useful in appraising companies whose value depends on new inventions and discoveries.

Chapter 10

Uses and Limitations of Narrative Disclosures

It shall be unlawful for any person, directly or indirectly, to make any untrue statement of a material fact or to omit to state a material fact necessary in order to make the statement made, in light of the circumstance under which they were made, not misleading ... in connection with the purchase or sale of any security.

—From SEC Regulation 10(b)5

Narrative disclosures are used in value investing as tools for gaining understanding of a business—its operations, values, problems, potentials, and long-term management direction. Except for occasional forays into risk arbitrage, the value investor does not attempt to predict near-term prices for securities traded in outside passive minority investor (OPMI) markets.

The principal purpose for using narrative disclosures in much of Graham and Dodd fundamentalism, in the efficient market hypothesis (EMH), in broker-dealer research departments, and among conventional money managers is as a tool aiding analysts in predicting market prices for common stocks trading in OPMI markets in the period just ahead. As do value investors, certain of these market participants use narrative disclosures as an aid in understanding a business. The primary objective of these market participants, however, remains to predict OPMI market prices over the near term rather than to understand a business. Still, understanding a business is desirable in all disciplines because it can help predict what OPMI market prices will be.

Given these differences in purposes, it is not surprising that corporate disclosures are used quite differently in value investing than they are used elsewhere. For value investing, no one type of disclosure is of overriding importance. The entire mix of information counts. The information that is most important varies on a case-by-case basis, so timeliness of disclosures is not a matter of material consequence in value investing, although it always is for other disciplines. Relative completeness of disclosures is always a matter of material consequence for value investing.

For EMH, Graham and Dodd fundamentalism and research departments and conventional money managers, how disclosures affect forecasted earnings or cash flows are matters of critical importance; there is a primacy of the income account. Timeliness of disclosures, at least those disclosures likely to effect near-term OPMI market prices—say, an outlook for the coming year—are also critically important. None of these analysts wants to be the last to get the news; many strive hard to be the first.

As far as mailings to securities holders and filings with the Securities and Exchange Commission (SEC) are concerned, there are two general types of disclosures made by corporations that are highly important for value investors:

- **Basically freewheeling disclosures from which management opinions and management styles become evident.** These documents include the letter from the chief executive officer (CEO) in the annual report to stockholders (ARS), product and activity descriptions in the ARS, press releases, conference calls with the investment community, addresses to security analysts' societies, and narratives in quarterly reports mailed to stockholders. The limits on what can be stated on a freewheeling basis by a management whose comments are reviewed by securities' counsel, as most of them are, loosely follow the strictures on free speech that are imposed by Regulation 10-b-5 of the amended Securities and Exchange Act of 1934. The scope of permissible insider disclosures has been expanded by the Safe Harbor Act (under the Private Securities Litigation Reform

Act of 1995) so that now, subject to hedge clauses, managements are freer to make forecasts. Regulation 10-b(5), however, remains a dominant consideration. The relevant portion of 10-b(5) states, "It shall be unlawful for any person ... to make any untrue statement of a material fact or to omit to state a material fact necessary in order to make the statements made, in light of the circumstances under which they were made, not misleading ... in connection with the purchase or sale of any security." Generally, CEO letters in ARSs allow management to take credit for what goes right while blaming uncontrollable circumstances for what goes wrong.

- **Basically stereotypical filings with the SEC.** These include Forms 10-K, 10-Q, and 8-K; proxy statements; registration statements; and Forms 3, 4, 5, 13-D, 13-F, and 13-G. These disclosures are prepared by attorneys who often follow slavishly the forms embodied in SEC Regulations S-K. A common mind-set in preparing these disclosures is that the quantity and quality of disclosures should be such that lawsuits are avoided. Certain disclosures are time driven (e.g., Form 10-K, an annual report; and Part I of Form 10-Q, a quarterly report); others are event driven, issued only when something occurs (e.g., registration statements, form 8-K, and Part II of Form 10-Q).

For more information on SEC forms, see the excellent booklet *A Guide to SEC Corporate Filings,* published in 1996 by Disclosure Incorporated, a document retrieval and research service.

In value investing, there is frequently a plethora of sources of readily available and useful disclosures in addition to SEC filings and security-holders' mailings, including the following:

- Court records, in connection with both litigation and Chapter 11 reorganization proceedings
- Filings with other regulatory agencies
- Competitor SEC filings and stockholder mailings
- Trade association reports
- The *Wall Street Journal*
- Other financial newspapers and magazines
- On-line summary services such as Bloomberg
- *SEC Daily News Digest*
- *Bankruptcy Reporter*

- Industry publications such as *Ward's Automotive Reports* and *Women's Wear Daily*

Some people may prefer to use hard-copy documents when they are available, but there are a number of excellent services that deliver documents by mail or on-line; including Disclosure Incorporated and EDGAR (Electronic Data Gathering Analysis and Retrieval). Filings with the SEC by corporations are available on the Internet through EDGAR.

Chapter 11

Semantics Counts

"When I use a word," Humpty Dumpty said in a rather scornful tone, "it means just what I chose it to mean—neither more nor less."

"The question is," said Alice, "whether you can make words mean so many different things."

—Lewis Carroll, *Through the Looking Glass*

The use of terminology is quite sloppy within the financial community. Rarely are precise meanings given to such words as *investor, speculator, value, price, company, risk, margin of safety, capital, earnings,* or *cash flow.* Even though it may not be that important in value investing to use financial semantics accurately, it is highly important to know precisely what specific terms and concepts really mean. For example, holders of common stock of certain Japanese commercial banks that followed unsound lending practices ought to be made and are likely to be made to suffer in 1998 and 1999 by having their percentage ownership interests in Japanese banks reduced or totally eliminated. This in no way means that any bank, as the bank, necessarily ought to or will suffer being put out of business or having its future activities curtailed. Put bluntly, the bank is not the bank's stockholders. The realization of this simplifies the task of financial reform for governments and regulators and also opens up paths to investment opportunities for investors from the private sector either as creditors or equityholders. Most current financial news items state that Japanese reforms will cause the banks to suffer, whereas what is really meant—and never seems to be articulated—is that the stockholders will find that their ownership interests are diluted or eliminated as a result of banking reform in general and of the restructuring of bank capitalizations in particular.

In learning about value investing, it is helpful to understand the sloppiness or unreality inherent in so much of Wall Street semantics; confusing stockholders with the company is not the only example of misinformation. This chapter compares what is commonly meant by certain terms used in the financial community with how those same terms are used or modified in value investing.

Speculator or Investor?

On Wall Street, every speculator is called an investor. This is bad semantics. The author agrees with Benjamin Graham who stated, in *The Intelligent Investor,* that "An investment operation is one which, upon thorough analysis, promises safety of principal and an adequate return. Operations not meeting these requirements are speculative." Furthermore, in equity investing other than risk arbitrage value investors believe *a priori* that any attempts to predict markets, to predict near-term securities prices, or to measure market results consistently (i.e., all the time) is speculation, not investment. On Wall Street, such people are called investors; in value investing, they are speculators.

The Company, the Management, the Common Stock, or the Holder of Common Stock?

In value investing the company, the management, the common stock, and the holder of common stock are each separate, distinct constituencies. Each has its own interests that usually combine elements of conflict of interest and communities of interest with each and every other constituency. The distinction among these four constituencies is rarely recognized on Wall Street.

In hostile takeovers and proxy contests, for example, the common description is that the company is pitted against dissidents or outsiders or raiders. It never is the company that in fact defends against outsiders; rather, it is the management (and an existing control group, or both) that is pitted against others.

All too frequently the company is referred to as the common stock, as in when it is said that General Motors closed at 60. It was not General Motors Corporation that closed at 60; it was General Motors common stock. Identifying the proper constituency becomes crucially important in the restructuring of troubled companies. For example, see the Japanese banking crisis described on pages 177–178.

Also too frequently the holders of the company's common stock are referred to as the company, as in when it is said that after a proxy solicitation, the company voted to elect certain people as directors. Not so. It was the holders of common stock who voted. It is probably unrealistic, though technically correct, to state that through the use of the proxy machinery, the stockholders voted for anything in an election that was not contested. The real election took place when proposals were made by those who controlled the proxy machinery—say, management or the nominating committee of the board of directors. Indeed, among populations of holders of common stock there are many different constituencies including short-term traders, long-term buy-and-hold investors, passive investors, and control investors. Each stockholder constituency has interests unique to itself, and each constituency has common interests with each other constituency. For example, both short-term traders and long-term buy-and-hold investors benefit if the company in whose stock they have invested is comfortably financed. On the other hand, short-term traders do not want management to follow courses of action that might interfere with short-term market performance (e.g., doing things that would reduce reported earnings per share [EPS] for the current quarter), whereas the buy-and-hold investor wants the company to undertake activities that will enhance long-term growth prospects (even while reducing quarterly reported EPS below what such earnings otherwise would have been).

Value or Price?

In Wall Street parlance, and according to the efficient market hypothesis (EMH), the words *value* and *price* can be used interchangeably. In these arenas, the common-stock price in an outside passive minority investor

(OPMI) market establishes a universal value; that is, the common-stock price multiplied by the number of shares outstanding on a fully diluted basis establishes the value of the equity capitalization.

In value investing, a price is one thing and a value can be something quite different. An OPMI market price can be a realization figure or a valuation figure for certain specific limited purposes, or both. A common-stock price, in value investing, never establishes a universal value, however.

A common-stock price in an OPMI market is for many purposes a realization figure: the approximate price at which a shareholder can dispose of his or her position or portions thereof. It is not necessarily a realization figure for all shareholders; some may not be able to realize because of blockage (the sale of the block would depress the market price) or because of restrictions on sale to public markets (whether contractual or legal). There are situations in which OPMI price is not a realization figure because the holder ought to be able to realize much higher prices in another market—say, sell at a control premium in the merger and acquisition (M&A) market.

In value investing, value can be determined by multiple measures, each appropriately weighted according to circumstances. Outside passive minority investor market price can be one such measure of value. Other value determinants include takeover—or change-of-control—prices; liquidating values; values in refinancings; in-use values (e.g., cash returns for investors holding nonmarketable performing loans); and values to those holders who obtain benefits from control, something off the top (SOTT), tax shelter (TS), and abilities-to-finance.

In value investing, then, it would be nonsensical to state that because Bill Gates owns 270 million shares of Microsoft Corporation common and because Microsoft common stock declined $2 yesterday, Bill Gates's net worth declined by $540 million.

Who Are Creditors?

Because EMH and Graham and Dodd analysts examine finance from the points of view of the common stock and holders of common stock, most Wall Street language describes debt as debt, with no distinction made among types of debt. Such a practice is usually appropriate only in the examination of things strictly from the point of view of the common stock, the low entity on the corporate capitalization totem pole.

In value investing, by contrast, finance is examined from the varied viewpoints of multiple constituencies. Whether something is debt depends on where you sit. Subordinated debentures are viewed properly as debt by the common stock and as equity by senior debt to which the subordinates are expressly junior.

What Is a Margin of Safety?

Margin of safety is a concept used by Graham and Dodd analysts. The Graham and Dodd margin of safety is strictly a quantitative—or price—approach. If investors acquire a security at a price deemed cheap enough on the basis of price-to-earnings (P : E) ratios, general market levels, and sometimes discounts from net net current assets or book value, they are deemed to enjoy a margin of safety.

For value investing, a margin of safety for passive investors has a qualitative aspect as well as a quantitative one. For there to be a margin of safety for a passive common-stock investment, the issuer has to enjoy exceptional financial strength measured first by a relative absence of liabilities, whether on or off the balance sheet; management has to appear to be reasonably competent and reasonably well motivated; and the business has to be understandable. In other words cheapness alone is not a sufficient condition, in value investing, to create a margin of safety. Safety as measured by what financial strength exists is also a necessary condition.

What Is Risk?

In the parlance of the EMH and Wall Street in general, risk refers strictly to market risk, which appears to mean strictly price fluctuations in OPMI markets.

In value investing, however, the word *risk* is never used unless it is preceded by an adjective, which means there are all sorts of risks, not merely market risk:

- Market risk: price fluctuation mostly in OPMI markets
- Investment risk: the prospect for a business that there will be a permanent impairment of capital
- Credit risk: the prospect that there will be a money default risk for a debt instrument
- Interest-rate risk: the prospect that increases in the cost of money will result in a depreciation for market prices of fixed rate debt instruments
- Failure-to-match-maturity risk: the prospect that those who both lend and borrow (i.e., those who are spread lenders) will suffer losses because, say, they lend long and borrow short
- Currency risk
- Inflation risk
- Loss-of-credibility risk

Currency risk is the risk of loss by changes in the relative prices of currency. For example, when the U.S. dollar appreciates in price relative to the Japanese yen and a U.S. investor holds a yen denominated security, the investor will suffer an unrealized loss in U.S. dollars attributable to the relative decline of the yen.

Inflation risk is the risk of loss in terms of real income because of rising prices. An investor holds a 5% long term U.S. Treasury Note. The consumer price index for a relevant period increases at an 8% annual rate. The investor, receiving only 5% annual interest suffers a real income (not money income) loss relative to the consumer price index.

Loss of credibility risk is the risk that an entity will no longer be trusted. For example, company ABC, because its top officers are charged with malfeasance, finds itself unable to raise capital any longer by the sale of common stock to the public market.

Are There Always Tradeoffs?

In value investing, there are tradeoffs involved in anything financial. Whether any financial action or practice is harmful or beneficial depends on nitty-gritty details. In general stock-market parlance, however, goods and bads tend to be absolute, with no appreciation of possible tradeoffs. In early 1998, popular OPMI market views were about as follows.

Inflation is bad. In fact under value investing, inflation ought to be a mixed bag. It is bearish for many companies in that the cost to replace depreciating assets will be higher than depreciation and amortization allowances. Inflation is bullish for many companies, though, in that higher costs tend to preclude new competition from coming into an industry. Also, inflation tends to foster M&A activity at improved prices as entities intent on expansion discover that it has become cheaper to buy assets in a market than to produce similar assets internally. A good example of this was in the upstream oil and gas industries in the mid-and late 1980s, when it was a lot cheaper to obtain oil and gas reserves by buying common stocks on Wall Street than it would have been to drill new oil and gas wells.

High interest rates are bad. In value investing there are a whole gamut of issuers whose future net income is enhanced any time interest rates increase. These are companies with portfolios of performing loans, especially portfolios expanding in size, that are financed by liabilities whose costs are unrelated to interest rates. These debt holders are not spread lenders. Insurance companies are a prime example of such companies: Their assets consist primarily of performing loans earning interest; their liabilities consist primarily of loss reserves, policyholder reserves, and unearned premiums; and costs, if any, are unrelated to interest rates. Since these companies rather continuously invest new funds into debt instruments and also reinvest maturing obligations, increased interest rates result in higher future income than would otherwise be the case. Offsetting this is the fact that assets consisting of performing loans decline in value on a mark-to-market basis as interest rates increase. For many companies and investors, though, the benefits are greater from increasing net investment income from operations compared with decreases in stated net asset values (NAV).

It is advantageous to have publicly traded common stock rather than to be a private company. In fact, in value investing, there are various advantages and disadvantages.

The advantages of being public are as follows:
- The company itself, and insiders who control timing, can take advantage of securities prices that are superhigh (by selling—say, in initial public offerings [IPOs]) and superlow (by buying—say, by going private).
- The discipline imposed by being public (e.g., the requirements for good recordkeeping) can be helpful to managements.
- Being public enhances liquidity and various exit strategies.

- Being public enhances prospects for M&As either as an acquirer or as part of exit strategy. Specifically, a company on the acquisition trail obtains an additional currency (a publicly traded common stock) with which to make acquisitions.
- The imprimatur of being public (especially with a well-regarded investment banker as lead underwriter) can be helpful to operations.
- Public or soon-to-be-public securities provide a method, by way of stock options, to provide an attractive compensation package to executives and employees.

The disadvantages of being public include the following:

- Being public means having an ill-informed, litigious partner—public shareholders.
- There is pressure to produce near-term results and increase EPS, rather than to build long-run values internally.
- There are potential liabilities from lawsuits over disclosure problems.
- Large expenses, especially for legal and accounting advice and for insurance.
- Pressure to have outsiders as board members, who might not understand the business.
- Discouragement of insiders from building corporate (and personal) wealth through internal means other than creating, for example, EPS and EBITDA (earnings before interest, income, taxes, depreciation, and amortization).
- Tendency of public companies to forgo long-term unrealized—and therefore unreported—appreciation.
- Tendency of public companies to forgo conservative accounting practices in regard to earnings from operations and thus lose opportunities to minimize income-tax bills.
- Possibility that public companies will opt not to undertake otherwise attractive projects because the projects have only long-term payoffs.

Does Investor Protection Equal the Public Interest?

In value investing, investor protection is not the same as the public interest. Public interest might be defined, at least in part, on expanding national productivity. There probably is too much mispricing in OPMI markets for OPMI market pricing to allocate national resources efficiently.

Can the Value of Benefits to a Recipient Be Equated with Costs to the Company?

In value investing, nothing could be farther from the truth than the idea that the value of noncash benefits to a recipient equals a cost to a company. The company is analyzed as the company; stockholders are a separate constituency. In no way can the value to a recipient of stock options equal a cost to the company for issuing such stock options.

Is Access to Capital Markets Cost Free or Low Cost?

In value investing, no transactions occur south of Chambers Street that are not damnably expensive both for issuers and investors.

Is Information Reflected in Market Prices Instantaneously?

Certain information, such as a change in earnings estimate, seems to affect market prices instantly while other information, such as a reduction in inventory and consequent increase in cash, may not affect market price at all. In value investing, the trick is not to obtain superior information but rather to use the available information in a superior manner.

Do Managements Work in the Best Interests of Shareholders?

Managements rarely work in shareholders' best interests. Witness the fact that virtually every public company in existence has charters and by-laws that entrench managements and control groups in office. When the author was an investment banker involved in going-private transactions in the 1970s, the vast majority of managements approaching him had a primary interest in paying as little as possible to outside shareholders. Donald Trump obtained voting control of Resorts International in the late 1980s by paying $80 per share for B stock. The A stock, publicly held, had the same economic rights as the B but had limited voting rights. Trump attempted to force out the A stock in a going-private transaction at $21 per share.

Is Ignorance without Cost?

An underlying tenet of EMH is that no investor can know as much as the market, so why try? Historically, this view has been an invitation to the defrauding of OPMIs and to misallocation of resources.

Is Mispricing Counterproductive?

Mispricing is not necessarily counterproductive in value investing. The ability to get superpricing from IPO markets drove the venture capital industry in the 1990s, especially after the defense industry cutbacks of the late 1980s. Such pricing drove U.S. high-tech small-cap industry and made the United States highly productive and thus the envy of the rest of the world.

Are There *Summum Bonum*s in Value Investing?

In value investing, there are no *summum bonum*s. Every financial phenomena with positive aspects also seems to have negative aspects:

- Great growth in earnings means low average earnings.
- High return on equity (ROE) spells a lack of operational leverage and frequently a lack of a margin of safety.

Is Filing for Bankruptcy Relief Always Bad?

For many troubled public companies, Chapter 11 relief makes much more sense than trying to reorganize out of court. Seeking Chapter 11 relief can be very bad for the common stock. It does not follow, though, that this is bad for the company, its creditors, or other constituents.

Is Market Regulation Bad?

Market regulation is not bad in all cases. The turmoil in Asia of the late 1990s can be attributed in great part to lax regulation, nonregulation, and stupid regulation.

Does Anyone Earn Excess Returns in an Efficient Market?

An efficient market means that excess returns will be earned if there are no external forces imposing disciplines. In an efficient market, each participant tries to do as well as he or she reasonably can under the circumstances.

Are High-Priced Common Stocks Sure to Perform Poorly?

Just because a common stock is high priced does not mean it will perform poorly. An overpriced common stock becomes a valuable corporate asset in the hands of a skilled management.

Is the Income Tax Rate What Counts in Examining How Burdensome Taxes Are?

How burdensome taxes are for a taxpayer is a function of three issues: (1) rate, (2) whether the taxpayer can control the timing as to when the tax should be paid, and (3) whether the event that gives rise to the tax also gives rise to the cash with which to pay the tax.

Are Certain Players in the Market Stupid?

In value investing, no one is stupid if the reasons behind his or her actions are understood. For example, almost full weight should be put on OPMI market prices rather than value investing considerations if the following conditions exist:

- The analyst is untrained in fundamental analysis.
- The analyst's job depends on near-term performance.
- A portfolio is operating with borrowed money and in mark-to-market deals.
- A company or an insider is seeking access to equity markets to sell common stock.

Are Generally Accepted Accounting Principles Supposed to Tell the Truth?

GAAP disclosures can have multiple meanings, depending on context. For example, large asset values can mean:

- Lots of overhead, lots of earnings potential, or both
- Sources of tax losses
- Separable and variable values from those of a going concern
- Lots of liabilities—many off the balance sheet—in owning non–passive investment assets

Do Earnings and Cash Flows Have Primacy?

In value investing, earnings and cash flows are not the main focus. Resource conversion and access to capital markets at superprices are at least as important.

Is the Goal of Most Corporations to Create Earnings?

The goal of most corporations should be not to create earnings but to create wealth in the most efficient manner, which may or may not be by way of taxable earnings from operations.

What Is Cash Flow?

Cash flow can mean many things, depending on context, but it usually means cash generated from operations. Analysts most often look at cash generation available for specific purposes. The low entity on the cash-flow totem pole is frequently cash generated that is available for distribution to shareholders. Next up is cash generated that is available to service securities (or their equivalents) that are part of the corporation's capitalization and are senior to the common stock. Third up are cash flows generated that can be used as a basis for expanding corporate activities. Such expenditures might be for property, plant and equipment, receivables, inventory, research and development, investments, or M&As. The first use of cash generated from operations is to make the same types of expenditures as are made for expanding corporate activities but that are made for the purpose of having a company maintain its competitive position. Exactly what cash generated from operations is useful for is a matter of detailed analysis of specific situations. The common definition of cash flow as EBITDA is a mere start. A good analyst then has to examine the use of proceeds from EBITDA, because EBITDA is one thing when it is available for distribution to the common equity but quite something else when it has to be used just to keep the company competitive and might not, as a practical matter, be available for debt service.

How Are Earnings Defined?

There are all sorts of definitions of earnings, with the most common being periodic net income as reported for GAAP purposes. Value investors' definition of corporate earnings refers to those corporate activities that create wealth for the benefit of the corporation, its securityholders, or both while consuming cash. This is what most prosperous companies do. Very few companies seem to be cash-flow companies (i.e., entities that create both cash and wealth at the same time).

What Is Capital?

Corporate capital refers to the amount invested in a business. Depending on the context, that amount can be measured by cost, by marks to market, by appraisal value, by replacement costs, or by combinations thereof.

Are United States Depositary Institutions Healthier Today Than They Have Ever Been?

Depositary institutions in the United States appear healthier now than ever before for three reasons:

- In commercial and real estate lending, banks, as senior lenders, no longer seem to be taking the risks they did before the junk-bond market exploded in size in the late 1980s. It now seems that many of the risks banks used to take have been assumed by junk-bond holders, especially nonbank financial institutions, such as pension plans and mutual funds.
- Lending risks, too, have been dispersed for individual banks, concomitant with the growth of loan securitizations.
- Fee income has grown, and spread lending is now much less important to banks than had formerly been the case. Indeed, in 1997 Citicorp derived 52% of its operating income, before other expenses, from the account "other income" and only 48% from the account "net interest income" (i.e., spread lending). Most of "other income" seemed to be in the form of cash fees from such things as mutual-fund management fees.

PART III

RESOURCE CONVERSION

In the investment disciplines—academic finance, Graham and Dodd fundamentalism, and conventional money management, exit strategies for outside passive minority investor (OPMI) holders of common stocks are visualized almost exclusively as sales at a subsequent date in the OPMI market. In value investing, however, it is assumed that at the time of purchase of a common stock, many—if not most—exits will involve resource conversion activities: mergers and acquisitions (M&As); contests for control; the restructuring of both healthy and troubled companies; and the acquisition of common stocks from OPMI shareholders by insiders and companies themselves in leveraged buyouts (LBOs), in management buyouts (MBOs), and in the repurchase of shares of companies that remain public by means of open-market purchases, private transactions, cash-tender offers, and exchange-of-securities offers. In addition, resource conversion includes the going public of companies for the first time through initial public offerings (IPOs).

Because of the prevalence of resource conversion activities, gaining understanding of what goes on in resource conversion should be helpful to readers of all stripes, especially OPMIs interested in understanding important activities that are the real lifeblood of what transpires in the financial community outside of trading areas. There are a number of good books describing certain resource conversion activities. The second half of one, *Big Deal,* by Bruce Wasserstein (Warner Books, 1998), describes various resource conversion activities.

The purpose of this section is to cover, from a value investing point of view, resource conversion activities that other literature does not cover or covers from a different point of view. The basis for this section is Chapter 12, "A Simplified Example," a road map to the types of activities that occur in resource conversion. Chapter 13, "Acquiring Securities in Bulk," reviews both the methods activists use to acquire public (and, in some cases, private) securities and the principal considerations that go into activists' decision-making processes. The following chapter "Restructuring Public Companies," covers a little-understood area that is not explained very well in the literature. If you understand the reorganization processes used to rehabilitate sick companies, you have a leg up in understanding investments in general and resource conversion in particular. Finally, this section concludes with Chapter 15, which discusses several selected topics that are highly important in most of the resource conversion activities that occur in the United States: pricing, the economics of stockholder litigation, the economics of statutory appraisals, IPOs, going-privates, and share repurchases.

Chapter 12

A Simplified Example

First fellow: "Did you know that Dave is a millionaire?"
Second fellow: "Dave is no millionaire. My goodness, you don't even know
　　　　　　what a millionaire is."
First fellow: "Oh, yeah, what is a millionaire?"
Second fellow: "A millionaire? Why a millionaire is someone who has at least
　　　　　　ten thousand dollars in cash."
First fellow: "You're right. That kind of money Dave ain't got."

The Saga of XYZ Company

A theoretical company, XYZ Company, can be used to illustrate how
resource conversion phenomena operate. This chapter examines various financial engineering techniques applied, in a simplified manner, to
XYZ. As a stand-alone, XYZ has the following characteristics.

XYZ is an ordinary non-growth public company with 1 million shares
of XYZ common stock outstanding. XYZ is debt free. The common
stock sells around $9\frac{1}{2}$ in the outside passive minority investor (OPMI)
market, giving the common stock an aggregate market value of around
$9.5 million.

Going forward for the next 5 years, XYZ is to have annual operating income of around $2 million including interest income of 6% on surplus cash held (i.e., cash holdings in excess of $500,000). During this 5-year period, the aggregate amount of receivables outstanding and inventory will remain constant at $2 million. Current liabilities remain constant at $600,000. Cash necessary for the operation of the business is assumed to be constant at $500,000. The value of the property, plant, and equipment (PPE) account will remain constant at $6 million, as capital expenditures for PPE will exactly equal charges taken for depreciation and amortization of PPE.

Prior to any financial engineering, the XYZ balance sheet and income account were as shown in Tables 12-1 and 12-2, respectively.

Then Promoter Group, via Newco, a newly formed corporate shell, acquires, in a newly formed wholly owned subsidiary of Newco, all XYZ

Table 12-1. Summary Balance Sheet

Variable	Value (000)	Variable	Value (000)
Cash	$1,000	Current liabilities	$600
Receivables and inventory	$2,000		
Property, plant, and equipment	$6,000	Net worth	$8,400
	$9,000		$9,000

Table 12-2. Summary of Income Account

Variable	Value (000)
Revenues	$7,000
Operating income, including interest income	$2,000
Income taxes at 40%	$800
Net income	$1,200
Earn per share for 1,000 shares	$1.20
Market value of equity at 8 times earnings	$9,600
Return on equity	+14.3%

assets, subject to all of XYZ's liabilities. The acquisition of these net assets is for cash, at six times operating earnings, or $12 million, equal to a 25% premium over the prevailing price of $9.6 million for XYZ equity in the OPMI market. Fees and expenses of the transaction are $500,000.

Newco obtains the $12.5 million cash needed to close the XYZ transaction, without recourse to Promoter Group, as shown in Table 12-3. Table 12-4 shows Newco's opening balance sheet.

Table 12-3. Financing for Purchase of XYZ Company

Source	Value (000)
XYZ surplus cash	$500
Funds borrowed from banks at 10%	
(5 times operating income, secured by various assets, such as receivables and property, plant, and equipment)	$10,000
Investment of cash by Promoter Group limited partnership	$2,000
	$12,500

Table 12-4. Approximate Newco Opening Balance Sheet (Consolidated)

Variable	Value (000)	Variable	Value (000)
Cash	$500	Current liabilities	$600
Receivables and inventory	$2,000	Secured borrowings	$10,000
Property, plant, and equipment	$6,000		
Intangibles	$4,000*	Net worth	$1,900
	$12,500		$12,500

*Most of the intangibles are assumed to amortize over 14 years for the purposes of both income tax and generally accepted accounting principles.

Newco's approximate, condensed income accounts, cash-flow statements, and balance sheets for each of the next 5 years are as shown in Table 12-5, assuming the secured borrowings are amortized at a rate of $500 per year.

Table 12-6 is a clone of Table 12-5, except that the equity investment into Newco is $1,000 rather than $2,000. The $1,000 cash needed to close

Table 12-5. NEWCO Forecasted Financial Statements (post LBO) ($2,000 Common Stock Investment)

	Opening	Year 1	Year 2	Year 3	Year 4	Year 5
Balance Sheet						
Cash	500	500	500	500	500	500
Accts Recv & Inventory	2,000	2,000	2,000	2,000	2,000	2,000
P, P & E, net	6,000	6,000	6,000	6,000	6,000	6,000
Intangibles	4,000	3,714	3,428	3,142	2,856	2,570
Total Assets	12,500	12,214	11,928	11,642	11,356	11,070
Current Liabilities	600	600	600	600	600	600
Secured Borrowing	10,000	9,286	8,529	7,726	6,875	5,973
Net Worth	1,900	2,328	2,799	3,316	3,881	4,497
Total Liabilities & Equity	12,500	12,214	11,928	11,642	11,356	11,070
Income Account						
Operating Income		2,000	2,000	2,000	2,000	2,000
Amortization of Intangibles		286	286	286	286	286
Interest on Debt		1,000	929	853	773	688
Income Tax @ 40%		286	314	344	377	411
Net Income		428	471	517	565	616
Sources and Uses of Funds						
Use of Funds						
Retire Debt		714	757	803	851	902
Sources of Funds						
Amort of Intangibles		286	286	286	286	286
Net Income		428	471	517	565	616
		714	757	803	851	902

Table 12-6. NEWCO Forecasted Financial Statements (post LBO) ($1,000 Common Stock Investment)

	Opening	Year 1	Year 2	Year 3	Year 4	Year 5
Balance Sheet						
Cash	500	500	500	500	500	500
Accts Recv & Inventory	2,000	2,000	2,000	2,000	2,000	2,000
P, P & E, net	6,000	6,000	6,000	6,000	6,000	6,000
Intangibles	4,000	3,714	3,428	3,142	2,856	2,570
Total Assets	12,500	12,214	11,928	11,642	11,356	11,070
Current Liabilities	600	600	600	600	600	600
Secured Borrowing	10,000	9,358	8,677	7,955	7,190	6,379
Subordinated Borrowing	1,000	1,000	1,000	1,000	1,000	1,000
Net Worth	900	1,256	1,651	2,087	2,567	3,092
Total Liabilities & Equity	12,500	12,214	11,928	11,642	11,356	11,070
Income Account						
Operating Income		2,000	2,000	2,000	2,000	2,000
Amortization of Intangibles		286	286	286	286	286
Interest on Debt		1,120	1,056	988	916	837
Income Tax @ 40%		238	263	290	319	351
Net Income		356	395	436	479	526
Sources and Uses of Funds						
Use of Funds						
Retire Debt		642	681	722	765	812
Sources of Funds						
Amort of Intangibles		286	286	286	286	286
Net Income		356	395	436	479	526
		642	681	722	765	812

is obtained by having Newco sell, for $1,000 cash, a new parent company issue of $1,000 principal amount of nonamortizing 10-year, 12% subordinated debentures. These junk bonds are a form of mezzanine finance.

Assume in Table 12-5 that at the end of 5 years, Newco goes public at eight times earnings, using the proceeds from the public offering (say

$2,000) to pay down secured borrowings. At eight times earnings, old equity would have an OPMI market value of $4,928, resulting in a compound annual return of 19.8%. Is this a comparison of apples and oranges here—$2,000 cash in 1996 versus $4,928 in restricted common stock in 2001? Would it not still be apples and oranges if all the Newco common stock became freely tradable in 2001?

Assume in Table 12-6 that at the end of 5 years, Newco goes public, as per preceding paragraph. At eight times earnings, old equity would have an OPMI market value of $4,208, resulting in a compound annual return of 33.3%. Assume in Tables 12-5 and 12-6 that with the secured lender's permission, Newco was able to dividend out $1,000 of surplus cash before going public. Returns of 19.8% and 33.3% would be increased materially.

In reality, Promoter Group, as the promoter, would have received much in the way of additional compensation from the XYZ deal:

- Part of that $500 initial expense incurred in connection with the acquisition of XYZ would have been an investment banking fee paid to Promoter Group. The actual promoters of the deal, as general partners (GPs) of Promoter Group, may or may not have shared that investment banking fee with the limited partners (LPs).
- Newco probably paid a home office charge to Promotor Group—say, $100 per year.
- The typical relationship between Promoter Group's GPs and its LPs is that the GPs, which run hedge funds, get a management fee of between 1% and 2% per annum of assets managed, plus 20% of the profits, sometimes after the LPs get a minimum return, say 7% or 8% per annum. The GPs are unlikely to have invested any of their own funds into Promoter Group; 100% of the funding would have been provided by the LPs.
- Instead of a 25% premium's being paid to OPMI investors (assuming that old XYZ was liquidated or that Newco had purchased XYZ common stocks rather than XYZ net assets), perhaps only a 15% premium was paid, with the missing 10% going to XYZ management and control people as bonuses and parachutes.

Why did the XYZ control group need to sell to Promoter Group? The control group could have accomplished a similar transaction itself in a strict going-private, in which case not only would it have extracted cash from XYZ, taxable on a capital-gains basis, but it would also have remained in complete control of XYZ.

Alternatively, important people at XYZ could have had interests in Promoter Group or Newco common stock. There is no need for Promoter Group to own 100% of Newco common. Indeed, PG might have actively sought XYZ management ownership of a minority interest in Newco common.

One of the big advantages Promoter Group has as the controlling entity of Newco is complete control of timing. Promoter Group chooses when to go public. Suppose the initial public offering (IPO) market heated up in 1998. Why not take Newco public then at, say, 12 to 15 times earnings, especially since at that time publicly traded comparables might be selling in the OPMI market at 16 to 20 times earnings? There are lots of institutional pressures to have buoyant IPO markets:

- A large number of Promoter Group–type entities are either associated with major underwriters (Merrill Lynch and Morgan Stanley) or have close relationships with them.
- Security salespeople love and need underwritings because of (1) large gross spreads, a substantial portion of which is paid to salespeople, and (2) exclusive products (Newco, now renamed XYZ, common stock as an IPO), designed to sell at premiums in immediate aftermarkets and usually unavailable to discount brokers.
- In going public, use of proceeds becomes a very important consideration. In Newco's situation, cash proceeds from an IPO could have gone in three general directions: the expansion of operations (i.e., investment in new assets), the paying down of senior borrowings, or payments on junior securities, subordinates or common stock. (If presently outstanding common stock is sold in the IPO, this is called a secondary.)

Assume that Newco had substantial amounts of net loss carry-forwards to shelter XYZ earnings before income taxes and that the $12,500 acquisition of XYZ net assets for cash left intact, for income-tax purposes, Newco's continuity of ownership and continuity of business. Cash flows available from the transaction would, of course, be increased materially. So would generally accepted accounting practices (GAAP) book value as per GAAP rules as promulgated in Financial Accounting Standards Board (FASB) 109. Under FASB 109, Newco would have capitalized as an asset the present value of estimated cash to be generated via use of the net operating loss tax carry forward.

As part of control of timing, suppose Newco goes public by way of an IPO and prospers, but the aftermarket is very poor, so that the OPMI market price is four times earnings. Promoter Group takes Newco private at six times earnings; stockholder suit is brought and settled on the basis of a $250 fee to class-action attorneys, and the stock price is increased by 25¢ per share. No Newco stockholder perfects rights to a statutory appraisal.

Suppose Newco falters and is unable to service debt to secured lenders, the trade creditors, or the subordinates. Either in court (Chapter 11 reorganization) or out of court (a voluntary restructuring), Promoter Group, as control people and as a debtor in possession (DIP), will have a tremendous amount of control over the reorganization processes.

Suppose Promoter Group wanted to acquire control of XYZ in a hostile takeover. It would have the benefit of not necessarily having to make a deal with XYZ management or control groups. If it owned a minority position in XYZ common stock, Promoter Group could serve as the catalyst that would put XYZ in play. The easiest way for XYZ control people to get rid of Promoter Group probably would be to have someone pay a premium for all XYZ common stock or to specifically buy out Promoter Group's position at a premium—greenmail. There would be many disadvantages to a hostile takeover, including quite high administrative expenses, whether Promoter Group seeks to acquire XYZ common stock, presumably for cash, or solicits proxies for control. There are always lots of uncertainties in engaging in hostile takeovers, and Promoter Group would be estopped from doing due-diligence research away from public records.

Suppose Newco were a public company selling at 25 times earnings and wanted to acquire XYZ in a merger transaction, exchanging a new issue of Newco common stock for all of the 1,000 shares of XYZ common stock outstanding. Newco currently has 1,000 Newco common shares outstanding and has net income of $1,000 and therefore an OPMI market capitalization of $25,000, or $25 per share. It acquires XYZ for $15 market value of a new issue of Newco common stock. This equals a premium of about 56% over the XYZ common stock OPMI trading price. It

Table 12-7. How Newco's Net Income
Increases in a Merger

Variable	Value
Newco net income	$1,000
XYZ net income	$1,200
Combined net income	$2,200
Earnings per share (1,600 shares)	$1.38

requires the issuance of 600 shares of Newco common stock. As a result of the transaction, Newco's net income will be increased from $1.00 per share to $1.38 per share, as shown in Table 12-7.

Conclusion

The tale of XYZ Company contains examples not of free lunches, but rather simplified examples of how activists engaged in financial engineering try to get other people to pay for their lunches. Getting someone else to pay for your lunch can, in the most general sort of way, fit into one or more of three categories:

- Something off the top (SOTT): whether promoter's compensation, managements' compensation, underwriting gross spreads, salespeople's participations, or free or cheap stock or options
- Other people's money (OPM): which is access to attractive outside capital, whether equity or debt, and access to attractive credit enhancements, whether for companies or other participants
- Tax shelter (TS) for companies and all participants with clout

Chapter 13

Acquiring Securities in Bulk

If after ten minutes at the poker table you do not know who the patsy is, you are the patsy.

An active investor seeking control or elements of control over a publicly traded commercial entity through securities acquisition can follow several different courses of action. From a securityholder's point of view, all acquisitions of securities are either voluntary or mandatory. *Voluntary* refers to situations in which each individual security holder can make up his or her own mind as to whether to take certain actions. *Mandatory* refers to voting situations in which all securityholders are forced to participate in some action once the requisite number of securityholders of that class vote in favor of the action. Each of the methods under which control and quasicontrol people acquire securities has advantages and disadvantages. This chapter discusses the advantages and disadvantages of each method in light of the following factors:

- Pricing issues
- Securities law issues

- Income-tax issues
- Accounting issues
- Other regulations
- Availability-of-information issues
- Ability-to-finance issues
- Financial-commitment issues
- Doability issues
- Social issues
- Speed
- Rates of return

The methods reviewed below are not mutually exclusive. For example, in seeking control of a company, an activist limited by other regulations (e.g., the need for Hart-Scott-Rodino filings if more than $15 million is expended on common stock purchase) might still gain a toehold position by acquiring target company common stock for cash in the open market, then follow up by commencing a cash-tender offer or by soliciting proxies seeking to elect a new slate of directors. Cash-tender offers frequently are preludes to mop-up mergers.

Methods for Acquisition of Common Stocks

There are four methods of acquiring common stock (or other securities) for cash:

- In the open market
- In private transactions
- In tender offers
- By use of proxy machinery (mergers, reverse splits, consents)

The first three are voluntary; the fourth is mandatory.

There are two methods of acquiring voting equities—common and preferred—by way of exchanges of securities:

- The voluntary method, in which each shareholder makes up his, her, or its own mind about whether to exchange.

- The mandatory method, in which the proxy machinery is used and in which, except for those who might perfect rights of appraisal, each shareholder has to participate in the proposed exchange provided the requisite vote of shareholders is obtained; even those who perfect rights to dissent cease to be shareholders.

Acquisition of Common Stock for Cash

Cash Purchases in Open Market

- **Pricing issues:** Acquisition is possible at outside passive minority investor (OPMI) prices, which tend to be far more irrational and frequently far lower than can be obtained in negotiated transactions.
- **Securities law issues:** No disclosure is required until the 5% ownership threshold is reached; no use of inside information is permitted. The Securities and Exchange Commission (SEC), though, is exceedingly tough on anything that smacks of OPMI market manipulation. The most important mandate to the SEC, ahead of providing disclosure and oversight of fiduciaries and quasifiduciaries, is protecting the integrity of OPMI market places.
- **Income-tax issues:** These are not a consideration.
- **Accounting issues:** These are not a consideration.
- **Other regulations:** Hart-Scott-Rodino applies when investing over $15 million.
- **Availability-of-information issues:** These are pretty much restricted to public information.
- **Financial-commitment issues:** Buy as little or as much as desired. Margin rules may restrict the ability to borrow.
- **Doability issues:** To gain control, investors probably need to acquire common stock by another—perhaps supplementary—method. (It may sometimes be possible, however, to "Tisch" a company, as in the takeover of CBS Corporation by Laurence Tisch soley by purchases of common stock in the OPMI market.) Also, owning cheap stock acquired as a toehold in OPMI market may afford very good returns for having put a company into play even if the acquirer never attains any element of control. On the other hand, if prices rise in an OPMI mar-

ket, future prices to acquire control by other methods tend to become more expensive than they otherwise would have been.

- **Social issues:** No social issues are involved.
- **Speed:** If the object is to obtain elements of control, the timing involved is likely to be long and indeterminate.
- **Rates of return:** The rates of return are usually plain vanilla.

Cash Purchases in Private Transactions

- **Pricing issues:** Prices reached in negotiated transactions are often far more rational, from a control point of view, than prices in OPMI markets. (From time to time, however, there are anxious or even desperate sellers—for example, the sale of Tejon Ranch common stock by the Times Mirror Company at a 25% discount from OPMI market price in 1997.)
- **Securities law issues:** Disclosure issues depend on privity. 10-b(5) always a factor in terms of implied remedies: When do courts decide that private transactions, market sweeps of OPMI markets, or a combination of the two are mere masquerades for cash-tender offers? Also, does the acquirer obtain restricted common or securities freely tradable in OPMI markets?
- **Income-tax issues:** Purchases of common stocks for cash are almost always straightforward taxable capital transactions for the sellers.
- **Accounting issues:** Purchase accounting prevails in business combinations involving the transfer of cash. Amortization of intangibles is an issue.
- **Availability-of-information issues:** Privity governs; the buyer can seek to know what the seller knows.
- **Ability-to-finance issues:** There is the possibility of seller finance; margin rules may be a factor when there is no change of control.
- **Financial-commitment issues:** What issues there are depend on the size of the block being acquired privately. Deal expense may or may not be minimal.
- **Doability issues:** Tying up large blocks tends to make obtaining control easier, whether the source of control is friendly, neutral, or hostile.
- **Social issues:** Sometimes as part of purchase, there are agreements about board representation and protection of incumbent managements.

- **Speed:** Purchase can be pretty fast—days to weeks.
- **Rates of return:** The rates of return are usually plain vanilla.

Cash-Tender Offers

- **Pricing issues:** A premium above OPMI market price must be offered. The basic rules are as follows: Immediately after the commencement of a tender offer, the bidder must file a tender offer statement with the SEC and the issuer identifying the bidder and setting forth the source of funds, the bidder's purpose in making the tender (free advertising?), the ownership of other securities of the issuer, and appropriate financial statements for those bidders that are not natural people if the bidders are material to a decision by security-holders of the target. The tender offer has to be open at least 20 days—10 days after an increase in price. Nobody of any consequence in the OPMI market tenders until just before a tender offer is to expire. If the tender is for less than all the shares, pro-rata shares must be accepted. The announcement is made promptly and payment is made within 10 days or so after acceptance of shares tendered. If a tender offer is extended, there must be an announcement of the approximate numbers of shares tendered.
- **Securities law issues:** With this method, securities law issues are considerably more onerous than open-market and private purchases but considerably less onerous than using proxy machinery or issuing new securities, which virtually always requires registration under the highly onerous as amended Securities Act of 1933. Portions of the Securities and Exchange Act of 1934, also known as the Williams Act, primarily govern here. In hostile takeovers, state court litigation, especially in Delaware, may take center stage. Even in a friendly takeover, there is likely the need to contend with the plaintiffs' bar representing OPMIs in both federal and state courts. These suits are usually easy to settle, as plaintiffs' bar is primarily driven by fee awards for counsel.
- **Income-tax issues:** These are as for other purchases for cash.
- **Accounting issues:** These are as for other cash purchases. If control is obtained, goodwill issues are likely to arise if there is a follow-on mop-up merger or if the acquired entity is to be part of an acquirer's consolidated financial statements.

- **Availability-of-information issues:** In hostile takeovers, only public information is available; in friendly takeovers, there is a prior opportunity to conduct due-diligence research.
- **Ability-to-finance issues:** Conventional finance may be readily available, starting with secured lenders and working south. Since a bidder can never obtain 100% acceptance for a tender offer, however, financing opportunities may be limited unless the bidder announces plans for a mop-up merger that would result in 100% ownership of the equity. It is far easier to finance a friendly takeover than a hostile one.
- **Financial-commitment issues:** There is almost always a multimillion-dollar commitment to purchase shares. Administrative expenses, including lawyers' fees, printing costs, information agent fees, dealer-manager/investment banker fees, corporate trustee fees, and transfer service fees, are also large.
- **Doability issues:** The key to doability is to offer a price premium above OPMI market price. During the pendency of a cash-tender offer, shares are likely to gravitate into the hands of risk arbitrageurs, who toward the conclusion of the tender-offer period will make market decisions (based on the current permiums over OPMI market prices) rather than investment decisions (based on perceptions of fundamental values). In hostile takeovers, there are always uncertainties about doability. There is a huge advantage (or sometimes disadvantage) over soliciting proxies or exchanging securities, in that tender offers are much quicker.
- **Social issues:** If the deal is friendly or the bidder wants to make a hostile or neutral takeover, it is frequently necessary to give terms that reward incumbent managements or other control people with clout.
- **Speed:** Making a cash-tender offer is infinitely faster than using proxy machinery or issuing securities, both of which require registration under the Securities Act of 1933. Further, in using proxy machinery, there is additional delay of, say, 20 to 60 days after effectiveness of a registration statement so that shareholder meetings can be held.
- **Rates of return:** If the cash-tender offer is successful, the present value of control becomes important.

Although cash-tender offers are classified here as voluntary (each shareholder makes up his or her own mind whether to tender), a cash-tender offer becomes mandatory when the offerer can present a meaningful threat that if enough shares are tendered, the company will deregister with the SEC and there will no longer be a public market for the shares. This can happen when common stocks are not traded on organized exchanges (the New York Stock Exchange [NYSE] or the American Stock Exchange [ASE]) and the company is left with fewer than 300 shareholders of record.

Cash Mergers through the Use of Proxy Machinery

- **Pricing issues:** Cash mergers through proxy machinery almost always offer a premium over OPMI market price, but there is nowhere near the same pressure as in a cash tender, because all that is needed here is the requisite vote of stockholders (e.g., anywhere from 50% of those voting to two thirds of outstanding holders once a 50% quorum votes) to bind 100% of the common stock to the transaction. Outside passive minority investors are a lot more attentive to sale situations at premiums over market than they are to voting situations. The price paid will be reviewed in state court, especially in Delaware, where there is a requirement for "entire fairness." The court will be heavily influenced, however, by OPMI market prices in determining entire fairness. Insiders control timing; they are free to pick depressed OPMI markets as the time for cash mergers.
- **Securities law issues:** It is much more difficult to comply with the provisions of the Securities and Exchange Act in soliciting merger proxies than it is in a cash-tender offer. The legal liabilities here, however, are far less onerous than when common stocks are acquired for securities rather than for cash. Issuing securities publicly gives rise to strictures existing under the Securities Act of 1933. The SEC clears proxy materials before they are mailed. Lawsuits by the plaintiffs' bar, both state and federal, are automatic in merger transactions, whether for cash or for securities. (Do insiders in merger transactions sometimes hold back some consideration initially so that they have reserve ammunition to settle stockholder suits?) In force-out mergers, state blue-sky laws, as they exist in California and Wisconsin for example, can be a problem. In part because of time-consuming delays, it tends to be more difficult to use the cash-merger technique in hostile takeovers than to use a cash-tender offer to be followed by a mop-up merger.

- **Income-tax issues:** These are as for other cash deals. After the investor owns 100% of target, however, it is easier to do subsequent tax planning on behalf of the surviving companies.
- **Accounting issues:** If 100% of equity is acquired and the company becomes private, reporting under generally accepted accounting principles (GAAP) tends to be far less important than when there are OPMI stockholders, present or potential.
- **Availability-of-information issues:** Control people can do due-diligence research. Disclosure to OPMIs, including making admissions against interest (e.g., providing rosy forecasts), becomes crucially important.
- **Ability-to-finance issues:** Generally, it is more easy to finance here than with any other cash purchase of common stocks.
- **Financial-commitment issues:** Usually, these involve megabucks both for the investment and for deal expenses.
- **Doability issues:** Cash mergers are very doable if the investor controls the proxy machinery, but see securities law issues above.
- **Social issues:** It is probably necessary to make a deal with the incumbent management and other control groups with clout.
- **Speed:** Cash mergers are much slower than cash-tender offers.
- **Rates of return:** These can be huge, including premiums for control. In the case of the use of proxy machinery for a hostile takeover, the expenditures incurred are probably better analyzed as an investment rather than as an expense. If the investor does fairly well in a hostile proxy solicitation—even if the investor loses—incumbents mostly will pay good-size amounts to get rid of the hostile solicitor. If the hostile solicitor wins, there is no doubt that he, she, or it will be reimbursed for expenditures.

Acquisition of Voting Equities through Exchanges of Securities

Voluntary

- **Pricing issues:** It is necessary to offer a premium over the OPMI market price in terms of the consideration to be received, whether that consideration is cash, debt, preferred stock, common stock of some issuer other than the target, or combinations thereof.

- **Securities law issues:** It is necessary to register under the relatively onerous Securities Act of 1933 (except for a Section 3(a)9 exemption, which involves different securities of the same issuer when no sales compensation is involved). Voluntary exchanges sometimes take a long time to clear the SEC, they are expensive, and their potential liabilities are large. The same problems with state lawsuit and plaintiffs' bar exist as for cash-tender offers and cash mergers, but voluntary exchanges are usually more difficult to defend.
- **Income-tax issues:** There are opportunities for tax planning. For example, the exchange of voting securities for voting securities might qualify for a tax-deferred reorganization under Section 368(b) of the Securities Act of 1933, and an exchange of voting common stock for net assets might qualify as a Section 368(c) reorganization.
- **Accounting issues:** Common stock for common stock might be considered a pooling rather than a purchase.
- **Availability-of-information issues:** The amount of information needed for Securities Act of 1933 registrations frequently makes voluntary exchanges a difficult tool to use in hostile takeovers. Sometimes voluntary exchanges can be used, however, when the investor is competing against a friendly exchange offer, because then the hostile bidder can clone the friendly bidder's registration papers in describing the target.
- **Ability-to-finance issues:** Exchanging securities means that the initiator is getting target companies' shareholders to finance, at least in part, the bid for control (e.g., the Worldcom bid for MCI in 1997).
- **Financial-commitment issues:** Usually, megabucks are involved for both investment and deal expenses.
- **Doability issues:** Voluntary exchanges are okay for friendly takeovers, but they are harder than buying for cash.
- **Social issues:** These tend to be huge, especially when the investor wants a friendly takeover and is willing to make a deal with the incumbents.
- **Speed:** Voluntary exchanges are often slow, although the SEC has been speeding up the clearance of registration statements. If clearance is required from other regulators (e.g., the Federal Communications Commission [FCC] or the Federal Trade Commission [FTC]), the process can be long.

- **Rates of return:** These can be off the charts, especially against the background that investor A will trade two of his or her $60 million of "funny money" common stocks or junk bonds for $100 million of investor B's solid underlying value, giving OPMIs a 20% premium over market.

Mandatory

- **Pricing issues:** These are much like those for cash merger, except that it is harder for the OPMI market to appraise the value of a securities package rather than cash. It is probable that premiums over OPMI market prices offered in exchanges are larger than for cash transactions, other things being equal. This may be especially true in voluntary exchanges.
- **Securities law issues:** These are much like those for cash mergers, except—and this is a big exception—that the issuer has to comply with the Securities Act of 1933 (see the Worldcom S-4 red herring). The S-4 is a combination proxy statement for voting purpose and a prospectus registering securities that are being offered publicly.
- **Income-tax issues:** There is more certainty regarding the use of Section 368 under the Internal Revenue Service code to effect a tax deferred reorganization than is the case for voluntaries. A Section 368(a) reorganization encompasses a merger transaction. Acquirers know they have 100% equity ownership at the conclusion of proxy solicitation.
- **Accounting issues:** There is more assured certainty than with a voluntary exchange to accomplish, say, a pooling, by virtue of 100% ownership.
- **Availability-of-information issues:** These are as for a voluntary exchange.
- **Ability-to-finance issues:** If senior debt is required from third-party lenders, it is easier to obtain here than for a voluntary exchange, in which the investor can never get 100% acceptance.
- **Financial-commitment issues:** Mandatory exchanges usually involve megabucks, both investment and deal expenses.
- **Doability issues:** These are just like those for cash mergers and voluntary exchanges. Mandatory exchanges tend to be hard to use for hostile takeovers.
- **Social issues:** These are likely to be highly important.

- **Speed:** Mandatory exchanges are as slow as voluntary exchanges of securities, and additional time is required for a stockholder meeting after definitive materials are issued—perhaps another 20 to 60 days.
- **Rates of return:** These are similar to the rates for voluntary exchanges, except here there may be less price sensitivity on part of the OPMI market, and as is stated above, it tends to be easier to get senior financing because acquirer will be a 100% holder of acquiree's common stock. Both these factors ought to improve returns over a pure voluntary exchange.

Acquisition of Control without Acquiring Securities by Using the Proxy Machinery

- **Pricing issues:** These are not relevant, but an outsider needs an issue or issues to obtain votes. The issue usually has to be the promise of improved future OPMI market prices.
- **Securities law issues:** These are a bitch. The investor needs SEC clearance and has to defend against lawsuits by incumbents in control. Incumbents have control of both the proxy machinery and the corporate treasury.
- **Income-tax issues:** Are proxy contest expenses always deductible for outsiders?
- **Accounting issues:** These are not relevant.
- **Availability-of-information issues:** These are not relevant.
- **Ability-to-finance issues and financial-commitment issues:** Securities are not acquired. The cost of hostile proxy solicitation usually runs well into seven figures for legal fees, printing costs (actual solicitation and fight letters), proxy solicitor fees, public relations (PR) costs, advertising costs, and the cost of courting large shareholders (e.g., Worldcom materials). If the attempt at the acquisition of control goes well, costs are likely to be recoverable because even if the hostile solicitor does not win, the incumbents are likely to pay to get rid of him or her. The situation may be different, however, if the outside solicitor is a strategic player in the industry rather than one engaged only in a financial transaction. Nonetheless, in terms of deal expense, the company finances all of the incumbents' expenditures and none of the outsider's expenditures.

- **Doability issues:** Such acquisitions are almost always highly uncertain.
- **Social issues:** These are usually extremely important, except when the raider can win without the necessity of making any deal with the incumbents.
- **Speed:** The transaction speed varies. In most instances, outsiders cannot call a special meeting of shareholders; they have to do their thing at an annual meeting. Such meetings are supposed to be an annual occurrence for listed companies, but sometimes they can be postponed almost indefinitely.
- **Rates of return:** This is an activity with a very high beta.

Chapter 14

Restructuring Troubled Companies

The Company has only two alternatives: go public or go bankrupt.

—Consultant to CEO

The conventional thinking has long been that if a borrower defaults on the payment of interest, principal, or premium and files for relief under the U.S. Bankruptcy Code, the game is over for both the borrower's business and for the lender. It is assumed that the borrower will cease operations and that the best the lender can do is either sell the loan at fire-sale prices or passively wait, hoping something might happen. In relation to larger companies, especially those that have issued publicly traded securities, this view is utterly unrealistic most of the time. These troubled companies stay in operation, and lenders are usually not wiped out—They either are reinstated or participate, frequently actively, in the reorganization process. At the end of a Chapter 11 case, they receive value in the form of new issues of securities and sometimes cash.

From the point of view of value investing, the existence of money defaults on credit instruments or the filing of a petition for relief under Chapter 11 of the bankruptcy code is the *beginning* of the game, not the end. The analysis for value investing purposes involves making judgments about the returns that might be earned in a workout, whether the credit instrument concerned is reinstated or participates in the reorganization. Returns are measured either by percentage of claims that might be paid relative to an investor's cost or by a yield to an event. It is rare indeed that a value investor acquires the common stock of a troubled company. Almost all analyses deal with debt instruments.

Acquiring the debt instruments of troubled companies prior to a reorganization is frequently attractive for control buyers, who, as participants in a reorganization, can obtain controlling interests in companies. This interesting topic, though, is beyond the purview of this chapter.

Because money defaults occur so frequently and always will be part of the investment scene, it is vital that practitioners of value investing have some sense of what reorganization processes consist. This is true even if these investors never deal in troubled companies, something likely to be the case if investments are restricted to more than adequately secured senior debt or to the common stocks of extremely well capitalized companies. Understanding the restructuring of troubled companies contributes to deeper understanding of various other chapters in this book: Chapter 5, "Corporate Valuation"; Chapter 6, "The Substantive Characteristics of Securities"; Chapter 13, "Acquiring Securities in Bulk"; and Chapter 15, "Other Resource Conversion Topics."

Probably the worst misconceptions about Chapter 11 reorganization in particular and about dealing with troubled issuers in general are promulgated by both the financial and legal academic literature on the subject. Scholars are way off base in four areas:

- **They misdefine *market*.** They seem to believe a market exists only when strangers who are buyers and sellers reach agreement as to price. They fail to understand that a market exists in any arena in which participants, striving to do as well as they reasonably can, arrive at agreements as to price and other terms. Thus, in Chapter 11, the agreements reached between and among claimants, and parties-in-interest in a Chapter 11 case after face-to-face negotiations constitute a market. Indeed, a very good market. Participants here tend to be experienced, well-informed professionals. As such, they probably create a far more efficient market for most economic purposes than is the case when market participants are mostly untrained outside passive minority investors (OPMIs) with a short-run point of view.

- **In attempting to ascertain the social values inherent in rehabilitating troubled companies, scholars tend strongly to think only in terms of value as measured by immediate market prices for outstanding securities.** They pay little or no attention to feasibility—the reorganized company's prospects of surviving and prospering without having to go through the reorganization process all over again. Implicit in the concept of feasibility is a long-term view of market prices for securities: what those prices will likely be in the years—not the days—ahead.

- **In thinking about values in reorganization, scholars tend to think in terms of cash values, not present values.** For many reorganizations, senior creditors ought to be cashed out before anything is given to junior creditors and the equity. In dealing with present values, though, creditors are not cashed out by the company. Rather, an important test is a feasibility test. *Feasibility* means that many creditors will have to take the claims to which they are entitled in the form of new securities that do not result in inappropriate cash drains on the company. From a feasibility point of view, the form of consideration paid to claimants is frequently as important as—if not more important than—the amount of consideration. Under a rule of absolute priority, most senior creditors participating in a reorganization are entitled to recover the full amount of their claims in present value, not cash value, before any consideration is remitted to junior securityholders, unless, of course, an appropriate percentage of the senior credits agree to accept less than full value.

- **Scholars seem to think that the costs of bankruptcy are huge, precluding many managements from seeking Chapter 11 relief.** The costs *are* huge, but they are borne by companies, not managements. The salient truth is that any resource conversion process involving attorneys, accountants, and investment bankers tends to be very expensive. These other hugely expensive activities include voluntary exchanges of securities especially for troubled companies, mergers and acquisitions (M&As), initial public offerings (IPOs), and leveraged buyouts (LBOs). Against this background, a Chapter 11 case may not be especially expensive. Here, the essential truth is that managements may be forced to have their companies seek Chapter 11 relief, whereas most M&A activity probably places no coercive pressures on managements. The understandable great reluctance of some managements to seek Chapter 11 relief is based not on expenses but on general ignorance, stigma, and, probably most important of all, the uncertainties and the forfeiture of some degree of control of the corporation that exist in Chapter 11 relief.

As long as the United States has a dynamic, industrial society, money defaults on credit instruments will always occur. It just goes with the territory. Any industrial society has to have a bankruptcy system—methodologies for realizing lenders' rights after a debtor has failed to meet its contractual obligations to them. The U.S. bankruptcy system is relatively unique, at least for larger companies. In the United States, the emphasis is on using reorganization techniques to rehabilitate debtors rather than on forcing debtors to liquidate, with proceeds of such fire sales going to creditors under a cash-out rule of absolute priority (senior creditors are paid in full before anything is left over for juniors). It is obvious that money defaults are going to occur from time to time because

- Overly optimistic forecasts are relied upon by both lenders and borrowers
- Businesses are unable to accurately predict future adversities, including competitive factors, general economic conditions, changes in technology, changes in fashion, and inability to access capital markets in bear periods
- Frequently, many debtors who have an ability to pay are unwilling to pay
- Many companies are badly managed, and any number are managed dishonestly

There are three methods that can be used to restructure troubled companies:

- **The company may seek to exchange new and more liberalized securities for the outstanding debt securities.** In connection with these voluntary exchange offers, the company almost always seeks consents from each creditor or securityholder to delete or amend restrictive covenants in the indentures or loan agreements under which the instruments were issued. Exchange offers and consent solicitations frequently do not work satisfactorily. A principal reason for this is that outside of a court proceeding—either Chapter 7 (the section of the Bankruptcy Code that requires the liquidation of the corporation by a court appointed trustee) or Chapter 11—no holder of corporate debt can be forced to give up the right to a money payment, whether for interest, principal, or premium. Exchange offers sometimes fail because they are premised on the often fallacious assumptions that creditors will accept an instrument with more immediate market value (as opposed to inherent or potential value) in exchange for outstanding debt securities that have a currently depressed market value. It is hard for most exchange offers to succeed unless creditors are shown that they will face considerable downside risk if they do not participate in a voluntary exchange offer. Downside risk exists when, with a requisite vote of the debt issue—usually 50% or two thirds of the outstanding issue, the creditor can be forced to accept a junior position vis-à-vis an exchanging creditor. Moreover, the proponent of a voluntary exchange will threaten to seek Chapter 11 relief if the voluntary exchange fails. Other than the rights to cash payments, virtually all indenture and bank loan provisions can be amended if the requisite amount of creditors consent. Typically, the company bears all the expenses of attorneys, accountants, and investment bankers who represent the creditor groups who are to be parties to voluntary exchanges.

- **The company may first file a bankruptcy petition under the Bankruptcy Reform Act of 1978 (Chapter 11, Title 11 of the U.S. code) and then attempt to recapitalize by soliciting acceptances of a plan of reorganization.** In most situations, this conventional approach to bankruptcy entails considerable risk and uncertainty for the company and its management. In a Chapter 11 bankruptcy, each of the company's creditors and stockholders is either a claimant (i.e., a creditor or its equivalent) or a party-in-interest as far as that proceeding is concerned with standing to object to any and all transactions outside the ordinary course of business. Unsecured creditors are represented by an official committee; other groups (e.g., the common stock) also might be represented by an official committee, although this is not required legally. In any event, claimants and parties-in-interest will have a significant voice in the administration of the bankruptcy and are generally well represented by active and aggressive attorneys, accountants, and investment bankers. Each of these claimants and parties-in-interest will likely press its own agenda. In addition, the company will end up funding huge administrative expenses because it will be required to pay not only the fees and expenses of its own attorneys, accountants, and investment bankers but also those of the attorneys, accountants, investment bankers, and other agents for all claimants and all parties-in-interest.

• **According to Section 1126(b) of the bankruptcy code, a prepackaged plan (also known as a prepack or preplan) may be used.** Here, the company solicits requisite consents to its bankruptcy reorganization plan *before* filing for Chapter 11 relief. If such consents are obtained, the company then will file for Chapter 11 for the limited purpose of getting the plan of reorganization confirmed by a bankruptcy court. Obtaining consents prior to filing for a Chapter 11 relief can dramatically reduce the uncertainty, time wasting, risk, and expense involved when a company attempts to recapitalize either through voluntary exchanges or a conventional Chapter 11. The basic problems with prepacks are that it is hard to obtain the prior consents of the various creditor classes. As long as there is more than one class of creditor that will participate in a reorganization, then unless a senior class is paid in full, the required vote to obtain approval of a plan of reorganization is two thirds, in dollar amount, and 50%, in number, of those voting. If a junior class fails to vote approval of a plan that a court deems to be equitable and feasible, that junior class might be "crammed down." A cram-down cannot take place within the context of a prepack in which the junior class will seek, at the minimum, an appraisal proceeding. When the author used to be active in restructurings, he promoted prepacks by telling the various players, "Look, we can fight for the next two or three years, after which we'll come up with a reorganization plan that looks pretty much like what is being proposed now. Why don't we just do the right thing now up front." This argument rarely worked. There are situations when it becomes possible to convert what originally started out as a voluntary exchange into a prepack. In addition, it is possible that a failed prepack can expedite the consummation of a conventional Chapter 11, especially when senior creditors agree to prepack terms but juniors dissent. In this instance, the juniors may not be very willing to resist the terms proposed in a prepack and risk the possibility that less favorable terms will be "crammed down" in a conventional Chapter 11.

Whether the company being recapitalized is healthy or financially troubled, the techniques used to recapitalize have to be either voluntary or mandatory. Voluntary techniques (such as exchange offers) are those in which each securityholder will make an independent decision whether to accept the offered recapitalization. If the securityholder does not elect to accept the voluntary offer, there will be no change to the entitlements to cash interest and cash principal in accordance with the terms of the holder's credit instrument even if the required threshold of acceptances is met so that other terms of a credit instrument are altered. Mandatory techniques almost always entail use of the voting process and proxy machinery, which is almost always within the absolute control of management when a healthy company is involved but is rarely so when a troubled company is involved.

Voluntary Exchanges

Voluntary methods for the recapitalization of troubled companies are attempted prior to a Chapter 11 filing. These voluntary methods usually involve offers to current holders to trade their existing securities or debt instruments for new instruments, usually with a lower principal amount (typically set at a small premium over the current market) and with less onerous cash service requirements. Those making exchange offers often seek forbearance on defaulted cash service to creditors, hoping that no creditor group forecloses on collateral, accelerates the debt, or files an involuntary Chapter 11 or Chapter 7 petition under the bankruptcy code. Occasionally, there are offers to buy out creditors for cash, with the consideration representing a substantial discount from the face value of the claim but at a premium over the then current market value. For example, the Petro Lewis Corporation and First City Bancshares transactions involved cash offers to public bondholders.

The biggest problem with exchange offers is the voluntary aspect of the offer. No creditor can ever be forced to give up rights to cash interest or principal payments outside of a Chapter 11 case or a similar state proceeding. There is a large and growing list of companies that experienced difficult and lengthy exchange offers or were totally unsuccessful in effecting recapitalizations through voluntary exchange offers.

The second biggest problem with exchange offers is they require that a registration statement and prospectus be filed with the Securities and Exchange Commission (SEC) under the relatively onerous Securities Act of 1933. Such filings are often expensive and sometimes time consuming.

It is frequently difficult to induce voluntary exchanges when the debt instruments are publicly traded and the market prices of these credit instruments are substantially discounted from their principal amount.

Put simply, when there is a voluntary exchange, creditors know two things: (1) they cannot be forced to give up their contractual rights to money payments and (2) if they refuse to tender their security and then become holdouts, the chances are that the market value of the non-tendered security will increase dramatically if other creditors accept the voluntary exchange offer and the troubled company elects to consummate the exchange, provided that the terms of the exchange offer do not result in considerable downside dangers for a nonexchanging creditor. This is true because without the downside threat, the creditworthiness of a nonexchanged instrument will be improved after the voluntary exchange is completed and the company's debt-service requirements are materially lessened. As a result, holders of public bonds are a different breed of animal than are holders of public stock when it comes to voluntary exchanges. Offer the latter a premium over market and they may stampede to exchange. This is not so for creditors if the issuer cannot show the creditors meaningful risks if they do not exchange. It is also true that many of the holders of large positions in the debt of troubled companies are secondary market purchasers and not the original purchasers of the debt. Professional investors in troubled securities are much less likely to rush to accept voluntary exchange offers than are bondholders who acquired debt securities in order to collect interest income.

Issuers invariably attempt to coerce creditors in a voluntary exchange by seeking nonmonetary consents or amendments to the indentures or agreements under which the outstanding debt instruments were issued. These amendments or consents usually are structured so that nonexchanging creditors will have their collateral invaded or their seniority reduced if the exchange offer succeeds. Exchange offers were structured this way by the advisors to Public Service Company of New Hampshire prior to that company's filing for Chapter 11 relief. This attempt failed because sophisticated investors acquired a sufficient dollar amount of credit instruments so that the required amendments to the indentures to permit the company to invade collateral or reduce seniority could not succeed.

Seeking Relief under a Conventional Chapter 11 Filing

A Chapter 11 recapitalization has a distinct advantage over a voluntary recapitalization because of the mandatory nature of the recapitalization. In a Chapter 11, the reorganization is implemented and becomes binding on all claimants pursuant to a bankruptcy court order of confirmation. A court is entitled to confirm a plan of reorganization if two thirds in amount and a majority in number of holders of each separate class of claimants who voted on the plan (e.g., holders of secured debt and unsecured debt) elect to approve the plan and two thirds of the amount voted by party-in-interest holders (e.g., holders of preferred and common stock) elect to approve the plan. In addition, if some classes of claimants and interest holders approve the plan and other classes reject it, the bankruptcy court may confirm the plan over those rejections via a cram-down if the court determines that the plan does not discriminate unfairly, that it is fair and equitable to each class, and that the rejecting classes will receive more under the plan of reorganization than they would if the company were liquidated. There can be no cram-down of a rejecting class, however, if (1) the rejecting class will obtain less than the full value of its claims and (2) a more junior class will receive any value at all under the plan of reorganization.

Notwithstanding the merits of a Chapter 11 bankruptcy as a tool to restructure a troubled company, most troubled issuers and investment banks have considerable reluctance to use Chapter 11. The reluctance is premised on factors such as perceived stigma, large administrative expenses, and loss of management control. Although the stigma issue and the expense issue (at least versus voluntary exchanges) seem to have little basis in fact, control issues are very real considerations in uncontrolled Chapter 11 bankruptcies.

With respect to the stigma issue, there appears to be little difference for large troubled companies whether a reorganization takes place within or without a Chapter 11. Troubled companies are stigmatized (if at all) when they are not able to discharge debts on a timely basis, and that stigma will last only so long as the troubled financial condition exists. Whether the recapitalization takes place in Chapter 11 is a detail that is beside the point because the stigma, if any, already exists. Is there any company that has been successfully recapitalized—by way of either a bankruptcy or an exchange offer—and then suffered a continuing loss of goodwill? Today, people do not seem to perceive Chrysler Corporation, Penn Central, Manville, Texaco Inc., A.H. Robins, and numerous smaller recapitalized companies as being stigmatized.

Ironically, an uncontrolled bankruptcy is often an expensive proposition for the debtor company. With court approval, the troubled company in Chapter 11 pays not only the fees and expenses of a whole host of professionals—attorneys, investment bankers, accountants, and sundry experts—who represent the company, but also the fees and expenses of various official creditors' committees, official equity committees, and such court-appointed officials as examiners. In addition, the debtor may be liable for the fees and expenses of others who have made "substantial contributions" to the reorganization of the company in Chapter 11. This heavy expense factor is offset to some extent by the existence of the automatic stay in bankruptcy that allows the company to forgo cash service on prebankruptcy unsecured claims and certain secured obligations. The same type of heavy expenses, however, exist for out-of-court voluntary exchanges, usually without the full benefit of an automatic stay.

There is little doubt that an uncontrolled Chapter 11 case usually poses large threats to continued control of a business enterprise by its current management and stockholders. The loss-of-control issue, however, must be viewed in context. Even without seeking Chapter 11 relief, troubled companies most often are required, in connection with exchange offers and other voluntary attempts to recapitalize, to cede large blocks of control to creditors and others. Prior to a money default, most troubled companies have to act as supplicants in order to obtain relief from bank lenders, trade suppliers, labor unions, government agencies, and so on. After a Chapter 11 filing, though, it is common for lending institutions and trade creditors to be quite agreeable to providing postpetition financing to a debtor. Nonetheless, once a company has filed for Chapter 11, there is usually an additional and material loss of control during the pendency of the Chapter 11: The debtor company generally lays bare its business and financial soul; the company cannot take any actions outside its ordinary course of business without requisite notice followed by a hearing and approval by the bankruptcy court; the company must share business and strategic plans with claimants and major parties-in-interest; and the company subjects itself to massive reporting, discovery, and testimony under oath. In an uncontrolled Chapter 11, the odds are that claimants and parties-in-interest will be organized and knowledgeable, and their opposition to any proposals by the debtor company will be financed by the debtor company.

In an uncontrolled bankruptcy, there is also a risk that a trustee or examiner will be appointed to run, oversee, or investigate the affairs of the company. The trustee risk is remote if there is an absence of fraud or gross malfeasance. Examiners have duties that clearly impinge on managements' ability to run the business and the reorganization. For practical purposes, though, the appointment of an examiner remains an unlikely event.

A key element giving management a certain amount of control inside of Chapter 11 is that during the first 120 days of the case, the debtor is granted the exclusive right to propose a plan of reorganization. During this period of exclusivity, the debtor is allowed an opportunity to negotiate with claimants and parties-in-interest to formulate a plan of reorganization. If a plan of reorganization is formulated, the debtor has an additional 60 days to solicit consents to its plan of reorganization. Most bankruptcy courts routinely extend the periods of exclusivity because they recognize that the exclusive ability to file a plan of reorganization is the key element of management control. Once the exclusive period is terminated, creditors can put forward their own plans that will likely result in a resolution of reorganization issues in a far different fashion than contemplated by management.

The ultimate loss of management control occurs if it is perceived that the Chapter 11 case is making no progress. Any claimant or party in interest may seek to either have the Chapter 11 dismissed or have the case converted to a Chapter 7 liquidation. If Chapter 11 is dismissed, the automatic stay is lifted and creditors are then entitled to move to assert their contractual remedies (i.e., foreclose on collateral and accelerate payments of debt). If the case is converted to a Chapter 7, a trustee is appointed and the company is liquidated. Liquidation proceeds are paid out to claimants and parties-in-interest in accordance with a strict rule of absolute priority under which secured creditors have first priority to the extent of their collateral and common stockholders come last. For large public companies, however, the vast majority of Chapter 11 cases have resulted in plans of reorganization rather than a dismissal or a conversion of the case.

The ability to control the timing of events is a key element of management control. Timing is a difficult thing to predict in a controlled Chapter 11 and impossible in an uncontrolled case.

Plans of reorganization also include corporate governance provisions as well as economic provisions. In most Chapter 11 cases, the corporate governance provisions adopted entrench existing management in office.

A conventional Chapter 11 has a number of tremendous advantages over a voluntary exchange. First, troubled companies are almost always troubled because they suffer from a cash shortage. Once a company files a petition for Chapter 11 relief, it can receive postpetition or debtor in possession (DIP) financing from financial institutions and trade creditors, which carries a superpriority and will be repaid before prepetition debts. Thus, a company in Chapter 11 has access to financing that is usually unavailable to companies seeking to reorganize out of court. The automatic stay that goes into effect when Chapter 11 relief is put in place insulates managements from continuous hounding by unpaid creditors, a common condition existing prior to any Chapter 11 filing. Furthermore, when a company emerges from Chapter 11, it is given a fresh start. Most claims against a company are resolved in the plan of reorganization, and most other claims not resolved are barred. By contrast, without court relief, a company is still stuck with all its old liabilities, known and unknown, contingent and fixed, in the financials or undisclosed anywhere. Hidden liabilities tend to be more of a real problem in analyzing troubled companies than is the case for healthy issuers.

Prepackaged or Preplanned Bankruptcy Reorganizations

Knowledgeable people in reorganizations go to great lengths to keep the reorganization process from getting out of control. This is not an easy thing to do when dealing with troubled companies, whether such companies seek to recapitalize voluntarily or seek Chapter 11 relief.

The events involving Public Service Company of New Hampshire are a good example of a needlessly uncontrolled bankruptcy. At the time of filing, Public Service had annual operating income before interest and taxes (EBIT) of around $130 million that was derived from stable operations unrelated to its interest in the deeply troubled Seabrook nuclear facility. Clearly, Public Service was easily reorganizable, whether EBIT was $100 million, $200 million, or something in between, because a company can easily reorganize on the basis of existing earnings without extinguishing any securityholders' ownership (existing holders of common stock would have had their percentage ownership reduced from 100% to around 2% to 5% of the reorganized entity). On January 28, 1988, however (and perhaps predictably), Public Service filed for bankruptcy relief without first attempting a prepack. The filing was precipitated by an adverse finding by the New Hampshire Supreme Court in a rate case. The filing resulted in an uncontrolled Chapter 11, and the scenarios outlined above for a hotly contested Chapter 11 reorganization were played out. In an analysis of Public Service, given its rate base, reorganization values ought to have ranged between $800 million and $1.2 billion in the absence of any rate increases. Since Public Service had outstanding only $741 million of mortgage debt, it seemed obvious that all mortgage loans would be made whole, receiving in present value cash, new securities, or both cash and securities that would have a reorganization value equal to mortgage principal plus back interest. The mortgage bonds could have been purchased prior to and just after the Chapter 11 filing in the low 70s. The result for Public Service after a 3-year case was a reorganization value of in excess of $2 billion, which contrasted with the perceived maximum $1.2 billion value prior to filing. The increase in value came about because the New Hampshire Public Utilities Commission allowed Public Service to benefit from massive rate increases. Put otherwise, the New Hampshire rate payers were subjected to cost increases so that unsecured creditors could be made whole and holders of Public Service common stock could participate in the reorganization in a meaningful way.

Had Public Service been willing to consider a prepack, it might well have been able to reorganize within 6 months, with each class of security-holders treated in a manner that complied with bankruptcy code requirements that the plan of reorganization must be fair and equitable to all parties. In addition, the plan could easily have been determined to be feasible (also as required by the bankruptcy code) because an agreement on retail rates could have been reached with the New Hampshire Public Utilities Service Commission in a less confrontational atmosphere than that which had existed prior to the Chapter 11 filing.

A prepackaged bankruptcy reorganization is provided for in Section 1126(b) of the bankruptcy code, which states, in part:

> For purposes of subsection (c) and (d) of this section [(c) and (d) describe the requisite votes to approve a plan], a holder of a claim or interest that has accepted or rejected the plan before the commencement of the case under this title is deemed to have accepted or rejected such plan, as the case may be, if—
>
> (1) the solicitation of such acceptance or rejection was in compliance with any *applicable nonbankruptcy law,* rule or regulation governing the adequacy of disclosure in connection with such solicitation...

In other words, a troubled company whose securities are publicly traded can use the proxy rules under Section 14 of the amended Securities and Exchange Act of 1934 to solicit consents of its creditors and equityholders to a Chapter 11 plan of reorganization before that company ever files for Chapter 11 relief. Again, in an uncontrolled Chapter 11, a troubled company is required to give seats at the negotiating and litigating table to all claimants and sometimes to parties-in-interest. In a prepack, the solicitation of acceptances of a plan of reorganization is conducted *before* creditors and equityholders are organized with official committees and aggressive attorneys and investment bankers, resulting in a much higher degree of management control. In essence, much of the infrastructure and massive cost of a bankruptcy currently provided for by the bankruptcy code can be avoided with a prepack. In addition, part of the beauty of a prepack is that the process deprives public bondholders of *any* incentive to hold out, because this is not a voluntary recapitalization technique.

As pointed out in Chapter 13, "Acquiring Securities in Bulk," the control of the proxy machinery of a public company is virtually always within the power of management. In a prepack, the management of a troubled company controls the timing of the solicitation and the content of the solicitation materials. Clearly, management of a troubled company will find it much harder to obtain the prebankruptcy consents to the plan of reorganization than, for example, to obtain shareholder consent to elect a slate of directors. The prebankruptcy consents should be much easier to obtain, however, than those same consents after the various creditor groups are organized inside Chapter 11. Finally, if the prebankruptcy solicitation fails, the troubled company will always have the option to pursue a conventional Chapter 11. In such an event, the company will have the added momentum that will be provided by its attempted prepack.

Valuation of Credit Instruments

In Chapter 5, "Corporate Valuation," there was a discussion of sources of value: flows, whether cash or earnings, on the one hand and on the other, resource conversion, which includes redeployment of assets to other uses, to other ownership, or both. This type of asset redeployment is known as liquidation under Chapter 7 and Chapter 11. Chapter 7 requires a liquidation, but under Chapter 11, no plan of reorganization can be approved unless the values available for creditors would be at least equal in a reorganization to what they would be in a liquidation. Thus the disclosure statement that accompanies plans of reorganization contains forecasts, usually 5-year forecasts, of future flows, as well as a liquidation analysis. These can be valuable tools for investors, although forecasts of future flows for companies undergoing Chapter 11 reorganization tend to be optimistic.

Since the debtor-in-possession (i.e., management) has the exclusive right to propose a plan of reorganization, the tendency is to propose plans that will most benefit the company at the expense of creditors. This becomes important when management chooses whether to reinstate a credit instrument or have a credit instrument participate in a reorganization. Reinstatement entails curing defaults, paying back interest plus compensation for any damages incurred as a result of reliance by the creditor on the contractual terms (perhaps equal to interest on interest), and resuming payments on the reinstated securities. Participating in a reorganization means that the creditor receives a new package of securities. Reinstated creditors have no votes on a plan of reorganization. Participants in a plan of reorganization can vote to approve or disapprove of the plan.

It is an important part of the analysis of a distressed company to decide whether a debt instrument will be reinstated or will participate in a reorganization. In reinstatement, return is measured by an investor by a yield to an improved credit rating. In participation, return is measured by dollar cost versus the amount of claim likely to be paid in present value.

Management will have the strongest voice in deciding whether to reinstate or have a creditor participate. Suppose interest rates generally are around 6%. If an investor holds a 4% senior note due in 15 years, the investor can be fairly confident that the instrument will be reinstated. If, on the other hand, the investor owns a 12% senior note due in 3 years, the investor can be fairly confident that the instrument will participate in the reorganization.

A Primer on Chapter 11

In late 1995, in his capacity as a fund manager, the author had a fund acquire a large position in Kmart senior credits at an average price of about

74. In that connection, he wrote a letter to stockholders of the fund explaining the reasoning behind the acquisition. That letter is a good explanation of the dynamics that take place in reorganizing troubled companies.

The Reasoning Behind the Acquisition of Kmart Credits

The U.S. economy in the past 20 to 25 years has been characterized by industry after industry going through difficult periods. Indeed, in many instances, conditions have been as bad as or worse than anything experienced by the particular industry during the Great Depression of the 1930s.... Look at the economic traumas in the last 20 years visited upon, among others, the energy industry, real estate, savings and loans, commercial banks, automobiles, steel, aluminum, machine tools, row crops, and airlines.

A factor that distinguishes the 1980 to 1996 industry depressions from the 1930s is that in modern times, the depressions are self-contained and confined to particular industries without a domino effect. The severe downturn in energy demand and energy prices after 1982, for example, did not lead to a draconian drop in gross domestic product (GDP), although by some measures, energy and related activities had accounted for almost 10% of GDP.

Retailing is now experiencing just such a devastating depression. The country is overstored, consumers in general have piled up much too much debt, and large numbers of retail chains are unsoundly financed with heavy debt loads, owing to financial institutions, trade vendors, and landlords. A huge number of retailing companies have recently sought relief from creditors by filing under Chapter 11 or Chapter 7 of the bankruptcy code, including Barneys, Jamesway, Merry Go Round, Bradlees, Caldor, and Ames. Many more seem bound to seek such relief in 1996. In addition, over the long term, there may well be dramatic changes in consumer shopping when, as, and if interactive shopping in cyberspace replaces, in part, in-person store shopping.

TAVF, and a previous fund also managed by the adviser, have fared well by acquiring securities of companies at the very time that these companies were going through economic hard times. Indeed, these purchases generally were made when immediate outlooks were quite bleak, as, for example, the purchase of secured bank debt issued by an oil service company in 1986 and 1987, the acquisition of real estate common stocks and depository institution common stocks in 1991 and 1992, the purchase of title insurance common stocks in 1994, and even the acquisition of derivative instruments—inverse floaters—in late 1994 and early 1995.

The strategy for faring well with the acquisition of securities of companies operating in ultradepressed industries or those that, like Kmart, also had troubles unique to themselves was twofold: restrict the ownership of such securities to the common stocks of issuers that enjoy exceptional financial strength and staying power or else own only those debt instruments which were senior enough so that in the event of a reorganization, either in Chapter 11 or out of court, those credit instruments would be likely to workout profitably compared with the fund's cost to acquire the credits. For practical purposes, Kmart Credits are currently the most senior issue of Kmart.

Kmart is a monster-size discount retailer operating approximately 2,500 stores in all 50 U.S. states, Puerto Rico, and Canada; in addition, the company has interests in retailing operations in Mexico, the Czech Republic, Slovakia and Singapore. Its retail facilities consist mostly of stand-alone big boxes of 100,000 or more square feet, of which about 70% are 6 years old or less, or have been extensively refurbished since 1990. Under prior management—new management has been in place since mid-1995—Kmart appears to have been dreadfully managed.

Annual Kmart revenues exceed $30 billion. Long-term debt, virtually all unsecured, is around $2 billion. Trade accounts payable and notes payable, both unsecured, probably approximate $3 billion during the low post-Christmas inventory period. Stated stockholder equity is well over $5 billion. Minimum lease rentals payable over the next 25 years or so probably aggregate $14 billion.

TAVF owns nine different Kmart Credits, one of which is a pool of trade payables and eight of which are debentures, each of which are governed by the same trust indenture. Fifty-seven percent of the principal amount of Kmart Credits acquired by TAVF mature within the next 15 months, 20% in 2 years to 10 years, and 23% in 26 to 27 years. The average price paid by the fund for the Kmart Credits was 74% of the principal amount of claim. The indicated yield-to-maturity (YTM) for the Kmart Credits was around 18%. This YTM compares with the YTM for the Standard & Poor's Bond Yield Index for Industrial Issues™ rated BB (the rating of Kmart Credits) of 9%. Except in the case of zero-coupon bonds, YTM is an artificial calculation because of the assumptions about the reinvestment of interest payments. However, YTM is an essential tool for comparing yields between and among different credit issues. The fund's YTM for the Kmart Credits it holds was, at the times of acquisition, about twice that of the most comparable index.

If Kmart were to seek relief under Chapter 11, and if, as seemed highly likely, the Kmart Credits were to participate in the reorganization rather than be reinstated, the key number to focus on in measuring return would be the dollar price—that is, 74% of the principal amount of claim. On the other hand, if the Kmart Credits were to continue to be performing loans, the key number to focus on is YTM—[that is], 18%.

At the times of acquisition by TAVF, mostly December 1995, I really did not have a good judgment as to whether Kmart would seek relief from creditors under Chapter 11. Whether Kmart would have to seek Chapter 11 relief really bottomed directly on whether Kmart would continue to have access to capital markets rather than specifically on how the business performed. Now a Chapter 11 seems relatively unlikely. Rather, Kmart seems to have good prospects for marketing a new issue of $500 million to $800 million of subordinated convertibles, which would result in all issues held by the fund benefiting from a material credit enhancement.

The one thing I had a strong judgment about at the time the fund purchased Kmart Credits was that if Kmart did file for Chapter 11 relief, the creditors in the reorganization would receive new securities with a value at least equal to the principal amount or, more likely, a value equal to the principal amount plus accrued interest. Assuming a $1\frac{1}{2}$-year Chapter 11 case filed in January 1996, at the end of which the principal amount would be paid on the Kmart Credits, the fund would earn an annualized return of around 22%. Assuming a 1-year case, and a return of principal plus 6% interest, TAVF's return would be 43%. While unsecured creditors are not, as a matter of law, entitled to post-petition interest, it is hard for me to see how Kmart Credits would be denied post-petition interest as a practical matter if, in the reorganization plan, any values were to be given to the existing Kmart common.

In a reorganization, the values to be paid on Kmart Credits would be in new issues of the reorganized Kmart, including new unsecured credits, and probably new Kmart common. Indeed, old Kmart creditors might well end up the control shareholders of a reorganized Kmart, if that is what it would take in reorganization value to obtain for Kmart Credits a value approximating the principal amount of the claims of creditors.

A potential Kmart reorganization would be one of the more simple ones. For practical purposes, there is only one class of creditors similarly situated—that is, the unsecured creditors and lease obligations. Insofar as lease obligations are rejected in a Chapter 11, the landlords mostly would become unsecured creditors entitled, at the maximum, to 3 years' unpaid rent. Kmart at present has no material secured debt and no subordinate debt outstanding.

Retail reorganizations under Chapter 11 tend to be relatively easy to do (compared with many other businesses) and Kmart strikes me as one of the easiest. In essence, Kmart consists of, say, 2,500 separate businesses (each store), some good, some bad. The reorganization process would give Kmart a way to get out of the bad businesses at minimal cost through disaffirming leases where the maximum obligations would be 3 years' unpaid rents. In addition, conducting GOB (going-out-of-business) sales in stores to be closed might generate substantial amounts of cash. Kmart might emerge from the reorganization process well financed, operating in its most profitable, say, 1,800 to 2,000 stores.

There could also be considerable value for Kmart if Kmart were to sublease various stand-alone big boxes—in such cases, these stores would be operated in the future as, perhaps, Home Depot, Toys 'Я' Us, or even Wal-Mart. Big boxes are the one type of retail real estate where demand continues to be good.

If Kmart Credits remain performing loans, I think the prospects are fairly good that returns to the fund will be better than an 18% YTM. TAVF, in that instance, might look forward to a yield to an improved credit rating, something that might result in substantial capital appreciation for the longer-term Kmart Credits held.

If Kmart were to seek Chapter 11 relief, there are quite a number of risks, or unpredictables, that TAVF would face. I'd enumerate them as follows:

1. There are huge market risks. A number of institutional investors have told me that they think I'm probably right about the workout values for Kmart Credits, but they think they will acquire them a lot cheaper if Kmart files. They would not buy just yet. Put otherwise, the Kmart Credits for which the fund paid 74% might become available at, say, 40% or 45%.

2. Kmart might just dawdle along for a few years with its credit rating gradually deteriorating as the company goes deeper and deeper into

debt, with most of the new debt being secured and effectively senior to the Kmart Credits. There are virtually no covenant protections for the Kmart Credits.

3.   In a reorganization plan, the proponent of the plan might attempt to reinstate long-term, low-coupon Kmart Credits rather than have such instruments participate in the reorganization. If reinstated, these Kmart Credits would remain intact as is; back interest, and probably the equivalent of interest on interest, would be paid. The appreciation potential of these Kmart Credits that were reinstated would be materially less than would be the case if the Kmart Credits participated in the reorganization. Since, for reorganization purposes, all Kmart Credits are similarly situated, it seems unlikely that a portion of such Kmart Credits could be chosen to participate while others would be chosen for reinstatement.

4.   Twenty-five million of the fund's $52.8 million of Kmart Credits represent an interest in trade account payables. In a reorganization, trade creditors might have a different agenda than TAVF in that it might be much more important to the trade to keep shipping to Kmart rather than pressing for full payment of their claims.

5.   There is really no way of knowing how long a Chapter 11 case will last. Time would be excruciatingly important insofar as a holder of Kmart Credits were not to receive post-petition interest or the claim were to be paid less than in full.

6.   The full value that I expect would be paid on the fund's holdings of Kmart Credits is a reorganization value, not a market value. The differences between reorganization value and market value tend to be quite small insofar as the securities issued in a reorganization are new debt securities. However, the differences in common stock prices can be huge. For example, say that in a reorganization plan, the reorganization value for a new issue of Kmart common, backed by an investment banker's opinion, is deemed to be $10 per share. This might not prevent initial market prices for the common stock from reflecting a trading value of $3 or $5 or $6.

When all is said and done, I just don't think the commitment to Kmart Credits is a high-risk venture for the fund as measured by investment—as distinct from market—risk. One of the important safety factors is that it tends to be a lot easier for trained analysts to deal in credits because so many of the variables revolve around understanding precise contract rights rather than predicting economic and financial outlooks.

While TAVF may have acquired its Kmart Credits on an attractive basis for the fund, it also was helpful to the sellers of Kmart Credits, who tended to have different agendas than TAVF. The different agendas for these other investors seem to encompass the following:

1. Investors unwilling to take market risk.
2. Investors required to sell securities that are no longer rated investment grade.
3. Investors unable to hold debt securities where cash service might be interrupted.
4. Investors, such as factors owing trade payables from retailers, who need portfolio insurance or diversification given the huge number of insolvencies and near insolvencies in the retail community.

An additional safety factor to consider is that the Kmart Credits are extremely unlikely to ever be wiped out. Suppose I am way off base about the economic values inherent in Kmart and that I completely misread what is to happen in a Kmart reorganization. Even so, considerable value ought to be left for Kmart Credits, even if substantially less than 74% of principal. Kmart common, on the other hand, could well become a wipe-out. I think there is a tendency in the financial community to reason that if Kmart common is high risk, then *ipso facto,* Kmart Credits are high risk. This is just not reality.

Finally, the investment in Kmart Credits certainly ought to be market neutral. How the fund fares with the Kmart Credits ought to be a function of how Kmart fares and not a function of what happens to the Dow Jones Industrial Average™ or other indices. Perhaps the Kmart Credits ought to be viewed as hedging against general market risk.

Chapter 15

Other Resource Conversion Topics

Your Problem, Marty, is that you overrate reality.

—disgruntled employee

Pricing

Once analysts escape from the straitjacket imposed by a substantive consolidation–structural subordination approach, they can bring a balanced approach to determining a fair price, or fair prices. Under a substantive consolidation–structural subordination approach, a fair price has two elements: First, that price—and only that price—has to give the outside passive minority investor (OPMI) justice (i.e., a premium over OPMI market prices) and second that price cannot give a bargain to the buyer in those cases in which the buyer causes the OPMI to be a forced seller and the buyer has a fiduciary or quasifiduciary obligation to the OPMI sellers. This is the situation that exists when management buyouts (MBOs) are contemplated.

A more constructive way to examine fairness is to appreciate the different agendas of different players in investment processes. Fairness involves a willing buyer and a willing seller, both with knowledge of the relevant facts and neither under any compulsion to act. Fairness to a willing seller who is an OPMI is a premium over market, whereas fairness to a willing seller is some price that represents a discount from what the asset is worth to the buyer. Since the OPMI seller and the control buyer have such different agendas and undertake valuation analyses using very different factors—or when they consider the same factors, weigh them differently—fairness can and ought to cover a very wide price range.

In a most meaningful sense, it is unfair and unproductive from the point of view of OPMIs to require that control buyers of OPMI interests pay the maximum amount a security might be worth to those buyers. The simple truth is that if a buyer cannot perceive that he or she is getting some sort of bargain, he or she will not buy at all. Outside passive minority investors, on the other hand, own portfolios of securities. The last thing they should want to do is to drive from the market groups or individuals that will offer premiums over OPMI market prices for control of companies.

Transactions are complicated. Agreements include many terms other than price, such as representations and warranties, indemnities, escrow arrangements, contingencies, marketouts, earnouts, and breakup fees. All of these contractual conditions are quantifiable by analysts, (i.e., they can be reduced to a present value so that analysts can estimate, from one or more points of view, a "true" price). That true price can be a materially different number than the OPMI market price.

In most resource conversion transactions, the forms of consideration to be received by participants becomes as important as—or even more important than—the amounts of consideration. Each form of consideration, whether cash or paper, has its advantages and disadvantages in terms of underlying-value issues, doability issues, income-tax issues, accounting issues, and securities law and regulation issues.

Cash, at least in U.S. dollars, has the advantage of certainty of measurement, usually with no—or only limited—restrictions on how funds are reinvested. (A no-compete clause, for example, could limit a cash recipient's opportunity to reinvest in the same industry.)

The receipt of cash, however, is almost always a taxable event, a distinct disadvantage to many recipients. Also, if the total consideration is in cash, the recipient's interest in the business is terminated. Payments of cash by an acquiring corporation diminish the amount of postmerger finances available for use by the combined companies. Payments in the form of non–dividend paying common stock leave intact the merged corporation's financial resources.

The receipt of common stock in a transaction has varied effects on the recipient. If there are restrictions on resale, the common stock may not be convertible into cash at anything approximating OPMI market prices.

If a merger transaction used pooling-of-interests accounting, insiders are restricted from sale for 2 years in order to preserve pooling accounting. In transactions in which publicly traded common stocks are to be traded after the transaction, most often pooling-of-interests accounting will be preferred by those interested in what the numbers *are* rather than what the numbers *mean*. If purchase accounting rather than pooling is used and if a premium over net asset value (NAV) is paid, goodwill will have to be amortized over not more than 40 years for the purposes of generally accepted accounting principles (GAAP), but not usually for tax purposes. This affects reported earnings even though it does not affect cash flows. Under pooling, the businesses are assumed to have been united all along and the financials for each party to the merger are joined as is. No goodwill is created for GAAP purposes because of the merger. In terms of taxability, equity for equity can give rise to a tax-deferred transaction, normally called tax free.

Market price is not the only factor a holder of a large block of shares will consider in determining the effective considerations received in a transaction. Percentage ownership, too, may be important. For control shareholders, degree of control of the merged company is likely to be a crucial consideration, frequently transcending in importance the OPMI market value to be received.

The form of consideration also becomes important depending on the agendas of constituencies with clout. Certain participants will be total-return conscious, other participants are cash-return conscious, yet other participants are seniority or safety conscious, and many want some or all of the above. Thus, there is room for all sorts of tradeoffs. The total-return players, for example, will desire common stock in a tax-free transaction, whereas the cash-return investor will seek a dividend-paying, voting, preferred stock convertible into common stock at, say, a 25% to 40% premium over conversion parity for the common stock.

The amount of premium to be paid over an OPMI market price to get a deal done is a function of myriad factors, the most important of which is probably the arrangements that are made with the parties controlling the seller. There are a few corporate finance rules that are helpful, however:

- The speedier the transaction, the less the premium. A cash-tender offer can carry a lesser premium than for an exchange-of-securities offer involving the issuance of new securities.
- Cash requires less of a premium than does paper, especially paper that may be hard to value, such as a non–dividend paying common stock whose resale would be subject to restriction.
- Voting situations probably require less of a premium than voluntary situations, in which each securityholder makes a decision to either sell or hold. Those who control the proxy machinery can usually have a great deal of confidence that they can obtain the requisite vote. In a cash-tender situation, on the other hand, holders will make market decisions. If the cash-tender offer price does not reflect a premium over the OPMI market price at the time the tender offer is due to expire, few or no shares will be tendered to the cash buyer.

It is occasionally possible to "Tisch" a company—that is, get control through open-market purchases without paying a premium over OPMI market prices. The Laurence Tisch group acquired control of CBS this way in 1987. Obtaining control through purchases in the OPMI market is a relative rarity, however, given the almost universal presence of "shark repellents," which insulate existing management in office.

In dealing with pricing, many analysts adopt an OPMI point of view and emphasize a conventional substantive consolidation–structural subordination approach. In this approach, there are usually three elements used to determine fair value:

- Discounted cash flow (DCF)
- Comparables: Outside passive minority investor prices; other resource conversion transactions
- Consequences as measured by future DCF forecasts alone

This conventional approach seems less constructive than valuing through the use of a more balanced approach in which quality and quantity of resources are recognized and in which recognition is given to the disparate agendas as well as to conflicts of interest and communities of interest between and among the various constituencies that participate in resource conversion activities.

Market Decisions versus Investment Decisions

A constructive way for an OPMI to gain a perspective on pricing from a value investing point of view is to realize that under certain circumstances, buy, hold, or sell decisions will largely be market decisions; that is, judgments will be based on perceived workout values compared with currently existing OPMI market prices. In other circumstances, buy, hold, or sell decisions will be primarily or exclusively investment decisions; that is, judgments will be based on comparing prices in OPMI markets with what the analyst believes to be the underlying value of the security (i.e., what the common stock would be worth were the business a private enterprise or a takeover candidate).

Frequently, both market decisions and investment decisions enter into a calculation. For example, in making a merger arbitrage decision, the analyst will have a view about the upside potential that will be realized if the merger transaction closes based on the announced terms or the expectation of improved terms. This is a market calculation. Also, the analyst will calculate what the downside might be if the merger transaction fails to close and there is no ready exit from his or her long position in the target company's common stock. Measuring this downside ought to have a huge investment decision component.

For most value investors, though, investment decisions will be far more important than market decisions most of the time. Indeed, the only time market decisions take precedence over investment decisions in value investing is when risk arbitrage situations exist (i.e., when certain resource conversion activities are announced or when it can be determined reasonably that these events will occur in the relatively near future). These activities include cash-tender offers, exchanges of securities, mergers and acquisitions (M & As), liquidations, and spinoffs.

Outside the realm of value investing, almost all OPMI participants focus on market decisions in all environments, not just risk arbitrage environments. This is demonstrated in this book in earlier chapters (in Part I) that examine the underlying approaches of modern capital theory

(MCT), Graham and Dodd, fundamentalism, and conventional money managers and research departments. This concentration on market decisions away from value investing is understandable and sensible most of the time, even given the author's strong belief that it is virtually impossible to make reasoned market decisions outside a risk arbitrage context. A market participant acts on judgments about markets, rather than on the underlying merits of the business and the securities it issues, when the following conditions exist:

- The analyst does not know much about the company being analyzed and its securities, something likely to be the case when the analyst concentrates on earnings, cash flows, or both, rather than on a balanced approach.
- A portfolio is financed with borrowed money and loans are likely to be called if OPMI market prices decline.
- Clients will redeem or otherwise leave a money manager that does not have good near-term market performance.
- The analyst's job, compensation, or both depend on near-term market performance.

These four conditions should not be the basis for any judgments in value investing.

Although value investing ought to result in above-average long-term performance and, for many periods, short-run performance ought to be okay, too, the very essence of value investing outside the risk arbitrage context is to pay no attention to short-run trading and short-run performance at all. Overtly attempting to perform well over the short run usually means having to be involved in activities that are the very antithesis of value investing:

- Short-run players attempt to buy what is popular or is believed likely to become popular, which usually means the immediate earnings outlook is favorable. Value investing bargains, on the other hand, are usually created when the near-term outlook is poor and the issuing company is unpopular. Short-run players tend to be outlook conscious at the expense of being price conscious.
- Short-run players have judgments about near-term macrofactors, such as the level of interest rates, the trends of stock averages (e.g., the

Dow Jones Industrials), the GDP, and national employment data, because general market conditions are bound to influence heavily the near-term performance of most nonarbitrage securities. In value investing, these macrofactors are ignored, or in any event, they are assumed to be utterly unpredictable.

- Many—if not most—short-run players pay attention to technical chartist factors they believe are likely to influence the supply and demand for securities over the near term. Value investing is not involved at all with technical chartist considerations. As far as value investors are concerned, there does not seem to be much rationality to technical chartist considerations. Market strategists and market timers are worlds apart from value investing.

The Present Value of Management-Entrenching "Shark Repellents"

It is claimed, almost universally, that "shark repellents" are put into corporate charters and by-laws to protect OPMI shareholders from raiders who, in the absence of such repellents, would obtain control of companies on the cheap. These repellents include "poison pills", blank-check preferred stocks, due on change-of-control covenants in loan agreements; staggered elections for members of boards of directors; restrictions on the ability of outsiders to convene stockholders' meetings; supermajority voting provisions in which changes of control may be involved; and certain fair-price provisions.

There is considerable merit to the observation that when an otherwise unwelcome acquirer has to negotiate at arm's length with an incumbent management and its board of directors, pricing for OPMI shareholders will be better than if all the acquirer had to do to obtain control was to buy directly from OPMIs enough common stock, either at the OPMI market price or at some premium over OPMI market price. This is far from the whole story, though.

The fact seems to be that when acquirers have to negotiate with managements, managements are likely to take some part of the premium paid for control for themselves, rather than giving it wholly to shareholders. If an otherwise unwelcome acquirer can obtain control by going directly to shareholders, he or she need not make special deals with management. If that acquirer negotiates with management, management is unlikely to work exclusively in the best interests of shareholders to the exclusion of seeking management's own rewards. This is just part and parcel of a financial world characterized by communities of interest and conflicts of interest.

Furthermore "shark repellents" should be looked at from the point of view of acquirers who might be unwelcome to an incumbent management. When potential acquirers see such repellents, they can assume that garnering control is likely to not only be more costly than would otherwise be the case but also—and perhaps more importantly—that it is likely to be uncertain, perhaps not doable at all. Many would-be acquirers conclude that attempting this takeover is not worthwhile. The existence of "shark repellents," in an efficient world, has to mean that there are fewer changes of control that would result in OPMIs receiving premiums over market than would otherwise be the case.

Intuitively, it would seem that the OPMI community is probably hurt more by repellents than it is helped. Given that OPMI market prices tend to be irrational compared with a balanced approach, however, it can be safely said that OPMI prices do not reflect managements' abilities to run businesses. Put simply, OPMI prices do not serve as a good test distinguishing between competent managements who deserve to be insulated in office and poor managements who ought to be removed from office. From a national interest or national productivity point of view, there appears to be ample justification for repellents despite disadvantages to OPMIs because the country would be a lot less productive if managements in general had to run companies by concentrating on the daily stock ticker and reported quarterly earnings per share. Although "shark repellents" seem justified from a national interest point of view, many repellents, including "poison pills" and Pennsylvania corporate law, seem to constitute overkill. The Pennsylvania antitakeover statutes, for Pennsylvania corporations opting to take advantage of Pennsylvania law, in effect bulletproof incumbents in office.

"Revlon rules" exist in Delaware, the leading state for the incorporation of companies whose common stocks are traded publicly. Put simply, these rules state that if control of a company is to change—whether hostile or friendly—the role of a board of directors changes. The board becomes an auctioneer and its duties are to obtain the best price, and other terms, that can be obtained for stockholders. The same trade off seems to exist under "Revlon rules" as exist under "shark repellents" from an OPMI point of view. "Revlon rules" probably result in there being better pricing than would otherwise be the case and probably also mean that there will be fewer deals at premiums over OPMI market prices than would otherwise be the case.

Speed

In all resource conversion transactions, speed, or timing, becomes important to OPMIs. How long until closing? How certain is the workout? The more time involved, the more monkey wrenches can be thrown in to screw up a deal.

The importance of speed can vary tremendously, however, depending on the characteristics of the transaction. If a transaction's price and terms are fixed, prompt closing can be crucial. On the other hand, if the consideration to be paid is continuously increasing, timing loses significance. The best example of this might be found in Chapter 11. Adequately secured creditors who know they will receive postpetition interest on their claims, either through reinstatement or participation in a plan of reorganization, probably will not be overly concerned with timing. A delayed consummation of a plan of reorganization may moderately reduce the overall return. On the other hand, unsecured creditors without any legal entitlement to postpetition interest will find that their rate of return will plummet as time elapses without consummation of a plan of reorganization.

The Economics of Stockholder Litigation

Almost everyone in the financial community is interested in stockholder litigation, but most people have little personal experience with these lawsuits. Understanding some of the economics of stockholder litigation ought to be helpful for many in a value investing context.

Stockholder suits, whether class or derivative, are not really brought by stockholders, and especially not by named plaintiffs, known on the inside as bodies. Rather, suits are brought and controlled by plaintiffs' attorneys, who originate, finance, and control cases. Class-action suits are actions brought on behalf of stockholders. Derivative suits are actions brought on behalf of the corporation.

Plaintiffs' attorneys tend to earn excess returns: Their rewards tend to be huge, their risks negligible. There are two factors that cause this. First, actions (lawsuits) are class actions, in which an attorney can represent a large class. Theoretically, a plaintiff holding, say, 10 shares of General Motors common stock can bring suit for the entire class of General Motors stockholders (on March 31, 1998, there were outstanding almost 6.7 billion shares of General Motors common) or the small shareholder can attempt to bring suit derivatively on behalf of General Motors Corporation itself. Second, the downside for the plaintiff's attorney is virtually nil. If the attorney's firm loses the case, the firm will not be responsible for defendants' costs. In only the rarest of instances do courts ever impose sanctions (i.e., money fines) against plaintiff's attorneys. The attorney's costs are limited to financing the case, which, at most, probably never costs more than several hundred thousand dollars, including office overhead. The more prominent plaintiff's law firms develop a portfolio of cases over the years. With a portfolio, the income stream can be pretty good—multimillions each year—even though the timing on when any individual case might pay off is indeterminate.

Normally, the plaintiff's attorneys or a group can look forward to fees in cash equal to 20% to one third of the dollar value of the recovery by the class. In good class actions, suits will be brought by several plaintiffs, each represented by a firm. Although all share in the fees, the lion's share will go to the firm chosen as lead counsel. Under amendments passed by the U.S. Congress in 1995 regarding federal cases, the attorney representing the largest named plaintiff is appointed lead counsel. Thus, it has become important to the plaintiff's bar to obtain as clients (i.e., as named plaintiffs) institutional shareholders because they tend to have large positions. Most institutional investors probably have no interest in becoming a named plaintiff, because first, the institution cannot control the case—the attorney does, and second, it cannot get paid fees off the top, but rather can participate in any recovery only as a class member *pro rata* with all other class members.

It is almost axiomatic that if a control group or corporation engages in resource conversion activities—M&As, initial public offerings (IPOs), goings-private—there will be stockholder lawsuits. This will also be the case when there appears to have been manipulation of OPMI market prices.

Probably most people who are the targets of stockholder suits—managements and outside directors—conduct their affairs on the basis of the criterion of "Let's avoid being sued." That is almost impossible to do under the American class-action system. Suits just go with the territory. The more appropriate criterion is "Let's avoid being sued successfully."

Being sued creates considerable discomfort for defendants. Records have to be turned over. Defendants are likely to be deposed under oath. Most suits never go to trial but rather are settled once defendants fail to be granted motions for summary judgment. Summary judgment motions cannot be granted if material factual questions are in dispute. Plaintiff's attorneys, though, want to spend large amounts of time on a case so they can build up fees. The granting of injunctive relief to plaintiffs before discovery is undertaken is usually not to be sought by the plaintiff's bar because it is hard to justify large fees if not much time has been spent on a case.

Many defendants do not have much will to resist settlement. There is discomfort during the pendency of a case. Although costs and expenses are probably paid for by insurance companies and D&O (director and officer) insurance policies, such might not be the case if there are court awards against defendants.

The plaintiff's bar works strictly on a contingency-fee basis. As such, its members are at quite a disadvantage compared with other attorneys who get paid by the hour, win, lose, or draw. This is true for defendant's attorneys hired by corporations, managers, control shareholders, and insurance companies. Before 1980, bankruptcy attorneys tended to work on a quasicontingent basis in Chapter X cases. They might be awarded fees by the court at the conclusion of a case. Under modern Chapter 11 and Chapter 7, the court awards fees to all attorneys during the pendency of a case in which fees are expenses of the debtor company.

Throughout this book, it has been pointed out that all financial relationships are combinations of conflicts of interest and communities of interest. This is also true of the relationship between plaintiff's attorneys and the class they represent. There also seems to be a combination of conflicts of interest and communities of interest between plaintiff's attorneys on the one hand and defendant's attorneys and defendants on the other.

Plaintiff's attorneys and their clients have a community of interest in that the larger the settlement or the award, the greater the benefit to both. Attorneys and clients frequently have a conflict in that the attorneys, to maximize the present value of their fees, might sacrifice present values that would be payable to the client. This is especially the case in large classes, in which the attorneys' fees are quite meaningful to the attorneys, but the awards to individual class members may be only pennies. The form of consideration also may give rise to conflict. Attorneys collect fees in cash; plaintiffs might get fees in kind—say, discount coupons if they buy a corporation's products. Fund managers often are not fans of the vast majority of plaintiff's attorneys, but a number of plaintiff's attorneys are aware of the conflict and quite a number seem to lean toward the community of interest side, working harder for their clients, rather than to the conflict of interest side, working harder for their fees. Class and derivative actions were pioneered by Abraham Pomerantz, now deceased, who was very friendly with the author. Abe's professional life seems to have been spent mostly working for the client class, not working for fees. It is dangerous to generalize about whole classes of professionals.

When a case is settled, or adjudicated, defendants obtain *res judicata,* that is, they are bulletproofed against further suits on the same issue. Since suits are so prevalent, defendants tend to have a community of interest with plaintiffs to obtain early and friendly settlements. Some defendants, indeed, may even promote suits they know can be settled on a reasonable or advantageous basis. *Res judicata* is important.

It is necessary to understand the tremendous abuses to which OPMI stockholders tend to be subjected in jurisdictions in which there are no class actions and the loser pays the winner's expenses after trial. This is the so-called English system. Under the English system, OPMI stockholders are grossly disadvantaged in comparison with insiders and they usually have no effective redress for management wrongdoing and insider overreaching. Obviously, both the American system and the English system are subject to abuse. It is apparent that all financial practices, including stockholder suits or an absence of them, not only are subject to abuse but will be abused.

The plaintiff's bar holds itself out to be a private cop, an essential part of the U.S. regulatory scheme. As a private cop, it is far more active than regulators, whether the Securities and Exchange Commission (SEC) or state blue-sky commissions, in rectifying alleged wrongs against OPMI shareholders. There may be something to this. It ought to be noted that the end result of American procedures is that the United States has the best, most honest, most efficient capital markets in history. Outside passive minority investors seem to be protected in the United States better than anywhere else. Perhaps the plaintiff's bar has made some contribution to this happy environment.

The Economics of Statutory Appraisals

For most investors, statutory appraisal rights arising when one dissents from a merger is an interesting but arcane area, but it is good to be curious about how appraisal rights work or do not work.

Unlike class-action litigation, statutory appraisals are relatively rare. The right to seek the fair cash value of a holding in a statutory appraisal proceeding arises when a shareholder perfects a dissent from a merger or similar transaction under which the shareholder is forced to give up his or her ownership of common stock. This occurs in voting situations, whether by use of the proxy machinery or a consent process.

Statutory appraisal proceedings are relative rarities largely because there is no meaningful class-action mechanism and it is possible that, after a proceeding, the dissenting shareholder might be liable for the respondent company's costs. Statutory appraisal proceedings are also relatively rare because the rights to an appraisal are not always present. For example, there are no statutory appraisal rights in Delaware if the consideration to be received by a dissenting shareholder is the common stock of a company either listed on an organized stock exchange or owned beneficially by 2,000 or more stockholders.

The dissenter incurs considerable expense in the form of attorneys' and experts' fees. Unless the dissenter is a very large shareholder and also has promise of receiving a very substantial premium over the value of the merger consideration, perfecting dissents does not seem to make much economic sense.

There is a built-in prejudice against awarding substantial premiums over the merger consideration in all states, including Delaware. Courts, in finding fair value, tend to give considerable weight to premerger OPMI market prices as well as to the OPMI prices of comparables. Further, in Delaware and other jurisdictions, the dissenter is not entitled to any value created by the transaction itself (i.e., the merger). In addition, there is an implicit view in many appraisal proceedings that dissenters are really entitled to no more than for what they would have sold their common stock in the open market prior to the merger proposal.

For a dissenter to receive a substantial premium over the merger consideration, there probably has to be a relatively simple showing that the business could have been sold or liquidated at a fair-size multiple over OPMI market prices—usually not an easy thing to do.

Once a dissent has been perfected, and before an appraisal award or settlement has been reached, the dissenter lives in a never-never land. He or she becomes an unsecured creditor of the merged company or a subsidiary of the merged company, but an unsecured creditor of the most amorphous sort:

- No loan documents exist.
- The principal amount of the unsecured credit is unknown.
- The interest rate to be paid on the unsecured credit is unknown, as is whether the interest is to be simple or compound.
- The maturity date is unknown.
- Protective covenants are nonexistent.

All this might make you wonder why statutory appraisal proceedings are not even more rare than they seem to be.

Initial Public Offerings

It is difficult to understand much of the IPO phenomenon without appreciating not only that private business values are different from the prices of publicly traded common stocks but also that the differences ought to exist because different tools and different variables (or different weights to the same variables) are used in the privates compared with publics. Put otherwise, investment value, the underlying worth of a business using a balanced approach, is different from market value, the price at which a common stock would trade in an OPMI market.

Given these differences between investment value and market value, the "great arbitrage" exists. There are times when public market prices are ultralow versus business values. At that time, businesses (especially well-financed public businesses) are taken private at a premium over market prices. Most deals probably are friendly (e.g., MBOs), with the attractiveness of hostiles limited by existence of "shark repellents," which diminish doability. In essence, publicly owned shares are acquired by insiders.

The great arbitrage works the other way as well. There are times when private business values are a fraction of the prices that would be paid for a common stock were the business public. In that instance, private businesses go public, either by being acquired by a public company that issues common stock or other equities as the acquisition consideration, or by the sale of common stock to the public for cash. The latter is an IPO.

The ideal theoretical pricing mechanism for a common stock in an IPO has two components, one indicating a high price, one pointing to a low price. First, the price of the common stock tends to be far above private business value or investment value for two reasons. If such attractive pricing were not available, insiders would tend to want to stay private, given the many disadvantages for insiders in public companies. Furthermore, if public market prices are below investment values, going public becomes a very hard sell; OPMIs are not that price conscious, focusing instead on the sizzle rather than the steak. For example, in mid-1998, prices for semiconductor equipment common stocks were highly depressed, as the industry was mired in a deep recession. There were no prospects then of going public with a new semiconductor equipment IPO, despite a buoyancy for IPOs in general. The internet was hot in an IPO context, but semiconductor equipment was stone cold.

Second, once market value is above investment value and a company is to be brought public, conscious efforts are made by those in the financial community bringing the company public to price the issue at a moderate discount from market value. This is part of the strong effort made to cause the new issue to sell at a premium over the issue price in the aftermarket that will exist after the company has gone public.

There are, of course, many exceptions to the norms described above for bringing companies public. For example, there are times when a company is so desperate for equity capital that a common stock issue will be sold publicly at prices below investment value. There are companies faced with the dilemma of going public or going bankrupt. These potential issuers are unlikely to be price conscious; their problem revolves around whether any equity issue, ranging from common stocks to high-interest junk bonds, is salable at all. Nonetheless, the great arbitrage appears to be a very useful generalization, even though its existence seems far from pervasive.

Initial public offering booms and boomlets keep recurring from time to time. Wall Street has great incentives to encourage and foster new-issue booms. They are needed to feed the financial community's huge selling machine. This has become increasingly so since the end of fixed commissions in May 1975. From the point of view of a Wall Street salesperson, an IPO has advantages:

- Huge commissions as a percent of the gross spread; payout may be from, say, 10¢ to 40¢ per share versus 2¢ to 5¢ for a negotiated commission in the secondary OPMI market.
- Status as an exclusive product.
- Status as an easy sell.

The great arbitrage has been the godfather of the U.S. venture-capital industry, in which the prospect of excess returns is driven by an exit strategy that contemplates creation of value through getting off an IPO at superprices. The venture capitalist strives to create a portfolio of positions in high-tech startups at average prices of 2¢ to 50¢ a share, in the hope that sometime hence, a fair percentage of these companies will market common stock in an IPO at $8 to $12 per share. High-tech startups are the engine that has driven the United States to unprecedented prosperity in the 1990s. New technology grew up as IPOs proliferated, probably concomitant with downsizing by large companies in defense and other industries that had employed scientists and engineers. Also, the United States has a terrific university system and trains many technology competent people to run high-tech businesses.

Going public via an IPO is not the end game for either the company or its promoters but rather a promising beginning. The nature of the IPO sizzle is such that going public means that the vast majority of the common stock marketed to the public will be a new issue sold by the company rather than a bailout by original shareholders, whether management or venture capitalists. In most cases, for the insiders to actually realize more than the paper wealth created for them by an IPO, the business has to actually prosper. This is not always the case, but it is a normative case. Usually, insiders own too much common stock to hope to be able to dribble out meaningful amounts of shares in the open market by way of the Securities Act of 1933 Rule 144 sales. To have a secondary public offering or to have the business acquired is frequently hard to do if the company has not prospered.

Going public does tend to give a company a leg up in its endeavor to become profitable. First, and probably most important, the IPO process results in the company's becoming well financed. The net proceeds from the IPO go into the business treasury. Second, the company has the imprimatur of being a public company, and perhaps a public company sponsored by a prestigious investment bank, be it Merrill Lynch or Raymond James. Newfound friends, whether bankers or stockholders, might be helpful to the company.

In marketing IPOs, institutional investors, such as large mutual funds, have become important figures that determine whether an IPO will be sold. Typical marketing is to try to have institutions give a "hard circle," in effect ensuring that the institution will acquire shares and ensure the success of the IPO. Marketing to institutions combines preparing documents that the institution's analysts will study, plus road shows, or meetings with institutions both in groups and one-on-one.

Leveraged Buyouts, Management Buyouts, Going-Privates, and Share Repurchases

The common factor among LBOs, MBOs, going-privates, and share repurchases is the acquisition of common stock from OPMIs. Most of these transactions involve the use of cash, but other considerations can also be involved: debt, preferred stock, pure-equity interests in another issuer. Leveraged buyouts and MBOs are going-privates when the resources of the target company are used to finance all—or the bulk—of the purchase by using the target company's resources to finance the purchase. Purchases of common stock from OPMIs can be voluntary or coercive. Coercion exists when OPMI stockholders can be forced to give up their position. There are two types of coercion:

- Proxy machinery, in which the requisite vote binds all shareholders to a course of action.
- Deregistration as a public company after insiders acquire voting securities in a voluntary buy for cash, or exchange of securities when, as a result of the acquisition of the voting securities of an issuer not listed on an organized exchange, there remain fewer than 300 shareholders of record.

Management buyouts and insider-led going-privates have lots of conceptual problems in that buyer is an insider with fiduciary or quasifiduciary obligations to the OPMI sellers. Here, the buyer has obligations to treat the sellers fairly. As pointed out in previous chapters, "fair" usually has to cover a wide price range.

In almost all going-private cases, fairness opinions are obtained from investment bankers. These fairness opinions do not comport with any objective standards, unlike audits must that are prepared in accordance with GAAP. Investment bankers are of course hired by buyers who control timing and set all conditions of purchase. Most investment bankers try to do a reasonable job, but their analyses tends to take place in a substantive consolidation mode, where the emphasis is placed on the premium over OPMI market price for the transaction. There frequently is a consequent downweighting of benefits to the buyer in arriving at conclusions about fairness. OPMIs have no control. All they get is a vote.

In going private, there cannot actually be a willing buyer–willing seller environment in which each party is well informed and under no compulsion to act. Rather, what exists is willing buyer–coerced seller environment, where the buyer tends to be much better informed than the seller. Fairness is that price—and other terms—that simulate a true willing buyer–willing seller environment. Courts tend not to look at matters this simply. A premium over OPMI market price tends to make OPMIs willing sellers.

Going private through an MBO results in an automatic class-action lawsuit in the United States. Most such suits are settled. I believe that many are welcomed by buyers who, for a relatively small increase in the acquisition price, obtain *res judicata*. Despite these conceptual problems, it seems not to be in the interests of OPMIs to discourage MBOs and going-privates. Frequently, these are important sources of buying interests that pay premium prices over OPMI market prices.

Dividends and Share Repurchases

Assuming that a company has superior uses for cash to expand its productive asset base and that the company has only uncertain access to capital markets to sell new issues of common stock, it is always far more productive from a long-term point of view if a company retains cash rather than distributes it to shareholders. For growth companies, distributions of cash to shareholders can be a good use of cash, but it frequently is not the best use of cash. It was far more productive for IBM, Xerox, Intel, and Microsoft, in their early days, to plow back cash into the businesses than it would have been to distribute that cash to shareholders.

Once a decision is made to distribute cash to shareholders, there are two ways of doing so: dividends and share repurchases.

The characteristics of a dividend are as follows:

- Dividends are mandatory; each stockholder is required to accept the cash payment.
- Dividends provide ordinary income for most recipients.
- For dividends, there is a 70% exclusion for stockholders that are qualified corporations.
- Many OPMI stockholders like dividends. Benjamin Graham and David Dodd were big fans of dividends.
- Dividend payments can improve access to capital markets, especially common-stock markets for those companies that need relatively regular access to outside equity financing. Companies that have needed relatively regular access to outside capital markets include electric utilities, finance companies, and real estate investment trusts.
- Shareholders receive cash without giving up any ownership interest.

The characteristics of share repurchases are as follows: On a short-term basis, they bring a buying group into stock. On a long-term basis, they are a far superior use of cash from the point of view of most corporations than are dividends.

The superiority of a program of long-term share repurchases for most companies over paying dividends is demonstrated in the letter (see Appendix), that the author sent to the chief executive officer of GATX Corporation in March 1985. At the time, the author was a member of the GATX board of directors. GATX never implemented his suggestions, but the letter is a very comprehensive analysis of the long-term effects of distributing cash to shareholders by the stock buyback route compared with those of distributing cash to shareholders by paying dividends. Thus, the letter is repeated here in its entirety.

Cash distributions to shareholders in any form are generally limited to adequately financed issuers. Creditors probably will prevent any meaningful amounts of cash distributions to shareholders in any form when the company is poorly financed, even if solvent.

Appendix

M.J. WHITMAN & CO., INC.

171 MADISON AVENUE

SUITE 1600

NEW YORK, N.Y. 10016

———

212 · 889-5150

March 29, 1985

Mr. James J. Glasser
Chairman of the Board
GATX Corporation
120 South Riverside Plaza
Chicago, Illinois 60606

       RE: Long Term Program to Repurchase GATX Corporation
            Common Stock

Dear Jim:

As you know, I think it would be highly beneficial on a long term basis, both for the Corporation and its stockholders, if GATX were to embark upon a program of repurchasing common shares from time to time as opportunities present themselves. Such purchases could take place either in the open market, in private transactions, or via tender offers.

A sound repurchase program, reasonably executed, could make GATX a growth stock, even assuming that future business conditions remain highly cyclical, or depressed. It also would be highly beneficial for the Corporation because it would reduce (or eliminate) the liquidity burden put upon the management and the Corporation to meet the de facto "fixed charge" in cash that a regular quarterly dividend represents.

The underpinning for my views becomes plainly evident by looking at GATX's actual experience during the 10 years, 1975 - 1984 (a very depressed period for the Corporation over-all), and comparing that with estimations of what GATX's experience would have been during that 10-year period assuming the following:

    a) The Annual Dividend on the Common Stock was only $1.20 per year
       and the difference between this $1.20 payment and the actual di-
       vidend disbursements was used to repurchase Common Stock each
       year at the average price at which GATX Common Stock traded dur-
       ing that year.

                     or

    b) No dividend was paid on the Common Stock; and all of the cash
       savings was used to repurchase Common Stock each year at the
       average price at which GATX Common Stock traded during that
       year.

EXHIBIT A

Results of the three 1975 - 1984 programs - Actual, $1.20 Dividend, and No Dividend - are measured by five factors:

1) Earnings Per Share 1975 - 1984.

2) Pre-Tax Earnings Per Share 1975 - 1984.

3) Net Asset Value Per Share 1975 - 1984.

4) Net Asset Value plus Deferred Taxes Per Share 1975 - 1984.

5) Aggregate Dividend Requirement for 1985.

In brief, relevant results for each of the three programs were as follows as per Exhibits 1, 2, and 3 attached hereto:

	Actual	$1.20 Dividend	No Dividend
1984 Earnings Per Share	$2.37	$3.43	$6.28
1984 Pre-Tax Earnings Per Share	$4.40	$6.37	$11.66
12/31/84 Net Asset Value Per Share	$30.35	$46.71	$85.49
12/31/84 Net Asset Value Plus Deferred Taxes Per Share	$61.90	$89.58	$163.96
1985 Aggregate Common Stock Dividend Requirement (Includes Common Stock Equivalents)	$16,900,000	$11,600,000	0

Operations, and operating results, were not altered, or otherwise affected, by the buy-in programs. In fact, though, there probably would have been net benefits to operations because of the added financial flexibility that would have arisen out of the absence of needs to pay a specific cash dividend every quarter. For example, in the 1983 downturn, there would have been no necessity for agonizing soul-searching before cutting the dividend from $2.40 to $1.20. Rather, management would have made a rational decision as to whether to retain cash in the Company, or use it to repurchase shares. Certainly, no repurchase could have taken place if either management felt there was a better use for cash within the Company, or if the price of the Common Stock was not relatively depressed.

When Warren, you, and I had lunch, you said that if earnings increased, you believed that a dividend increase would be in order because that is what the shareholder constituency would want. I disagree. I think, by this time, the relevant GATX shareholder constituency is seeking to maximize total return rather than dividend income. Insofar as long term investors seek steady, and rising, dividend income, their investment orientation is toward issuers such as Ameritech Common Stock and Commonwealth Edison Common Stock – not GATX Common Stock. Given the nature of the GATX business and shareholder constituency – highly cyclical; important subsidiaries are cash flow companies; conventional securities analysts find the company hard to understand – I'm convinced that the shareholder seeking total return is far better served by distributing cash to stockholders via buying in the common stock periodically rather than by paying dividends.

There obviously are a few things wrong with my statistics. First, operationally, 1985 – 1994 ought to be a lot more prosperous than 1975 – 1984 – but who really knows. Second, if the per share growth occurs as would be the case in my hypotheticals, the prices at which shares would be repurchased could well be at materially higher prices than those I've used – the mean between the high and low for each year. Again, who knows. In any event, if the next 10 years are much better operationally than the last 10 years and/or stock prices are considerably higher in the future than they have been in the past – those are high class worries.

In a very meaningful economic sense, I consider these long term buy-backs as modified LBO's, or better yet, BO's, where the principal beneficiaries are the long term stockholders, themselves, and where the financial position of the company is never jeopardized but, rather, is enhanced.

If you like, and accept, the idea of a long term Common Stock repurchase program, management might consider recommending one of the following approaches to the Board:

1) Make a so-called 23(c) announcement of Board authorization to purchase X number of shares of Common Stock from time to time in open market or private transactions if such shares are available at prices which management deems to be attractive.

2) Announce the elimination of all Common Stock dividends for the foreseeable future stating that the Company is embarking on a 23(c) program as outlined above. In connection with this announcement, GATX would also announce, and implement, a 13e4 self-tender under which the Company would expend, say $40 million to $50 million, to acquire Common Stock at, say $37.50 to $40 per share. This would be an offset to the disappointment that would be felt by those stockholders who are dividend income conscious, or feel vitally affected by day-to-day stock price fluctuations. I don't think spending, say $50 million for the repurchase would jeopardize GATX's strong financial position, especially against the background that there would be an elimination of "fixed charges" for Common Stock dividends which, given the present $1.20 dividend, amounts to some $16 million per year.

My guess – and it can't be more than that – is that management would get high marks from the financial community if it implemented a relatively aggressive buy-back program provided that management explained it well. I have no question but that such a program can be explained well by you.

GATX would be far from a pioneer if it undertook an aggressive buy-back program. John Chlebowski, you and I once talked about the long term results achieved by Crown Cork & Seal, Tandy and Teledyne, all of whom buy back shares rather than pay dividends. All have had times of operational adversity during the past 10 years but, yet, their reported results compare with GATX's as follows:

Issuer	Earnings Per Share 1984	1975	Net Asset Value Per Share 1984	1975
GATX	$2.37	$3.47	$30.35(A)	$32.22
Crown Cork & Seal	4.98	2.43	40.61(B)	14.32
Tandy	2.75	0.25	10.64(A)	1.33
Teledyne	20.61	2.57	123.36(B)	9.57

(A) Excludes the value of extraordinary distributions of the common stocks of subsidiaries.

(B) 10 years to 12/31/83.

I'd be happy to discuss the pros and cons of buy-back programs in detail with you and other members of management if you think I can be helpful.

Regards.

Sincerely yours,

Martin J. Whitman, C.F.A.
President

MJW:mh
Encls.

Exhibit 1. GATX 10 Year Data 1975–1984 (Actual)

Year Ended	Average No. Common Shs. Outstanding (000)	Dividend Per Sh.	Approx. Common Dividend Paid (000)	Net Income (000)	Pre-Tax Net Income (000)	Net Asset Value Attributable to Common Stock (000)*	Net Asset Value Plus Deferred Taxes Attributable to Common Stock*	Per Share Data				Trading Range of Common	Average Price of Common
								Net Income	Pre-Tax Net Income	Net Asset Value	Net Asset Value Plus Deferred Taxes		
12/31/74	13,335	—	—	—	—	—	—	—	—	—	—	—	—
12/31/75	13,508	$1.80	$24,300	$40,900	$73,800	$429,800	$609,900	$3.25	$5.46	$32.22	$45.15	35–24	29 ½
12/31/76	13,508	$1.80	$24,300	$28,900	$64,000	$440,800	$654,800	$2.13	$4.74	$32.83	$48.47	35–25	30
12/31/77	11,960	$1.80	$21,500	($7,000)	$30,300	$401,700	$646,500	($0.58)	$2.53	$30.60	$54.06	34–24	29
12/31/78	13,516	$1.80	$24,300	$59,600	$92,900	$440,900	$785,100	$4.62	$6.87	$33.71	$58.09	32–22	27
12/31/79	13,535	$1.00	$17,000	$70,100	$116,700	$487,000	$843,100	$5.39	$8.62	$37.57	$62.29	46–24	40
12/31/80	13,573	$2.20	$29,900	$64,800	$121,800	$523,400	$921,800	$4.97	$8.97	$40.75	$67.91	44–25	34 ½
12/31/81	13,600	$2.40	$32,600	$67,900	$118,100	$555,400	$993,700	$5.16	$8.68	$43.74	$73.07	41–30	35 ½
12/31/82	13,166	$2.40	$31,600	$29,400	$51,100	$486,300	$949,500	$2.40	$3.88	$39.48	$72.12	33–20	26 ½
12/31/83	11,956	$1.10	$25,100	($90,800)	($33,800)	$442,500	$839,300	($7.84)	($2.83)	$29.41	$70.20	37–25	31
12/31/84	14,084	$1.20	$16,900	$33,400	$62,000	$454,600	$871,800	$2.37	$4.40	$30.35	$61.90	34–26	30
12/31/85			$16,900**										

* As stated per books.

** Dividend requirement at $1.20 per share including Common Stock equivalents.

Exhibit 2. GATX 10-Year Data 1975–1984

Year of Activity	Number Shares Outstanding Beginning of Period (000)	Dividend Requirement at $1.20 (000)	Actual Dividend Paid (000)	Difference (000)	Average Price of Common	No. Shares Repurchased (000)	Average No. Shares Outstanding During Period (000)	Per Share Data on Average Shares			
								Net Income	Pre-Tax Net Income	Net Asset Value	Net Asset Value Plus Deferred Taxes
1975	13,335	$16,200	$24,300	$8,100	29 ½	275	13,198	$3.10	$5.59	$32.57	$46.21
1976	13,060	$15,700	$24,300	$8,600	30	287	12,917	$2.23	$4.95	$34.12	$50.69
1977	12,773	$15,300	$21,500	$6,200	29	214	12,666	Deficit	$2.39	$31.71	$51.04
1978	12,559	$15,100	$24,300	$9,200	27	341	12,389	$4.81	$7.50	$35.58	$63.37
1979	12,218	$14,700	$27,000	$12,300	40	308	12,064	$5.81	$9.67	$40.36	$69.89
1980	11,910	$14,300	$29,900	$15,600	34 ½	452	11,684	$5.54	$10.42	$44.80	$78.89
1981	11,458	$13,800	$32,600	$18,800	35 ½	530	11,193	$6.06	$10.55	$49.62	$88.77
1982	10,928	$13,100	$31,600	$18,500	26 ½	698	10,579	$2.78	$4.83	$45.97	$89.75
1983	10,230	$12,300	$25,100	$12,800	31	413	10,024	Deficit	Deficit	$44.14	$83.73
1984	9,817	$11,800	$16,900	$5,100	30	170	9,732	$3.43	$6.37	$46.71	$89.58
1985	9,647	$11,600	$16,900	$5,300							

Pro-forma per share data assuming (1) there had been an annual dividend of $1.20 Pershare; (2) difference between $1.20 dividend and actual dividend used to buy common stock at average trading price.

Exhibit 3. GATX 10-Year Data 1975–1984

Year of Activity	No. Shares Outstanding Beginning of Period (000)	Actual Dividend Paid (000)	Average Price of Common	No. Shares Repurchased (000)	Average No. Shares Outstanding During Period (000)	Net Income	Pre-Tax Net Income	Net Asset Value	Net Asset Value Plus Deferred Taxes
1975	13,335	$24,300	29 ½	824	12,923	$3.16	$5.71	$33.26	$47.19
1976	12,511	$24,300	30	810	12,106	$2.38	$5.28	$36.41	$54.09
1977	11,701	$21,500	29	741	11,331	Deficit	$2.67	$35.45	$57.06
1978	10,960	$24,300	27	900	10,510	$5.67	$8.84	$41.95	$74.70
1979	10,060	$27,000	40	675	9,723	$7.21	$12.00	$50.09	$86.71
1980	9,385	$29,900	34 ½	867	8,952	$7.24	$13.61	$58.47	$102.97
1981	8,518	$32,600	35 ½	918	8,059	$8.42	$14.65	$68.92	$123.30
1982	7,600	$31,600	26 ½	1,192	7,000	$4.20	$7.30	$69.43	$135.57
1983	6,408	$25,100	31	810	6,003	Deficit	Deficit	$73.71	$139.81
1984	5,598	$16,900	30	563	5,317	$6.28	$11.66	$85.49	$163.96
1985	5,035								

Pro-forma per share data assuming (1) no dividend; (2) savings from no dividend used to buy common stock at average trading price.

Epilogue: The Values of Value Investing

With all thy getting, get understanding.

Obviously, value investing is not for everyone. With the exception of risk arbitrageurs who rely on relatively determinant workouts in relatively determinant periods of time, value investing just does not work for people deeply involved in trying to predict near-term stock prices or general trends for securities markets or commodities markets. Value investing is not very useful for nonarbitrage short sellers, stock-market technicians, those involved with academic finance, and money managers whose job, compensation levels, or both depend on outperforming an index or peer group.

For most investors, though, whether private business people, control investors, or passive investors seeking a long-term accumulation of wealth, the principal tenets of value investing are either what is done as a matter of course—as for private business people and most control investors—or a more comfortable, probably much more profitable way to employ long-term passive investment funds.

There are many advantages to value investing. It is often a much easier technique for analysis than is any other investment technique: all the value investor does is reach judgments about the underlying value of a business and about the business's probable dynamics. By contrast, for analysts using other techniques, these same analyses are merely prerequisites for trying to determine the price at which a security might sell. These analysts then undertake another whole series of analyses that have nothing to do with underlying business values, including near-term earnings forecasts, dividend estimates, prognostication about the general market, prognostication about specific indices, technical chartist considerations, insider buying and selling, institutional buying and selling, and broker-dealer recommendations. To the value investor, these market considerations constitute excess analytic baggage, and many such considerations—say, predicting the outlook for the general market or gauging investor psychology—may be impossible to judge meaningfully. The author certainly thinks this is the case.

Value investing is probably how most fortunes have been made by strictly passive investors who receive no promoters' compensations whatsoever.

The companies whose common stocks investors obtain using value investing criteria are usually ones with which the investors can live in comfort. Because these businesses all have high-quality resources (e.g., surplus cash on the balance sheet or seemingly unassailable franchises), they have the wherewithal—if reasonably managed—to expand, refinance, make massive cash distributions to shareholders, acquire attractive companies and properties, be acquired at premium prices, and, above all, survive the vicissitudes of dramatic and unpredictable business downturns.

Value investing comports with the balanced approach that is the lifeblood of control investing away from Wall Street. There is little balance on Wall Street, however, in the evaluation of common stocks. Rather, there is a primacy of future flows—whether earnings or cash flows—and a consequent denigration of balance sheet factors. Control investors and private businesses often adapt a primacy of future flows approach only when trying to take advantage of the dominant climate in financial community securities analysis and academic finance. Since value investing is mainstream, value investors may have a better understanding of various types of financial phenomena, including the Asian financial crises or the economic collapse of Russia.

Value investing is relatively noncompetitive. There are thousands of very bright analysts focused on predicting near-term outlooks and on attempting to outperform one another. It is comforting to buy-and-hold value investors to be above this fray.

In value investing, the goal is essentially to earn satisfactory long-term returns rather than to outperform peers consistently or almost consistently. Performance is something that deserves weight in value investing, but never 100% weight. Although value investors ignore market risk on an individual security basis, they are quite conscious of market risk on a portfolio basis. If a portfolio's performance is rather negative for an extended period—say, a year or so—a value investor probably ought to conclude that the fundamental analyses of the securities in the portfolio were poor. In such a case, the value analyst probably ought to be fired, should reexamine what he or she is doing, or both.

Value investors do not think in absolutes. They know that there are no perfect investments. Rather, they figure out what is wrong with any particular investment and may proceed to invest if what appears to be wrong does not seem to be a showstopper. Problems normally encountered in value investing include the following when looking at attractive securities:

- Near-term outlooks are generally poor.
- The industries are depressed and unpopular.
- Managements tend to be conservative and nonpromotional.
- What is attractive on a going-concern basis may be unattractive on a resource conversion basis—for example, a portfolio of performing loans.
- Good past market performance may mean a dearth of good present investments.
- Strong growth trends spell low average earnings.
- The best evidence of growth prospects may not necessarily lie in the past growth record most of the time but in qualitative reasoning, including subjective appraisals of managements as well as forecasts of long-term results for companies whose current operating results are depressed.
- A large amount of resources—say, as measured by book value—may mean large profit potential or large overhead or both.

Disasters seem far less likely for value investors than for others. First, value investors are far less likely to be victimized by fraud than are growth investors. Second, value investors are unlikely to be victimized by having too much leverage, as was the case in 1998 for Long Term Capital Management, and value investors are unlikely to suffer the fate of Long Term Capital Management, where judgments seemed to be based solely on technical quantitative analysis unleavened by any qualitative judgments.

An underlying assumption of value investing is that for value investing purposes, the investor knows more than the market. The market was personified by Benjamin Graham, not as anyone knowledgeable or sagacious but rather as "Mr. Market," an irrational person constantly bidding and offering at various prices for equity interests in businesses. The author could not agree more. Knowing more than the market for one's purposes seems essential for those who like to sleep soundly every night and also want to avoid worrying not about facts on the ground in securities markets but about what John Maynard Keynes called "the average opinion of the average opinion."

Regulators face a real problem in deciding whether the focus of their regulation ought to be value investing principles or an attempt to require a Wall Street–type emphasis on *truthful* statements of periodic operating earnings. The dilemma arises because part of regulators' task is to ensure the maintenance of orderly markets and another part is to provide adequate disclosure and transparency. In maintaining orderly day-to-day markets relatively free from manipulation, what the numbers *are*, especially earnings numbers, becomes crucial. In providing disclosures to those who want to analyze a business in depth, what the numbers—all numbers—*mean* tends to be crucial.

The Securities and Exchange Commission (SEC) seems to be emphasizing what the numbers *are* rather than what the numbers *mean*. In November 1998, the SEC pressured Sun Trust Banks, Inc. to restate its earnings upward by decreasing its loan-loss provisions by $100 million. The SEC believed that Sun Trust was overreserving for loan losses and that its earnings thus did not represent truth. For value investing purposes, though, Sun Trust's conservative loan-loss policy went primarily to an appraisal of management showing the conservative manner in which it accounts for something that is really unpredictable: what future loan losses might be.

Many outside passive minority investors might be interested in following a value investing approach but do not want to do it themselves. The author manages the Third Avenue Value Funds and Whitman Advisors, both of which follow a value investing approach. Fortunately, there are a number of other mutual fund and investment advisors who are basically value investors, even though many are also market-risk conscious, and many probably place less emphasis on high-quality assets than does the author. Here is a partial list of highly recommended funds and investment advisors for value investors:

Mutual Fund Families
- Baron Capital   *BPTRX*
- Davis Selected Advisers
- Gabelli Funds   *GATAX*
- Longleaf Partners   *LLPFX*   *FRANKLIN*
- Mutual Series
- Oakmark Funds   *OAKLX*
- Sequoia Fund
- Sogen Funds
- Third Avenue Funds
- Tweedy Browne Funds   *TWEBX*

Investment Advisors
- Baupost Group, Inc.
- Chieftain Capital
- Peter Cundill & Associates
- Delafield Asset Management
- Kahn Brothers Investment Management
- Ruane, Cunniff and Co.
- Walter & Edwin Schloss Associates
- MJ Whitman Advisers

You do not have to be a player in speculative markets in order to be a successful passive investor. Knowing a lot about the companies with which you are involved, the securities issued by those companies, and being price conscious should be good enough. In the final analysis, think Main Street not Wall Street.

Index